CHICAGO ORIGINALS

A CAST OF THE CITY'S COLORFUL CHARACTERS

KENAN HEISE   ED BAUMANN

Bonus Books, Inc.

94 93 92 91 90   5 4 3 2 1

Library of Congress Catalog Card Number: 90-83080

International Standard Book Number: 0-933893-94-9

Bonus Books, Inc.
160 East Illinois Street
Chicago, Illinois 60611

Printed in the United States of America

If a man does not keep pace with his companions, perhaps it is because he hears a different drummer. Let him step to the music which he hears, however measured or far away.

—Henry David Thoreau

Contents

Foreword

As a boy growing up in Old Town, in the years before Old Town became the quaint/arty/dear area it is today, I would sometimes wander over to a saloon on North Avenue and sit around with Paddy Bauler.

I did this not because Paddy had any special affection for the youth of his 43rd Ward—hell, he didn't even treat his relatives with kindness and kids, with rare exception, didn't vote—but because my best friend then was Paddy's namesake and grandson, Mathias Bauler, whom we all called Ty.

We would go over to Paddy's saloon, just west of Sedgwick, because we knew that if we sat and listened to the alderman talk for a while, his hands sitting atop his huge stomach, he would give us each a dollar and tell us to go spend it at the nearby ice cream parlor owned by a crony, which we wouldn't always do. Sometimes we spent it on candy at the Economy grocery store on Wells or at the dime store farther west on North.

Except that he was generous and fat, there was nothing particularly special about Paddy then, and even though I learned otherwise through the years, the uniqueness of his character—the "Chicago ain't ready for reform" basis of his legend—was something that seemed perfectly normal.

That's the thing about Chicago's characters. They don't try to be eccentric, unique, wacky or weird. They just are and the fit is perfect.

Chicago has always been a fertile and nurturing environment for those who march not to the beat of a different drummer, but to a different symphony. Loud and proud, Chicago's distinctive personality has less to do with its gloriously distinctive architecture than it does with the sum of its people. Most of the people you'll meet in this book are not mere Bughouse Square babblers, fly-by-night fads. They were the movers and shakers and brokers and bandits who not only made the city tick but rang its bell.

Unlike any other city in the land, Chicago accomodated its characters, celebrated them, in fact. In reading the profiles compiled by Kenan Heise and Ed Baumann, one can't help but be awed by the range of Chicago personalities. And they come at you in this book with dizzying delight.

Many of them seem too good to be true, too wild to be real. If they had never existed surely some fiction writer would have had to create them.

But could they? Some of Chicago's characters absolutely defy the imagination. That familiar phrase, "larger than life," applies to most of them, of course. But one is also struck, having swallowed whole the morsels of this book, by the city's legacy of lively lives, and moved to ask, Where are the new originals?

Let's face it. Ryne Sandberg, for all his transcendent talent, lacks the panache of Hack Wilson—and Sandberg will never tally 190 RBIs in a season.

Indeed, the collection of contemporary Chicago characters appears pale beside this "Chicago Originals" package. Modern times do not take as kindly to peculiarities and peccadillos. Facelessness is in.

There are still a handful of the real thing around: Royko, Studs, Kup and, for worse, Gus Savage. But on the whole, we settle for less these days: Oprah, Fast Eddie, Seka and Helmut Jahn.

There's style, to be sure, but substance?

And so, in the same manner that David Lowe catalogued the city's vanished architectural glories in his brilliant *Lost Chicago*, so have Heise and Baumann captured a vanishing breed.

Heise and Baumann, newspapermen to the core, have done a fine job. It must have been an incredibly frustrating, even painful task, and there is good reason they have subtitled their book "A" cast of characters, for a gathering of "The" cast would fill volumes. (Not a bad idea, fellas. Just think of the characters you had to leave on the cutting room floor.)

But what they have given us in the following pages is more than enough to engage and entertain. It's a gallery, written in a breezy, inviting manner.

What they have done is make me yearn for the chance to have rubbed barroom elbows with people now dead. It evokes for me some memories I don't really have, reminds me of lazy afternoons at Paddy's saloon and compels me, I'm getting out of my chair right now, to walk down the halls to Royko's office and hear what he has to say.

Rick Kogan

Preface

I t is doubtful that you will find anywhere a more unlikely collaboration of writers than Edward Baumann and Kenan Heise.

Heise spent his pre-journalism years in a Catholic monastery, while Baumann, a former construction worker, picked up his press card after service in the jungles of New Guinea and the Philippines during World War II.

The one thing they both have in common is an undying love for Chicago and a fascination with the people who made—and make—the city both unique and enchanting.

The late Robert J. Casey of the *Inter-Ocean, Daily Journal, Examiner, Evening American* and *Chicago Daily News* once said, "Journalists meet such interesting people, and they're all in the newspaper business."

Most of them are, to be sure, but every now and then a reporter meets someone who is not in the business who is also more than a little bit interesting.

Baumann, who worked for the old *Chicago Daily News, Chicago's American, Chicago Today* and the *Chicago Tribune*, got into the business early enough to have clasped the hand of Ben Hecht. He knew Sally Rand, drank beer with Yellow Kid Weil, and once talked Aurora Mayor Paul Egan out of swimming to shore for supplies when they ran out of brew on a fishing tug 10 miles out in Lake Michigan.

Heise, one of the city's most knowledgeable historians, started as a reporter for *Chicago's American* in 1963. For 17 years as Action Line editor, first for the *American/*

Chicago Today and later for the *Tribune,* he helped solve the city's problems and answer its questions. Since 1982 he has been the *Tribune's* obituary writer. His collection of 9,027 books on Chicago has become part of the Chicago Public Library. He has written or co-authored 10 books and two plays, including such divergent titles as *They Speak for Themselves: Interviews With the Destitute of Chicago* (1965) and *The Chicagoization of America: 1893–1917.* He was the 1986 winner of the Vicki Matson Award from the Friends of American Literature. Heise also owns Chicago Historical Bookworks, a bookstore in Evanston specializing in used, rare, and out-of-print books on Chicago.

The men and women described in this book are all people Heise and Baumann have known during their combined 65 years of newspaper reporting in Chicago—or wish they had. They are the makers and the fakers, the builders and the bilkers, the schemers and dreamers, madams and madonnas, prostitutes and presstitutes, freebooters and free spirits.

Line them all up and you will have, indeed, a parade of different drummers.

These are characters who gave you character, Chicago. They made you what you are today. We hope you're satisfied.

Very Early Chicago

Pierre Moreau
(The late 1600s)

One of the first two residents of Chicago (1674) whose names history has recorded was a bootlegger. Pierre

Moreau, known as "The Mole," and a fur trader, sold liquor to the Indians. He came here with a companion called "The Surgeon."

In first exploring the territory, these French voyageurs came down the St. Lawrence River from Quebec in canoes. These two built a log cabin approximately 50 miles south of the Chicago River, according to the diaries of missionary explorer Jacques Marquette. In 1674 the Jesuit priest wintered at Chicago along the South Branch of the river. He was plagued with serious illness and diarrhea. The Mole and The Surgeon, who knew he was coming, had made preparations for him, including setting aside a cabin near their own. When they learned of his illness, The Surgeon rushed across the frozen prairie to care for the sick priest and to bring him some corn and blueberries.

History does not tell much else about The Surgeon than his presence in the area and his act of kindness.

About "The Mole," however, we know more. Moreau probably had been along with Marquette and Louis Jolliet, when they first visited Chicago in 1673. He represented Count Frontenac, the governor of New France, as an agent in his illegal liquor trading with the Indians. And there was no Eliot Ness to try to stop him.

Jean Baptiste Point du Sable
(1745–1813)

An 1880 history of Chicago wanted to inform residents of the burgeoning city that its first permanent resident had been black. With gross bias and ignorance, the author used an illustration portraying him as a three- or four-year-old black child with a happy, but mindless look riding a log down the river.

Even the serious historians and scholars of the late nineteenth century (and many from the twentieth) ignored Jean Baptiste Point du Sable to the extent that they could not even get together on how to spell his name. The focus was rather on John Kinzie, who moved into du Sable's house and whom they called the "Father of Chicago." Kinzie was not a very noble character, and owned slaves in Chicago despite it being illegal under the Northwest Ordinance. One eventually escaped and went to the South, where Kinzie pursued him. The man, nevertheless, won his freedom in a New Orleans court because of the provisions of the Northwest Ordinance.

One of the reasons for Kinzie's favorable image is that the history books relied on Juliette Kinzie's accounts of him in *Wau-Bun*. She was his daughter-in-law.

The competition between these two men for preeminence in the history books took a decided turn in 1913, when historian Milo Quaife discovered a document in the records at Detroit. It was the bill of sale from 1800 for du Sable's home and property to Kinzie's

3

assistant, Jean LeLime. The document represented an extraordinary property list, full of unexpected indications of du Sable's sophistication and affluence. Quaife outlined what was involved in the transaction:

> Besides the "mansion," described by Mrs. Kinzie (22 by 40 feet in size), there were numerous outbuildings: two barns, 24 by 30 and 28 by 40 feet, respectively; a horsemill, 24 by 36 feet; a bakehouse, 18 by 20 feet; a poultry-house, a workshop, a dairy, and a smokehouse, each of smaller dimensions.
>
> The equipment included 8 axes, several saws, 7 scythes, 8 sickles, 3 carts, and a plow. There were 2 mules, 30 head of full-grown cattle, 2 calves, 28 hogs, and 44 hens. A moment's reflection will suffice to show that these figures indicate an extensive civilized establishment. One does not build and equip a mill and a bakehouse unless he has grain to grind and flour to bake. Corn might be bought from the Indians, but to have wheat for his mill Point Sable must have raised it himself. This, and the cutting of hay for his live stock, explains the use to which his seven scythes and eight sickles were put. . . . Evidently, Point Sable produced the lumber used in the erection of his buildings: 8 axes, 1 plank saw, 1 large ripsaw, 1 crosscut saw with 7-inch blade, 1 cooper's handsaw, and a kit of carpenter's tools, tell their own story. Noticeable in this connection is the inventory item "1 horse stable—all the wood for a barn." This can only mean that prior to selling his establishment Point Sable had planned to erect a third stable, and had already manufactured the lumber for it.
>
> Within the house, two items attract our particular attention, a large number of copper kettles (eleven in all), and a cabinet of French walnut, 8 by 4 feet, with four glass doors.

Quaife in his later book, *Checagou*, pointed out that the list of eight axes, seven scythes and eight sickles implied the presence of a considerable number of workers. Du Sable was an Indian trader and was often absent from Chicago. He had little chance or time to do all the manual labor and farming his storehouses and implements called for.

The paintings and the French walnut cabinet were even more extraordinary, not only because of the wilderness setting of Chicago, but also because of the extreme difficulty in bringing these items to the area.

4

The only means of transport was a bateau, a wide French canoe, with part of the trip being by portage. This meant that both the shipment and the canoes had to be carried for miles.

Additional research eventually focused on du Sable and his place in Chicago history. Allan Eckert in *Gateway to Empire* speculated on two interesting aspects of the du Sable story. He discussed what is known of the trader and argued that du Sable had the vision to foresee Chicago's future, but grew impatient for it to happen and that is why he sold out. Secondly, Eckert's research established that du Sable did not want to sell his property to Kinzie, so the latter used LeLime to be his front man in the transaction, buying it from his assistant in 1803. The jealousy and frustration this created in LeLime, according to Eckert, led to a fight between him and Kinzie in which the Frenchman was killed.

Du Sable, a native of Haiti, settled at Chicago sometime in the 1770s. He was apparently fully accepted by the Indians, marrying the daughter of a Potawatomi chief and raising a family with her. The color of his skin and his mutual and open respect for the Indians won their confidence.

During the Revolutionary War, he was imprisoned for a time by the British at Detroit, indicating his sympathies with the Colonies.

Every reference in the sketchy records indicates he was quite a human being, a bridge from the city's wilderness past to its urbanized future. He successfully established his home and business at Chicago three decades before Fort Dearborn was built and more than half a century before it became a village. If he came back today, however, he would find the site of his home on a street named after John Kinzie.

Gurdon Saltonstall Hubbard
(1802–1886)

To the Indians he was Pa-pa-ma-ta-be, "The Swift

Walker." To Chicago he would be Gurdon Hubbard: fur trader, pioneer, entrepreneur, shipping and insurance magnate, and eventually, author.

When Hubbard first arrived in Chicago on Oct. 1, 1818, it was a tiny garrison settlement. He had just turned 16 and was an apprentice fur trader with John Jacob Astor's American Fur Company. His companions were rugged voyageurs, who had been employed by the firm's French predecessors. He had come to northern Illinois to spend the winter, to trade with the Indians, and, he would learn, to try to stay alive. Not all his associates succeeded in doing so. A young fur trader with whom he had traded assignments that first year froze to death, as did Hubbard's companion on a long, bitter cold trek through the area.

Hubbard, on the other hand, would live to be 84 years old and to see Chicago grow to a city of a million residents. His ability to master the harsh northern Illinois climate and its environment would become legendary.

A native of Vermont, the man Indians called "The Swift Walker" learned survival in the wilderness as part of an industry specifically adapted to it, the American fur trade. The daily food allotment for the voyageurs with whom he worked consisted of "one pint of lyed or hulled and dried corn, with from two to four ounces of tallow, except on Saturday flour was given for Sunday pancakes." They had learned, he said, that they could endure more hardships on this diet than on one which included bread and meat. The more experienced traders ridiculed apprentices who ate meat as *mange-du-lard* or "pork eaters."

When people doubted Hubbard could have ever walked 75 miles in a day, he told of Pierre Le Claire, who had traveled from St. Joseph, Mich., to Chicago, a distance of 90 miles in "one continuous walk." Le Claire was carrying news of the outbreak of the War of 1812 to his uncle, John Kinzie, at Fort Dearborn. He wanted to warn the garrison of an imminent attack by the Indians aligned with the British. He had started at daylight and arrived at nine o'clock at night.

When the local Indians questioned Pa-pa-ma-ta-be's legendary walking speed, they chose their fastest man to start walking alongside him and try to outdistance him. They then placed bets among themselves. The Indian lost, literally by miles, and could barely move the next day. The young fur trader felt no ill effects.

Part of his speed came from his ability to travel straight through the roadless wilderness. His route directly south became known as "Hubbard's Trail." He used it on a famous Paul Revere-type horseback ride in 1827 to recruit residents of the settlement at Danville, Ill., to come to Chicago to help protect against a possible Indian attack.

Hubbard in the early 1830s would serve in the Illinois General Assembly and lead the fight to make the Chicago River, rather than the Calumet, the end of the Illinois and Michigan Canal. His argument was that Indiana would benefit more than Illinois if the Calumet were chosen. It was effective logic with his fellow state legislators.

The lanky, friendly Hubbard eventually took over completely the fur trade in the area. He also rounded up hogs from farmers in the state and brought them to Chicago to supply the men at Fort Dearborn, making him the city's first meatpacker. It was so cold in Chicago that year that he simply froze their carcasses along the bank of the river and stored them there.

Several years later, he built a large, brick warehouse along the south bank of the river (near La Salle Street), which his fellow Chicagoans promptly labeled "Hubbard's Folly." Not only was it the first such structure of its kind in Chicago, but it was also so large that it was beyond comprehension of the people to see how it could ever be fully utilized.

Hubbard was involved in building and running the first waterworks in the city, and owned the *Lady Elgin*, that sank with a tragic loss of lives in 1860.

His main focus, however, was to become insurance. He believed in the future of Chicago, and as the city's first underwriter and the owner of several insurance companies, in effect, bet on it. In 1871, he came close to losing that wager as the Chicago Fire wiped out his insurance companies and nearly bankrupted him. He

7

was personally devastated, but he had made friends as well as a fortune and they helped him recover his old spirit.

And, in his eighties, the man who had outwalked everyone in his youth did another amazing thing. He wrote a book, his autobiography. In it, he reconstructed what it had been like in this area when Indians lived here. He told of his experiences and his feelings and ultimately why he walked so fast: Gurdon Hubbard was going somewhere and got there.

The Indian Tribes of Chicago
(Removed 1835)

The Indians who got snookered out of Chicago did not want to have to say they were happy about it, especially when the white commissioner tried to get them to do so.

The scene was the Council of Chicago and the year, 1833.

A visitor from England, Charles Latrobe, described the gathering of commissioner, traders, Indians and land speculators "as numerous as the sand." He wrote:

> You will find horse-dealers and horse-stealers—rogues of every description, white, black, brown, and red—half-breeds, quarter-breeds, and men of no breed at all;—dealers in pigs, poultry, and potatoes;—men pursuing Indian claims, some for tracts of land, others, like our friend Snipe, for pigs which the wolves had eaten; creditors of the tribes, or of particular Indians, who know they have no chance of getting their money if they do not get it from the government agents;—sharpers of every degree; peddlers, grog-dealers; Indian agents and Indian traders of every description, and contractors to supply the Potawatomies with food. The little village was in an uproar from morning to night, and from night to morning; for, during the hours of darkness, when the housed portion of the population of Chicago strove to obtain repose in the crowded plank edifices of the village, the Indians howled, sang, wept, yelled and whooped in their various encampments. With all this, the whites seemed to me to be more pagan than the red men.

It was a raucous, disorderly gathering. Not only were the tribal leaders there; but, because the U.S. government was providing ample food, the whole tribe, including children.

The frontier philosophy of Indian removal (westward); forcibly, but by treaty if possible, was the policy of the United States.

President Andrew Jackson told Congress in 1830:

> It gives me pleasure to announce to Congress that the benevolent policy of the government, steadily pursued for nearly 30 years, in relation to the removal of the Indians beyond the white settlements is approaching to a happy consummation.

In the spirit of such words, Governor George B. Porter of the Michigan Territory told the assembled council of Indians:

> . . . as your great father in Washington had heard that you wished to sell your land, he had sent commissioners to treat with you.

The Indians replied:

> . . . the great father in Washington must have seen a bad bird which had told him a lie, for that far from wishing to sell our land, we wish to keep it.

They continued seeing "bad signs, " and making the white negotiators wait as long as they felt they could, but they did not keep their lands. They signed away 5 million acres with their "X"s and agreed to move west to Iowa by 1835.

A local resident who had witnessed the occasion said:

> You or hardly any other man, can imagine what was done, or how ridiculously the whole thing was carried on or closed up. It should have been conducted upon the principles of truth and justice; but the whole thing was a farce, acted by those in office in our government.

The Indians, who lived here for 10,000 years, departed two years later, leaving behind their name for the place, *Chicagou*, "smelly onion."

Mark Beaubien
(1800–1881)

Mark Beaubien, ferryman and inn keeper in the very early days of the settlement of Chicago, was known for turning the too-often mud-mired and discouraged town into a spot of gaiety and revelry.

Always happy-go-lucky, he arrived at Chicago in 1826, when the population of settlers was less than two dozen.

"There was no town; didn't expect no town," he is quoted in Hurlbut's *Chicago Antiquities*. "When they laid out the town, my house laid out in the street."

In the days before bridges in Chicago, he had the license as ferryman. He charged residents from out of the county, but had to ferry locals free. He built The Sauganash Tavern, a lean-to log structure. It was named for his Indian friend, who was also known as Billy Caldwell. When settlers voted to incorporate Chicago as a town in 1833, the first election of trustees was at his tavern, which was a favorite resort both for business and pleasure.

Another contribution he made to the population of Chicago was the fathering of 23 children by two successive wives.

Lloyd Lewis and Henry Justin Smith, in *Chicago, the History of Its Reputation*, described him:

> Mark was a capital "mine host," wearing nankeen trousers, letting the kitchen run itself, gossiping with the half-breed loungers, scraping his fiddle at dances; singing an endless ballad about the surrender of Detroit, neglecting his hotel (as he had his ferry) to race horses.

He lived in Chicago for several more decades and was the light-house keeper, having received the appointment from President Buchanan.

Beaubien was a frequent companion of the local Indians, and in their treaty with the U.S. government, they conveyed "to their good friend, Mark Beaubien" a reservation at the mouth of the Calumet River. He was unaware of the gift for more than 20 years, finally receiving a deed from President Martin Van Buren for it in the late 1850s.

He wore his famous nankeen trousers in the summer. In the winter, his dress, especially on great occasions, was a swallow-tail coat with brass buttons.

Paul Gilbert and Charles Lee Bryson in *Chicago and Its Makers*, said of Beaubien:

> In all the history of Chicago there is no more delightful figure than that of the rollicking, fiddling, singing innkeeper, merchant, ferryman and good fellow, Mark Beaubien. From the year, 1826, when a gay, careless, adventurous young blade from Detroit, he came to this city, he wove a brilliant thread of gaiety into the somewhat somber fabric of social life of the settlement until, at the age of 81, he died peacefully at Kankakee.

William B. Ogden
(1805–1877)

William B. Ogden, Chicago's first mayor, had a philosophy of "get on with it."

His friend, Isaac Arnold, said that if a thousand picked men were cast upon a desolate island, Ogden "would, by common, universal, and instinctive selection, have been made their leader."

Arnold also said Ogden was the man you would want along on a long stage ride because he made

> . . . the longest day short by his inimitable narration of incidents and anecdotes, his graphic descriptions, and his sanguine anticipation of the future.

Ogden had a lot of reasons not to be sanguine about the future. He was, nevertheless, the incurable optimist the young town needed to jumpstart it and keep it pushing along. The 4,000 residents (or rather, the 706 voters) of Chicago who selected him as mayor in 1837 thought so. He defeated the son of furtrader John Kinzie, John H. Kinzie, who had grown up outside of Fort Dearborn and who had escaped the massacre in 1812.

When Ogden first arrived two years earlier, he was unbelievably disappointed. He was born in Delaware County, upstate New York, in 1805, and loved the mountains, streams and rivers of his native place. By contrast, Chicago was frantic and mired in mud. He came to Chicago on a business trip to look after some property that his brother-in-law, Charles Butler, and several others had earlier purchased for $100,000.

Ogden wrote back to the men whom he represented and told them that they had been taken. In a land auction, however, he recouped the $100,000 by selling off one-third of what they had bought. He expressed his new attitude to a friend:

> When you are dealing with Chicago property the proper way is to go in for all you can get and then go on with your business and forget all about it. It will take care of itself.

The land speculation bubble burst during Ogden's term as mayor. The situation became exactly what it was called, "a panic." He pushed hard for the city not to go bankrupt and renounce its debt. Comparing the situation to a city besieged, he argued passionately:

> . . . many a fortress has saved itself by the courage of its inmates and their determination to conceal their weakened condition.

His optimism and fight carried the day.

Ogden stayed enthusiastic. He designed the city's first swing bridge, donated the land for its first medical school (Rush Medical College), dealt in real estate, twice served on the City Council, built a fine home and established a literary and cultural tone for the community.

Chicago's first railroad had been started in 1836, and abandoned the next year, when hard times hit the city. It faded for almost everyone; not, however, for William Ogden.

When Ogden wanted to resume building the railroad, William F. Weld, a Boston financier, told him to do so, but that it would go broke and then he and other Eastern financiers would finish it. Ogden climbed on a horse, rode out to the farmers along the proposed route and got the money from them, a few dollars at a time.

His Galena & Chicago Union Railroad in 1848 purchased a third-hand engine, The Pioneer, and started operation from Chicago to a point 10 miles west. It never reached Galena, but it became the first spoke in the great railroad system that within a decade made Chicago the railroad hub of North America.

He later formed another line, the Chicago & North

Western, which subsequently purchased the Galena & Chicago Union.

His vision was broader than his midwestern lines, however. In 1850 Ogden became chairman of the National Pacific Railway Convention. He would serve in 1862 as president of the Union Pacific Railroad, a position he held until 1866. He would later help drive in the golden spike at a place named after him, Ogden Flats, Utah, when the country was finally spanned by a railroad line in 1869.

As a man who steeled himself to handle adversity, William Ogden would need all that strength to face what was ahead. As his railroads spread throughout Wisconsin, he invested in the lumber trade that dominated sections of the state. The focus of his interests was the town of Peshtigo, where large numbers of the residents worked for Ogden companies.

On Oct. 8, 1871, major fires burned both Chicago and Peshtigo, devastating the cities and killing 1,000 people in Peshtigo and 300 in Chicago. The former mayor lost his home in Chicago as well as his investments. In the Wisconsin fire, he lost close to $1,000,000 plus the lives of friends and workers.

He stayed in Chicago only four days to handle business and personal matters. He then spent two months in Peshtigo, helping to save the city with the same optimism for its future that he had for Chicago in 1837.

In 1875, at the age of 70, the busy and determined Ogden finally married.

David Kennison
(1736?–1851?)

David Kennison claimed to have been involved in the Boston Tea Party (1773), Valley Forge (1777), and the Fort Dearborn Massacre (1812), dying in 1851 at the age of 115 or 116.

Early Chicagoans, furthermore, believed in David Kennison and his unbelievable history.

He is buried in Lincoln Park, one of the few graves left after the City Cemetery vacated the land in 1865. A grave marker was erected near the Academy of Science on Clark Street. It read:

> In memory of David Kennison, the last survivor of the Boston Tea Party, who died in Chicago February 24, 1852. Aged 115 years, 3 mos., 17 days and is buried near this spot. This stone is erected by the Sons of the Revolution and the Daughters of the American Revolution.

Kennison's claims were to say the least farfetched; his motives, obvious; and his supporters, confused.

He said he was born in Scotland on Nov. 17, 1736. That would have made him 36 during the Boston Tea Party and a 75-year-old soldier at the Fort Dearborn Massacre Aug. 15, 1812. Considering the difference in longevity for people today, his age claim of 115 would be comparable to at least 150 today.

A. T. Andreas in *History of Chicago* (Vol. I, p. 487) quotes the following ad from Mooney's Museum for the 8th of November 1848:

> I have taken the Museum in this city, which I was obliged to do in order to get a comfortable living, as my pension is so small it scarcely affords the comforts of life. If I live until the 17th of November, 1848, I shall be 112 years old, and I intend making a donation party on that day at the Museum. I have fought in several battles for my country. All I ask of the generous public is to call at the Museum on the 17th of November, which is my birthday, and donate to me what they think I deserve.

Andreas comments:

> It is unfortunate that no authentic account of the proceedings of the 17th can be found, for the amount donated might serve as a criterion of Chicago's estimate of a patriot's services.

Kennison not only profited from the museum that was donated to him by the town's fathers, but had a day for himself.

Newspaper editor (and later Mayor) John Wentworth was a Kennison supporter and heralded his return to Chicago in 1848 thus:

We had a call yesterday from David Kennison, the only surviving participant in throwing the tea overboard in Charleston Harbor. He was a soldier in the war of the Revolution, and in the last war with Great Britain. He draws a pension of $8.00 a month. He is 111 years old, and bids fair to live many years yet. He has a son over sixty years old. We consider him the greatest curiosity of the day, and almost the last link between the American colonies and the United States.

The Boston Tea Party, according to Wentworth, happened in Charleston harbor. Various sources list three dates for Kennison's birth and even two different years for his death.

Kennison—whatever his age or claims to it on his grave marker—now plays second fiddle to the nearby dinosaur exhibit at the Academy of Sciences. If it had been there in his day, who knows what claims might have been made in his name?

1850s

G.P.A. Healy
(1813–1894)

George Peter Alexander Healy was known as one of Chicago's most distinguished citizens in the nineteenth century.

During a long and phenomenally busy career as a portrait artist, old G.P.A., as he was known, painted kings, queens, popes, statesmen, generals, authors, musicians, women of fashion and some of the most prominent Chicagoans, beginning with William B. Ogden, the city's first mayor.

The son of an Irish sea captain, he was born in Boston in 1813. He opened his first studio there in 1830 at the age of 17, posting a sign with a self-portrait of himself in front of the shop.

He sailed for France in 1834, hoping to meet and perhaps paint his boyhood hero, the Marquis de Lafayette. Lafayette died on the day of his arrival, however, and Healy watched his funeral procession from a Paris sidewalk.

Over the next 20 years he traveled about Europe, painting the nobility, before he decided to make Chicago his world headquarters, thanks to Ogden.

He was living in Paris, where he was one of the most celebrated painters of the crowned heads of Europe, when the former mayor encountered him while on vacation in 1855, and asked him to do his portrait.

As Ogden posed and Healy painted, the two men talked, and soon became good friends.

"Come out to Chicago, which is thirsty for culture

and growing like a green bay tree," Ogden told him. "Come and do portraits of the prominent citizens and get rich quick.

"Mr. Healy, if you will honor me with your presence as my guest in my Chicago home for one year, I can guarantee that at the end of that time you will bring your family over and make a greatly needed addition to our community."

Ogden was a good salesman. Healy did get rich painting portraits of the city's business and civic leaders, including the Blairs, McCormicks, Ryersons, Farwells, Fairbanks, Kinzies and a host of others.

He purchased a home on a tree-shaded lot surrounded by flowers on Ontario Street, not far from Ogden's mansion, and sent for his family. His wife, Louisa, arrived with their six children in 1856.

With Chicago as his headquarters, Healy radiated to Washington, Baltimore, Philadelphia, New York, Boston, or wherever he was called to paint a prominent citizen. Every U.S. President from John Quincy Adams to Ulysses S. Grant sat for Healy, who was especially noted for his portraits of Abraham Lincoln.

He also painted a number of Civil War generals, including William T. Sherman and Robert E. Lee.

He once accepted a tract of land from a Chicago businessman, in lieu of the $1,000 asked for a portrait. The property ran from State Street to the lake, and from the Water Tower near Chicago Avenue to Elm Street. While paying the $10 fee to have the deed recorded in his name, a clerk in the recorder's office told Healy, "Why, that land on the lakefront isn't worth $10."

Between 1855 and 1867 Healy painted an estimated 500 portraits, of nearly every person in Chicago who was anyone. Most of his works were destroyed in the Great Fire of 1871.

He was not present when fire raged through the city. He had gone back to Europe in 1867, sailing aboard the French steamer *Pereire*, for Le Havre. He settled his family in Paris, and for a time commuted to America for portrait assignments. He kept a home in Chicago on Wabash Avenue, and stayed there during his frequent visits to the city.

When the Art Institute was rebuilt after the fire, Healy presented it with its first painting, *The American Fathers.*

By 1882 he found Europe no longer to his liking, and told his wife over breakfast, "We sail next month. Yes, we shall leave Paris. It is changing and we are not. We had better settle in America . . ."

"Where?" she asked. "Boston? New York? Washington? Chicago?"

"Chicago, I think. We have so many friends there—and the property."

Upon his return he bought a new home on Ontario Street in the same neighborhood in which the family had formerly lived. The home, during the World Columbian Exposition of 1893, became a focal point for French visitors and exhibitors.

He was past 80 by then, but continued to make daily trips to his studio, where he put more and more Chicagoans on canvas. One hot June day in 1894 he started for the nearby studio but turned back and went to bed. On June 24th he lapsed into unconsciousness and died in his home on Ontario Street at the age of 81.

Long John Wentworth
(1815–1888)

Long John Wentworth, according to a legend he probably started himself, strode into Chicago six feet, six inches tall, barefooted, carrying his giant shoes—fourteen inches long and six inches wide—and clinging to a jug of whiskey "with which to bathe my blistered feet."

He would balloon to 300-plus pounds as he grew to become a dominant figure in early Chicago.

Emmett Dedmon in *Fabulous Chicago* said of him:

> In the history of Chicago there was never another man
> cut to so individual a pattern as John Wentworth.

His culinary habits would have earned for Long John a pre-eminent place on any list of the city's characters. He drank a pint of brandy or other "ardent

Long John Wentworth

spirits" every day of his long life. He usually stayed in a hotel rather than in his home in Summit. His meals—eaten alone at his special table—were carefully ordered by him ahead of time so the food would be on the table when he arrived. He selected and ate as many as 30 or 40 items at one sitting.

Wentworth did more, however, than eat his way into the history books.

A graduate of Dartmouth University, he took over the editorship of the city's first newspaper, the *Chicago Democrat,* and plunged headlong into the city's politics.

He was in the U.S. Congress for six terms. His vote was a big one when the Territory of Wisconsin wanted to change a controversial border decision and claim Chicago was in its limits to meet the statehood population requirements. He turned the down the offer of a U.S. Senate seat if he would go along with the plan.

But it was more his office-holding as a Republican mayor that made him what Lloyd Lewis and Henry Justin Smith called "an eccentric politician."

Norman Mark in his excellent book, *Mayors, Madams & Madmen,* observed:

> Long John was certainly colorful. If he were any more colorful, Chicago might not have been standing after he finished his terms as mayor.

The previous mayor, Thomas Dyer, had started in office with a parade in which the town's prostitutes had ridden in open carriages, followed by "a miscellaneous crowd."

Long John, on the other hand, came down hard on the less socially acceptable citizens of Chicago. Criminals were taken out of jail and put to work in ball and chain on the city streets. A public outroar ended this Chicago version of a chain gang.

He hired a spy, George "Beast" Brown, to report on what was happening in the city's bars and brothels. When this caught up with him during the next administration, the *Chicago Tribune*—a life-long enemy—chortled, "The days of Johannes Elongatus in politics are over." The paper was wrong. He would return to the mayorality.

One of his more infamous acts was to attack the Sands, Chicago's redlight district, north of the river near where the Tribune Tower now stands. The land was claimed by his friend, William Ogden. Wentworth, on his part, wanted the brothels and gambling dens closed. He personally led a raid in 1857 that burned down the Sands' buildings while the men of the area were away at a dog fight.

He also launched an attack against merchants who had signs hanging over the sidewalks. At six foot six, Long John had almost bumped into many of them and took pleasure in tearing them down. Merchants who had praised his raid on the "undesirables" of society now called him a tyrant.

Wentworth, praised on one hand as "completely independent and honest," has also been called, "truly a mayor to inspire personal malice." The *Chicago Times,* less restrained than the *Tribune,* accused him of such vices as dishonesty, drunkenness, lechery and habitual use of vile language. It also made sneering references to the fact that his wife, Roxanna, declined to live in Chicago.

The comments about his wife were true. She preferred to live in Troy, N.Y. There he visited her regularly during their 26 years of marriage and the birth of five children.

As he grew older, his interest focused on history, and even more, his place in it. He published a three-volume genealogy of the Wentworth family and gave speeches on the city's history, which were published in the *Fergus Historical Series* of pamphlets. One person who was writing a history of the city lent a copy to Long John for comment. The former mayor crossed out all of the material where his name did not appear and said, "There, young man, is a correct history of the city."

Long John was the mayor of Chicago when the Prince of Wales visited the city. Someone asked him how it felt to be seated next to the heir to the throne of England. His answer was:

He sat next to me.

1860s

Allan Pinkerton
(1819–1884)

Ironically, Allan Pinkerton, who would become Chicago's first police detective, and America's first "private eye," had fled to this country from his native Scotland to escape imprisonment.

The road was a rocky one.

The youngest son of a Glasgow police sergeant, young Pinkerton was a skilled barrelmaker—a cooper. He was also a champion of human rights and belonged to the Chartists—an organization known as the People's Charter, that advocated the use of arms in winning equal rights for the masses.

On the day of his wedding to Joan Carfrae, he was warned that the Crown was about to arrest him as a conspirator. He and his bride hastily boarded a steamer with third-class tickets to Nova Scotia (New Scotland). The ship was wrecked on a shoal about 200 miles from Halifax, and a passing schooner picked up the Pinkertons and other survivors in lifeboats. They were delivered to the mouth of the St. Lawrence River, and from there the newlyweds took a boat to Detroit.

Unable to find work there, Pinkerton spent the last of his savings on a horse and rickety wagon and traveled overland to Chicago. He arrived in the city in 1842 at the age of 23. He sold the horse and wagon to pay for lodging for him and his wife, and went to work making kegs at a local brewery for 50 cents a day.

A year later the Pinkertons moved to the Scottish

settlement of Dundee, 40 miles northwest of Chicago, where he prospered as the only barrelmaker in town.

While gathering poles for barrel hoops on an island in the Fox River one day, Pinkerton found a small piece of a burned $5 bill. Through natural powers of deduction he determined that the island was a counterfeiters' meeting place. He passed the information on to the Kane County sheriff, and the outlaw band wound up in jail.

Lawmen throughout the area began consulting Pinkerton, who put his inborn detective ability to work solving a number of puzzling cases. His fame spread, and in 1846 Cook County Sheriff William Church talked him into moving back to Chicago to serve as his special agent. Pinkerton sold the cooperage works and became a lawman. In 1850, the young City of Chicago hired him away from the sheriff's office to become the police department's first and only detective.

A hands-on lawman, Pinkerton was a master of disguises. He later reported that he had become a country bumpkin to catch a swindler; a bearded waterfront thug to nail warehouse thieves; a railroad ticket agent to apprehend an embezzler; and a grimy workman to catch a jewel thief.

The Chicago newspapers were full of accounts of his deeds, and by the end of the year he established Pinkerton's Detective Agency to deal with the railroads and other private industries that were clamoring for his service. The Rock Island Line alone guaranteed him $10,000 a year to protect the railroad from theft.

The agency consisted of nine men, all trained by Pinkerton. Clients were charged $3 a day for an ordinary detective; $8 for a supervisor; and $12 for Pinkerton's personal service. He also set up a corps of watchmen, and soon every building in the business district was being protected by his men.

A friend of Abraham Lincoln through his work with the Illinois Central Railroad which Lincoln represented as a lawyer, Pinkerton became his bodyguard during the Presidential campaign and helped protect Lincoln from an assassination plot in Baltimore in 1861. He was also active in the Underground Railroad, harboring escaped slaves in his house on Adams Street on their way to Canada.

Pinkerton was engaged as a Union spy during the Civil War, traveling through the South posing as a Confederate sympathizer. He was almost exposed in Jackson, Miss., when he was recognized by a German barber who greeted him by name and bubbled, "I cut your hair many times in the Sherman House on Randolph Street."

Serving under General George McClellan as Lincoln's chief of espionage and intelligence, Pinkerton was subsequently sent to Washington, where he organized and became head of the United States Secret Service.

Returning to Chicago after the war, Pinkerton resumed his detective agency, with his two sons, William and Robert. With Chicago as their headquarters, Pinkerton and his agents roamed the country on the trails of the James brothers, the Youngers, the Daltons, and other gangs of bank robbers and highwaymen.

The gang wars ended for Pinkerton in 1882, when he suffered a stroke. He died two years later at the age of 65.

The motto of Pinkerton's private detective service was "We never sleep," and its trademark was a wide-open eye—thus giving birth to the term "private eye."

Today the Pinkerton organization has more than 33,000 employees in 101 cities in the United States and Canada.

And it all started in Chicago with the barrelmaking sleuth who became the city's first detective—and America's first private eye.

John B. Rice
(1809–1874)

Few, if any, mayors of Chicago have ever done anything more preposterous than John B. Rice did 15 years before he was mayor (1865-9). Even Big Bill Thompson and Jane Byrne couldn't outdo his deed.

Rice, an actor, had come to Chicago in 1847 to entertain its people and all the politicians gathered in the city for its first national convention, "The River and Harbor Convention."

Even though Chicago's population was only 16,859, he was determined to establish a permanent theater, named, of course, Rice's Theater, after himself. He ran the place and would fill in when any actor was drunk or absent.

He proved on July 30, 1850, that he had more audacity than common sense, according to A. T. Andreas in his *History of Chicago*. In the midst of the opera, *La Somnambula*, according to the historian:

> "The appalling cry of fire rang through the house. The audience started to their feet in terror. Serious injury to many might have ensued had it not been for the presence of mind evinced by Manager Rice. Hastening to the footlights, he cried, 'Sit down. Sit down. Do you think I would permit a fire to occur in my theater? Sit down.'

And obedient to his command, the panic-stricken people paused half assured by the peremptory tone that all was safe. But, while Mr. Rice was still standing on the stage, someone from the prompter's place said, 'Mr. Rice, the theater is on fire.' The alarm spread and soon the building was cleared of its audience."

The theater was totally destroyed, at a loss to Rice of about $4,000. A benefit at City Hall to help him recoup was a failure netting him only $60, and he retreated to Milwaukee.

In 1851, a stubborn Rice returned to Chicago and built another theater—this one a brick structure—on Dearborn Street, just south of Randolph. He hired James McVicker as his manager and remained active with it until 1857, when he "retired" to other business interests, including management of the by-then very valuable property he

29

owned on both Randolph and Dearborn Streets in a
burgeoning real-estate market.

On April 18, 1865, Rice, a very conservative Republican, was easily elected mayor of Chicago. The Union
victory in the Civil War and Abraham Lincoln's assassination a week before the municipal election ensured his
win.

His political bent saw him veto the revolutionary
idea of an eight-hour day for city employees. A large
spontaneous rally on May 1, 1867, to protest his action
led to the world celebration of May Day as a day for
working men's and women's protests. Returning Civil
War vets wanted the eight-hour day because they
needed jobs spread to those who couldn't find work.
The Council eventually overrode his veto.

That same Council had developed a system of
rings, similar to a committee system, to collect payoffs.
The city of Chicago was meanwhile earning an international reputation for its corruption with 250 brothels and
a gambling area along Randolph Street known as "Hair-
triggers Block" and "Gamblers' Row."

The citizens of Chicago threw Rice out in a wave of
reform in 1869 and put in Mayor Rosewell B. Mason,
who would become famous as the mayor of Chicago
when the city burned down in 1871.

Mrs. Kate O'Leary
(1835–????)

Alas, alack! Poor Mrs. O'Leary. She was blamed, oh was she blamed, for burning the whole town down!

And her son, Jim, he turned out to be a good-for-nothing gambler!

What's an Irish mother to do?

History books tend to blame the Chicago Fire of 1871 on Mrs. O'Leary's cow. A few say it was rather Pegleg Sullivan, a neighbor, while a recent book says it was all the result of a comet hitting Chicago.

One erroneous newspaper account in the *Chicago Times* immediately after the fire directly accused the poor woman, claiming she had threatened the whole city, saying, "I'll show everybody" after being cut off the dole administered through her parish. The article said she wanted revenge and made it clear she was Irish and poor, thus capitalizing on the anti-foreign and anti-Catholic sentiments that existed in Chicago.

Catherine O'Leary was, indeed, guilty of being Irish. She and her husband, Patrick, lived on the Near Southwest Side of Chicago at 137 DeKoven St. (by the newer numbering system, 558).

The O'Learys were not on the dole, a fact of which she was proud. The couple owned not only their own home, but also the house in front of it on the same lot, which they rented to another family. A plump woman, 35 years old, she possessed five cows, a calf and a horse.

She had a route in the neighborhood and sold milk to the immigrants new to the area.

Obscurity was not to be hers.

The Chicago Fire started on Sunday evening, Oct. 8, 1871, and continued burning until Tuesday, the 10th. All versions agree that it started in the O'Leary barn. The Chicago Fire Department Academy and a sculpture by Chicago artist Egon Weiner are now located on the spot.

Chicago in 1871 was, for the most part, made up of wooden buildings. That fall had been especially dry and the city's fire-fighting force was worn out from a major fire that occurred the evening before.

The popular theory has been that one of Mrs. O'Leary's cows kicked over a lantern and started the fire, some versions and illustrations having her milking the cow at the time. The papers claimed that she denied this because of the immense damage which the fire did.

The impression that all of Chicago, except the Water Tower, burned to the ground in the fire is simply not true. The conflagration did not touch the South Side or most of the West Side. North, it stopped at Fullerton Avenue. The destruction covered an area 3.32 miles square. The number of lives lost was said to be 300, although only 75 bodies were ever found. The total figure on buildings destroyed was 17,450, and the estimated cost of the fire was $200 million.

The commercial center of Chicago faced near, if temporary, extinction. Among the losses were: City Hall, homes, hotels, banks, stores, office buildings, theaters, the Opera House, churches, brothels and gambling houses.

But Kate O'Leary could not have foreseen this when she was telling neighbors about her barn burning. She said, as did witnesses, she was in bed or at least in the house. It would have been inconsistent for such an industrious woman to leave her barn and animals and run into the house without having tried to save them.

Two versions have come down to us about the fate of the allegedly guilty cow. One said it was stolen or disappeared. The other is that it was slaughtered by a local butcher.

The weary firefighters, when they did come, were

unsuccessful in checking the fire, and it was some time before anyone had a sense of what a conflagration the city was in for.

The O'Learys did not lose their home, a fact that was later held against them. The fire, however, burned northeast with the wind and headed straight for downtown, leaping everything in its path as the heat intensified the wind. The O'Leary's house was southwest of its route.

Attention for decades focused on Mrs. O'Leary. She was called to testify at hearings on the fire and related that she was in bed and did not know how the fire started.

A reporter of the old *Chicago Journal* was the only one to succeed in interviewing her. Following is his report:

Reporter: Are you the lady of the house?

Mrs. Leary: I am, sir.

Reporter: Have you lived here long?

Mrs. Leary: Going on five years.

Reporter: Do you own this place?

Mrs. Leary: I do.

Reporter: Did the fire start in your barn?

Mrs. Leary: It did.

Reporter: What was in it?

Mrs. Leary: Five cows, a horse, and about two tons of hay in the loft.

Reporter: Is your husband an expressman?

Mrs. Leary: Indade, he is not. We all knocked our living out of those five blessed cows, and I never had a cint from the parish in all my life, and the dirty Times had no business to say it.

Reporter: How about that kerosene-lamp story?

Mrs. Leary: There is not a word of truth in the whole story. I always milked my cows by daylight, and never had a lamp of any kind or candle about the barn. It must have been set afire. Two neighbors at the far end of our alley saw a strange man come up about half-past nine in the evening. He asked them was the alley straight through. It was not five minutes till they saw the barn on fire. Before we had time to get out the horse or any of the cows it was all gone, and the fire was running in every direction. The boys turned to and saved the house. I hope to die if this isn't every word of it true. If you was a priest I wouldn't tell it any different.

Her son, Jim, later operated a major gambling house and saloon on South Halsted Street.

"I been raided a thousand times, but I've never had a real raid," he boasted.

Finally, at the age of 53, he was raided, convicted and fined $100 as a first offender. He died three years later without being caught a second time.

Big Jim O'Leary died in 1925, in the parlance of the time, a Chicago "Gangster."

Myra Bradwell
(1831–1894)

In 1868, Illinois' first woman lawyer, Myra Bradwell, founded *The Chicago Legal News*. She is credited with using her paper to prod lawyers constantly to be more honest and professional as well as with initiating the drive that created the Chicago Bar Association in 1874. Yet, both the Illinois and the U.S. supreme courts stopped this woman from practicing law in Illinois simply because she was a woman.

Mrs. Bradwell—she was the spouse of a judge—made it very clear where she stood on the issue of women's rights in a time when men felt it was up to them to decide all such questions.

"We have never said anything in the columns of the News and never intend to, from which any person could tell whether we were in favor of the Democratic or Republican party—the Methodist, Baptist, Universalist or Catholic churches. But one thing we do claim—that woman has a right to think and act as an individual—believing that if the Great Father had intended it to be otherwise—he would have placed Eve in a cage and given Adam the key."

Unfortunately for Myra Bradwell and for the legal aspirations of other American women in the early 1870s, the high courts supported a position that did believe the Great Father had put women in a cage and had given men the key to it, concluding therefore that she should not be admitted to the bar to practice law.

Myra had studied law, more to assist her husband James, a Cook County judge, than to practice law herself. But she passed the bar exam and her aptitude and self-respect drove her to become the first female candidate in Illinois certified to the Illinois Supreme Court for admission to the bar.

"No," the state's highest court responded to her in 1869.

In his book, *The First Century: The Chicago Bar Association 1874–1974*, Herman Kogan repeats the answer as stated by the court's reporter:

> The court instructs me to inform you that they are compelled to deny your application for a license to practice as an attorney in the courts of the state upon the ground that you would not be bound by the obligation necessary to be assumed where the relation of attorney and client should exist, by reason of the disability imposed by your married condition—it being assumed you are a married woman.
>
> Applications of the same character have occasionally been made by persons under twenty-one years of age, and have always been denied upon the same ground—that they are not bound by contracts, being under a legal disability in that regard.
>
> Until such disability shall be removed by legislation, the court regards itself powerless to grant your application.

She responded with a scholarly brief, citing cases holding contrary views on the subject of women. She called the words, "The disability imposed by your married condition," as:

> . . . a blow to the rights of every married woman in the great State of Illinois who is dependent on her labor for support and say to her, you can not enter into the smallest contract in relation to your earnings or separate property that can not be enforced in a court of law.

The state supreme court got the message, but not

the meaning. It then responded that the problem was rather that she was a woman.

The U. S. Supreme Court in 1873 affirmed the judgment of the Illinois court, stating that being a lawyer was not "one of the privileges of women citizens." Abandoning any adherence to the concept of law and democracy and miring themsevelves in contemporary platitudes, their response referred to the "Laws of the Creator" and stated:

> The peculiar qualities of womanhood, its gentle graces, its tender susceptibilities, its purity, its delicacy, its emotional impulses, its subordination of hard reason to sympathetic feeling are surely not qualifications for forensic strife. Nature has tempered women as little for judicial conflicts of the courtroom as for the physical conflicts of the battlefield. Woman is moulded for gentler and better things, and it is not the saints of the world who chiefly give employment to our profession.

No person offered better proof that such thinking was softheaded than Myra Bradwell. She named names when she assailed lawyers for their corruption, lack of professionalism and even their drinking in her publication. She got in the middle of battles in her writing and pushed for solid and meaningful reform based on the best study and use of the law.

Another woman, Alta M. Hulett, with Myra's help and encouragement, took another direction to be admitted to the bar after having been refused. She prepared and got passed a bill that provided that no person be excluded or debarred in Illinois from any occupation, profession or employment except military service on account of sex. Alta was admitted to the bar in 1873.

Myra focused on her newspaper and on women's rights and did not apply again for the bar. In 1890, however, the Illinois Supreme Court on its own motion granted her a license, and two years later she was admitted to practice before the U. S. Supreme Court.

The lawyers for whom she helped make the legal profession a better one in the city and state included a son and, yes, a daughter. Both enjoyed the kind of professional reputations of which their mother and her publication would have approved.

Bertha Palmer
(1849–1918)

Bertha Palmer, in the latter part of the nineteenth and the early part of the twentieth century, was indisputably the queen, the *grande dame* of Chicago society.

The authors of the 1979 book, *Who Runs Chicago,* said with their tongues in their cheeks that she was still No. 1 on the list of current Chicago socialites. They wrote:

> Yes, Bertha Palmer did pass on to that great drawing room in the sky in 1918, but no one has ever come close to the style, wit, grace, spunk and majesty with which she presided over Chicago society in the wild and woolly days. Discussing her successors is like discussing the queens who came after Elizabeth I.

Mrs. Potter Palmer, as she was referred to in the style of her day, had both the requisites and the prerequisites for her unofficial title. These included family, education, and husband, and ultimately, charisma and self-confidence. She arrived in Chicago in 1855 at the age of six, a member of the prominent Honore family from Louisville. Miss Bertha was schooled at Chicago's Dearborn Seminary and then at the Convent of the Visitation in Georgetown, Washington, D. C. There, she excelled, the school reported, "in the profane subjects."

She married Potter Palmer in 1870. He had started the store now known by the name of the man who bought it from him, Marshall Field. He had also developed State Street, drawing the city's attention away from the formerly exclusive Lake Street. He had almost finished constructing the Palmer House, the most sumptuous hotel in town. The Chicago Fire in 1871 destroyed both his new hotel and his State Street real estate, but he confidently and resolutely rebuilt them.

In addition to wealth and a successful husband, the place at the top of the city's social pecking order required Bertha to have the *sine qua non* of being a *grande dame,* the willingness at times to be preposterous and the ability to get away with it. And she did.

Her comments about art were an example. She was

unquestionably the major American patron of the French Impressionists, as her subsequent contributions to the Art Institute of Chicago would prove. Yet, it was Bertha who said:

> What is art? I cannot argue with Loredo Taft who is a pundit, but in my limited conception it is the work of some genius credited with extraordinary proclivities not given to ordinary mortals. Speaking of art . . . my husband can spit over a freight car.

In the early 1880s, she and her hotel-owning husband built a mansion, more a castle, on North Lake Shore Drive. At the time, Chicago society lived on the South Side (Prairie Avenue) or the West Side (Washington Boulevard.) While many were aghast at her switch and held a fierce loyalty especially to Prairie Avenue, most eventually moved to her domain. Some would remain aloof for decades and refuse to call on any who followed her north.

The turreted structure she called home was designed by Henry Ives Cobb and Charles Frost, and stood in contrast to the developing trend of the simple, direct architecture of the Midwest. One of the bizarre aspects of the Palmer mansion was that none of the entrance doors had outside knobs on them. They had to be opened, usually by a servant, from the inside.

Bertha is remembered for running the social event of the nineteenth century in the United States, the social side of the 1893 World's Columbian Exposition in Chicago. She was chairman of the Board of Lady Managers. As such, she chaired meetings and greeted visiting women ranging from the royalty of the world to members of the newly-burgeoning class of women professionals, writers and artists.

At the Exposition, the haughty Infanta Eulalia of Spain expressed her disdain for Palmer and for her husband's profession by referring to her as "that innkeeper's wife." The irate Bertha retorted among her friends by referring to the Spanish princess as "this bibulous representative of a degenerate monarchy." Years later, however, the two became friends.

William T. Stead, who wrote the extraordinary 1894 exposé, *If Christ Came to Chicago*, saw her, along with

Jane Addams, as a shining hope for change and amelioration in the city. In such a spirit, Bertha offered her eldest son, Potter, as a reform candidate for alderman in Chicago and worked hard for his election. As with other sons of Chicago's wealthy who became aldermen, he proved a dilettante in city council politics.

According to *Tribune* columnist Michael Kilian, she had an affair with King Edward VII of England. Other biographies describe her rather as a "favorite" of the king.

After having spent considerable time in England and Europe, she returned for a while to Chicago. There was speculation about her social status in the city. The *Chicago Inter-Ocean* in 1907 pronounced its judgment:

> Mrs. Potter Palmer returned home yesterday, and at once resumed her undisputed sway and sceptre as sovereign leader of Chicago society. During her absence in Europe there have been many speculations as to who would wear the crown this winter; each section of the city, each particular faction of society had its aspirants, its heirs-apparent, its pretenders, and its claimants to the throne. But they all faded in a flickering glimmer yesterday morning when the Pennsylvania's eighteen hour flyer rumbled into the Union Depot and Mrs. Palmer was in Chicago again.

She was a clever person of whom it was said she was never upstaged. That is not exactly true. Newspaper reporter Charles MacArthur did it. He wagered with a friend that he could get her on the phone. He won the bet after having his call announced as coming from newspaper publisher William Randolph Hearst. After a moment on the phone, she realized she had been had. She determined not to let it happen again and built an even higher wall against the press, one that included even its moguls.

Fittingly, the forever queen of Chicago's society is buried along with her family in the grandest tomb in Graceland Cemetery.

George M. Pullman
(1831–1897)

George M. Pullman, in the 1850s, thought he knew how to lift Chicago up, and he did—literally. In the 1880s and 1890s, he believed he also understood how to uplift the working people. He did not, and the results were tragic, both for him and for the city.

Born March 3, 1831, in upstate New York, he was one of eight children of a ne'er-do-well carpenter. He dropped out of school at the age of 14 and took a job as a clerk in a general store for $40 a year plus room and board. Three years later he went to work as a cabinet-maker for his older brother.

Hardly an auspicious beginning for the man who would make his mark in history as one of Chicago's most influential—and controversial—citizens.

A medium built, round-faced man, standing five feet, seven inches and weighing 160 pounds, Pullman arrived in Chicago in 1855 at the age of 24.

In the 22 years since the town was incorporated, the area around old Fort Dearborn had mushroomed to a bustling community of 30,000. What Pullman found, however, was that America's fastest growing city was wallowing in a sea of mud.

The only solution was to raise the streets in the heart of the city four to seven feet. The problem was, what to do about the buildings—some of them brick structures standing four and five stories high—which had sprung up in the low lying areas.

The answer, according to Pullman, who had helped

his late father move homes for the widening of the Erie Canal, was to jack the buildings up to the new street levels and stick new foundations under them.

Working with two other contractors in 1857, Pullman proved it could be done by raising an entire block of stores and office buildings on Lake Street, between Clark and LaSalle, in one incredible operation.

Massive timbers were propped along the cellar walls and ceilings of the buildings. He then placed six thousand jackscrews under the row of structures and engaged an army of 600 laborers to turn the screws. The late Emmett Dedmon described the operation in his book, *Fabulous Chicago:*

> At a signal, each man gave the eight or more screws of which he was in charge a half-turn, raising the buildings a fraction of an inch. As the block rose slowly into the air, it was shored up by timbers. In this way the block, with its sidewalk, was raised four feet into the air in a period of four days without interrupting the business of any of the stores in the block.

Not even one pane of glass was broken.

The following year Pullman engaged up to a thousand men to raise the Tremont House, a four-story brick hotel, at Lake and Dearborn Streets, without disturbing its occupants.

Such accomplishments soon won Pullman more business than he could handle, and by year's end the 27-year-old entrepreneur found himself on the way to becoming one of Chicago's wealthiest and most respected citizens.

Still mindful of the jolting train ride from New York, he next determined that he would build a comfortable sleeping car, and completed his first Pullman in 1864.

Assembled by a carefully selected crew of carpenters and mechanics, the palace on wheels, called the "Pioneer," boasted brocaded fabric-covered seats, highly polished woodwork, and gilt edged mirrors reflecting the light of silver-trimmed oil lamps. Hinged upper berths, cleverly concealed behind ornamental paneling, were used to store bedding during the day.

The prototype cost $20,000—five times the cost of

an ordinary rail car. At Pullman's suggestion, the "most elegant railroad car in the country" was used to carry the remains of President Abraham Lincoln to his resting place in Springfield.

With the martyred President serving to showcase his new product, Pullman was on the way to becoming one of the richest men in America.

The demand for Pullman sleepers on railroads throughout the United States soon outstripped production facilities in the shop on the site of the present Union Station, and Pullman built a new plant at 105th Street and Cottage Grove Avenue.

Because of its distance from downtown, he decided to build a company town on the shores of Lake Calumet, where his employees could live near their jobs. Thus was born the town of Pullman, with its own arcade, market, post-office, shops, theater, parks, an elegant hotel and even a library.

Few of the 5,000 families in Pullman could afford to use the library, however, since Pullman assessed an annual fee of $3 for adults for $1 for children. Gas and water were bought from Chicago and resold to Pullman householders at a profit. Cottages in the community rented for $18 a month, or $3 more than workers had been paying for similar housing in Chicago.

When the sleeping car business fell off in 1894, Pullman cut jobs, wages and working hours. But he did not lower rents, or charges for gas, water or products from the company stores.

Some workers ended up with as little as 7 cents a week cash after these charges were deducted from their paychecks. Others ended up with nothing.

When Pullman refused to meet with exasperated workers, a bitter strike ensued, and 3,000 employees left their jobs. President Grover Cleveland eventually sent Army troops from Fort Sheridan and broke the strike.

Technically, Pullman had won, but he died three years later, a broken-spirited man.

Normally his achievements in helping to pull Chicago out of its own mud, founding one of its great industries and developing a model community might have won him an imposing statue on the lakefront.

Unfortunately, it was the bitter, violent strike that stuck in people's minds when Pullman died in 1897 at the age of 66. Instead of a statue to his memory they built a grave, the likes of which had never been seen.

After a private funeral in his Prairie Avenue mansion, his lead-lined mahogany casket was lowered into a room-sized pit, with walls of reinforced concrete a foot and a half thick, that had been prepared for him in Graceland Cemetery.

Heavy steel rails were criss-crossed atop the coffin and tons of cement were poured into the hole to prevent anyone from ever desecrating the body.

He will lie for all eternity, under all that weight.

Carter H. Harrison I
(1825–1893)

In 1855 a gutsy 30-year-old land owner from Kentucky named Carter Henry Harrison rode into the frontier town of Chicago and liked what he saw. "I think Chicago is destined to be the greatest city on this continent," he told his new bride. "I have decided to cast my lot with it."

Harrison, a Yale man who had studied in Paris and Berlin, moved into a fine home on Ashland Avenue. The street was originally called Reuben, but its socialite residents chafed at being called Rubes by the hoi polloi, and renamed it Ashland after Henry Clay's Kentucky estate.

The far-sighted Harrison did well in real estate, and soon became known as the Squire of Ashland Avenue. He stabled a black bay near his home at the corner of Jackson Boulevard, and took pleasure in riding up and down the street like a plantation owner surveying his acreage.

An aristocratic man with a large head, white beard and flowing mustache, the popular Harrison was elected mayor in 1879 and would serve four consecutive terms, until 1887.

His reign was wide open. Harrison believed the

desire of each and every Chicagoan was first to make money, and then to spend it—"how and why is nobody's business."

Saloons, gambling dens and whore houses flourished during his administration. The city boasted so many vice districts that special maps had to be printed to enable visitors to find their way from one sin palace to another.

"The young city is not only vigorous but she laves her beautiful limbs daily in Lake Michigan and comes out clean and pure every morning," Harrison said.

The "Mickey Finn" was invented during this period by a saloon owner of the same name, who dropped a mysterious white powder into well-heeled customers' drinks to render them unconscious while he investigated the contents of their pockets.

Historian-journalist Emmett Dedmon called Harrison, "a man who personified this combination of wickedness and piety." In his book, *Fabulous Chicago*, he wrote:

> Harrison's aristocratic background and southern upbringing, plus a period at school in Europe, had given him a sense of noblesse oblige toward the workingman and infinite tolerance for the weaknesses of all human beings. He believed that vice was as durable as virtue, that no law ever written could prevent gambling or prostitution and that a workingman had as much right to have a glass of beer on Sunday—his only day of leisure— as on any other day of the week.

Even Harrison's severest critics, who argued that he had made Chicago the "Gomorrah of the West," conceded that he was good for business; and his most ardent enemies never questioned his personal integrity.

As the city's mayor he weathered some of Chicago's most troubled times.

He headed city government during the violent McCormick Reaper strike and the Haymarket massacre.

In fact, in 1886, on the night of the Haymarket speeches, Harrison walked unmolested through the crowd. He found the gathering orderly, and personally advised police not to antagonize the multitude. The fact that the anarchist meeting turned into a massacre was the direct result of a police inspector disobeying the mayor's instructions.

After the riot a delegation of prominent merchants called upon the mayor to demand action against the rioters. Their spokesman, Marshall Field, said, "Mr. Harrison, we represent great interests in Chicago . . ."

"Mr. Field," Harrison interrupted, "Any poor man owning a single small cottage as his sole possession has the same interest in Chicago as its richest citizen."

An uncommon man who favored silk underwear, Harrison had somehow become a champion of the common man.

People on the streets cheered as their 225-pound leader, astride his chestnut steed, galloped by, waving his slouch hat as his white beard flowed in the wind. He enjoyed riding into the city's ethnic neighborhoods, where he would climb down from the saddle and chat with the citizenry, inquiring about their children's health and listening attentively to their personal complaints.

The Democrats called him "Our Carter," and with the coming of the World's Columbian Exposition of 1893 they called him back for a fifth term, feeling nobody could better represent Chicago, with the eyes of the world upon the city by the lake.

Back in City Hall after an absence of six years, Harrison let out the word that a genuine Chicago welcome awaited visitors to the fair—which meant that gambling would be wide open, and whiskey would flow by the barrel. Harrison even appointed First Ward Alderman "Bathhouse" John Coughlin to the official reception committee.

The Exposition indeed brought Chicago unprecedented prosperity and international acclaim.

And, by all accounts, Harrison had become Chicago's all-time favorite mayor.

On October 28th, three days before the closing of the fair, Harrison proudly addressed a gathering of mayors.

"Genius is but audacity," he proclaimed, "and the audacity of the 'wild and wooly West' and of Chicago has chosen a star, and has looked upward to it, and knows nothing that it cannot accomplish."

"The World's Fair Mayor," as Harrison had become known, went home that night a happy man.

Later that same evening a gaunt young man rang Harrison's doorbell and asked to see the mayor. Harrison, whose house was always open to visitors, went to the door to see what he wanted.

The caller pulled out a revolver and fired three shots at point blank range. Harrison collapsed bleeding on his own doorstep, and was dead within 15 minutes.

His assassin, Patrick Eugene Prendergast, turned out to be a disappointed office seeker who felt that he should have been corporation counsel. On July 13, 1894, he paid for his deed on the gallows.

Three years later the martyred mayor's 36-year-old son, Carter H. Harrison II—known as Carter the Younger —was elected mayor in his father's place. The first native-born mayor in Chicago's history, he also was elected to five terms.

John W. "Bet A Million" Gates
(1855–1911)

John W. Gates was a native of DuPage County who made enormous fortunes at the end of the last century in both barbed wire and steel, but he is best remembered for the million dollars he made betting on a single horse race.

Gates was a salesman, a seller of barbed wire.

Three DeKalb men—Joseph Glidden, Jacob Haish and Colonel Isaac Ellwood—had seen an exhibit of a strip of wood with barbs on it "to keep cows in." Having agreed that the same thing could be done with wire, they then invented such a barbed wire. Gates, leaving his job in a hardware store, went to work as a salesman for Ellwood. At age 21, he was sent to Texas to sell ranchers on the idea that barbed wire, rather than cowboys, could be used to keep cattle from straying.

After watching Doc Lightfoot and his Diamond King medicine show, Gates figured out how to sell his product. He set up a rodeo in Military Plaza in San Antonio, and took bets that not one cow would break through his barbed wire. Using the tamest of cows and highly-secured wire, he won his bets and repeated his rodeo week after week. It sold barbed wire for Gates and it brought a land revolution to Texas and the West.

Making money enthralled Gates. He moved from selling to manufacturing barbed wire, starting as a pirate operator who ignored others' patents. In court, he successfully challenged what seemed an airtight patent monopoly. He became the top manufacturer of barbed wire in the country and opened offices in the Rookery Building in Chicago.

On the floor above Gates' headquarters in the 1890s was the Illinois Steel Company, beset by a violent strike, a sag in orders and questions about stock watering. For Gates this was opportunity. Marshall Field I and the other directors let him take over and invest the firm's money in new ideas. With a lot of help from a turned-around economy, the firm soon became second only to the vast Carnegie Works in producing steel.

Working at his office all day did not keep "Bet A Million" from playing poker all night.

"Life is a gamble," he always said.

Gates' nickname, "Bet A Million," came from a bet he made in England on the horse Royal Flush. How much was actually bet is not clear, but his winnings were judged to be over $1,000,000 and the British press picked up on it.

His battles with J. P. Morgan included several victories and often struck at the heart of the financier's steel, railroad and banking trusts. Ultimately, in a show-down with Gates out of the country, Morgan won and ended a dream "Bet A Million" had of creating the great steel empire. Gates, when he died in 1907, left between $40 and $50 million dollars, not as much as he had wanted to accumulate, but enough to bet on a few horse races.

Vina Fields
(the late 19th century)

How is one to judge Vina Fields, the madame of the largest brothel in Chicago in the 1890s?

Certainly, as kindly as history has the Everleigh sisters, who operated the most famous such house from 1900 to 1911.

Vina was black and so were all her "boarders." There were never less than 40 of them between when she opened in "The Levee" red-light district in the mid-1880s and the late 1890s when she closed. In 1893, while the World's Columbian Exposition was in full swing, she had as many as 80 young women working in her establishment.

It was said of Vina that she gave her boarders a larger percentage of their earnings than any other madame in Chicago.

Vina also enforced decorum and what William T. Stead in *If Christ Came to Chicago* referred to as "decency." He wrote:

> The rules and regulations of the Fields house, which are printed and posted in every room enforce decorum and decency with pains and penalties which could hardly be more strict if they were drawn up for the regulations of a Sunday School.

What was forbidden, according to *The Gem of the Prairie*, by Herbert Asbury, included hustling at the windows (a common practice in the Levee), drunkenness, and indecent exposure in the parlors and hallways. Twice a week, she held court. Those who had transgressed or fought were fined, set to menial tasks, refused the privilege of the parlors or expelled. The latter included the notorious strong-arm woman, Flossie Moore.

Stead left us this description of Vina:

> Strange though it may appear, [she] has acquired the respect of nearly all who knew her. An old experienced police matron emphatically declared that "Vina is a good woman," and I think it will be admitted by all who knew her, that she is probably as good as any woman can be who conducts so bad a business . . . She is bringing up her daughter who knows nothing of the life of her mother in the virginal seclusion of a convent school, and she contributes of her bounty to maintain her unfortunate sisters whose husbands down South are among the hosts of unemployed. Nor is her bounty confined to her own family. Every day this whole winter [1893–4] she had fed a hungry, ragged regiment of the out-of-works. The day before I called, 201 men had had free dinners of her providing.

How wealthy her business made her, history has not recorded. She did not make the *Chicago Tribune*'s list of self-made millionaires published in the 1890s. But, then, the exclusion might have been for other reasons than the amount of her wealth.

Louis Sullivan
(1856–1924)

"Louis Sullivan was a relative, my father's cousin."

The woman on the phone sounded to be in her eighties, a fact confirmed by the story she was telling.

"I read what you wrote in the *Tribune*," she told the reporter, "and I wanted to share with you a personal experience with him."

It was before World War I. Her family, she said, was "quite well off." They had a cook and on this special occasion, her mother hired an additional servant to help prepare and serve the meal.

"My father had built an apartment building," she said. "Bay windows at the time were the latest thing and

he had put one in. He wanted to show it off to his cousin, the architect."

Her mother scheduled a dinner party for the occasion, inviting another couple and a woman friend to match up with their guest, who was separated from his wife at the time. The additional servant was taken on and the meal meticulously planned.

Guests were scheduled to arrive at six. Louis Sullivan showed up at five.

"To get him out from under foot, my father took him to see the new apartment building," the woman reported. "He proudly showed him the bay window."

Sullivan had a one-word comment, "Hurumph!"

The two men then returned to the apartment.

Sullivan put on his coat and left.

"My mother was furious," the phone caller said. "Her eyes were blazing. She looked at my father and said, 'I never want that man to come into this apartment again.'"

The story was pure Louis Sullivan. He was gruff; at times, anti-social; and had no tolerance for the latest nuance in a style of architecture he despised.

This same man, so ungracious in this long-remembered vignette, is considered by many architectural historians to be the "Father of modern architecture."

Sullivan's profoundly radical and pivotal concept was democracy in architecture. Sullivan did not believe the measure of architecture had to be what imitated the past the best, what was awesome because of its proportions or what was trendy. He was convinced form follows function. By that he meant the purpose and use of a building should determine its shape, appearance and style. He hated architecture that overawed and tried to impress people, and loved a more democratic concept in which it pleased and served humanity.

His Transportation Building at the World's Columbian Exposition in 1893 stood out as the only piece of creative, new architecture on the world's fair grounds. His design for what is now Carson, Pirie, Scott & Co. offered Chicago a store, and not a generic building used as one. Its windows dramatically framed the merchandise they attempted to sell. His Auditorium and the Schiller Building are two of the greatest, and most functional theaters ever designed. Sullivan designed the Getty Tomb in Graceland Cemetery that Frank Lloyd Wright called a "symphony in stone." His creative works include, in addition, homes, banks, hotels and office buildings.

Sullivan's writings, especially *Kindergarten Chats* and *The Autobiography of an Idea,* have guided young architects in creating a revolution in the field that replaced the imitative, neoclassical designs with the lean, meaningful styles of modern American architecture.

Frank Lloyd Wright, who started his career working for Louis Sullivan, called him, "Der Meister" (The Master).

Sullivan's gruffness and his hurumphs cost him not only invitations to dinner parties but also commissions later in life. But his final years, in which he also developed a drinking problem, were not entirely lost ones. He turned to writing and fulfilled the role that Wright saw him best at, teaching.

James "Sheriff Jim" Brown
(18??–1892)

James Brown was a popular horse race figure in the Chicago of the 1890s. Known as Sheriff Jim, because he had once served as a sheriff of Lee County, Texas, he still paraded around with a six-shooter that had 12 notches in the handle.

The last track Brown ever saw was the one in Garfield Park, which Republican Mayor Hempstead Washburne vowed to shut down in 1892 because of neighborhood complaints about the unwholesome characters it attracted.

The mayoral threat caused near panic in the heart of First Ward Alderman John "Bathhouse" Coughlin, whose very mission on the City Council was to protect the racing interests.

"You can't do that!" bellowed the Bath, who owned several horses at the track. "You can't do that! It's unfair. It's . . . it's . . . un-American, that's what!"

Despite his eloquence, the license to operate the track was denied.

The track opened without a permit nevertheless, and racing got underway during the month of August with Democrat Coughlin and his other Council cohorts thumbing their nose at the mayoral authority.

The fun ended on September 2nd, when a score of police officers descended upon Garfield Park with billy clubs swinging and arrested all the jockeys and Pinkerton guards hired by track operators, hauling them off to the Desplaines Street station.

The next day police did it again, arresting every track employee they could lay hands on, while ignoring the fuming Coughlin, who shouted insults at the law. The alderman then went down to the jailhouse and bailed out the arrestees.

Sunday was a day of rest, but Alderman Coughlin personally announced there would be racing the following day, the police and the mayor be damned.

On Monday the track swarmed with fans as five wagonloads of police rolled up, only to find themselves locked out. The cops broke down the gates and rounded up 800 track employees and customers, the biggest bust in history up to that time. Again Coughlin posted bail for his friends.

The following day, Garfield Park opened for business once again, with 1,500 people in the bleachers. Sheriff Jim Brown had had enough, and decided to personally see that the fans were not disappointed.

Climbing atop the barn in which he kept his horses, the one-time Texas lawman, who had killed a dozen men in his day, jumped up and down on the roof, twirling his .44 caliber revolver and shouting, "By God, these police ain't goin' to stop these races no more!"

But at 3 o'clock sharp the lawmen surged through the gates, as Brown denounced them from his perch on the roof.

"Come down here! We want you!" a police officer commanded.

"You got no warrant, you sons-a-bitches!" bellowed Brown.

Police fired several shots into the air, and Brown scampered down from the barn and took off down the track like a racehorse. The Texan pointed himself toward the track entrance, with six police officers in hot pursuit.

Halfway around the oval Police Officer John Powell caught up with Brown and clamped his arm on the fleeing man's shoulder. Brown spun free, however, pulled his .44, and shot the policeman through the head.

As Officer Powell fell to the track dead, Brown took off as fast as his Texas legs could carry him with a small posse on his tail. Two blocks from the track Brown darted around a corner and ran smack into Officer William Jones.

The desperate Brown again drew his revolver and pulled the trigger, but this time the .44 failed to fire. Jones pulled his service revolver and fired two shots, killing Brown instantly.

In the dead man's pockets police found $7,420 in cash, and the extra bullets he had neglected to reload into his gun. The Texas pistol, with 12 notches cut into the handle, lay at his side. The 13th man Brown killed had proved his undoing.

According to Herman Kogan and Lloyd Wendt in *Lords of the Levee*, the public was outraged at the murder of Officer Powell, but Bathhouse John took the floor at the next City Council meeting and praised Sheriff Brown as a brave man and true.

"Jim Brown was a good man and I don't think he meant to shoot that policeman," Coughlin argued. "This thing that happened the other day is a—a—a onslaught on a perfectly law-abiding amusement."

He fought to keep the track operating, but this time the gates to Garfield Park were locked once and for all. And the loud-mouthed Texas lawman who tried to keep Chicago's horses running with a six-gun was carried to his grave.

Little Egypt
(????–????)

"Little Egypt" introduced the Hootchie Kootchie to America in the Streets of Cairo exhibit on the Midway at the World's Columbian Exposition in 1893. Or did she? Or did they?

The controversy has continued for a century.

It was long a matter of faith that there was a Little Egypt and that she gracefully entertained customers at the Chicago world's fair in Jackson Park. As the years went by, the number of men who "remembered" seeing her seemed to increase. Others, however, said such claimants may have seen Little Egypt dance, but they did so in the burlesque and vaudeville houses on South State Street long after the World's Columbian Exposition.

Old newspaper files contain two obituaries and one divorce notice for individuals who claimed to have been the "original" Little Egypt. The deaths were Katherine Devine in 1903, and Frieda Spyropolous or Fahreda Mahzar in 1937. The woman claiming the title at the time of her divorce was Gertrude Warnick. Oh yes, and we shouldn't forget Seida De Kreko, who subsequently owned an amusement park and beach in Rome, Ill.

A letter writer told the newspaper he had seen two different women on the same block of South State Street billed as Little Egypt.

Columnists in the *Chicago Tribune* and the *Sun-Times*, 30 years apart, challenged the existence of Little Egypt. So did a hotel, the Water Town Inn, that wanted proof of her existence to put on its wall.

The most famous claimant to wiggle was Frieda or Fahreda Spyropolous or Mizhar or Mahzar (depending on which news story you were reading). She sued Metro-Goldwyn-Mayer over its movie, *The Great Zeigfield*, in which Little Egypt is portrayed as dancing in the buff. She was also bold enough to perform at the age of 62 at the A Century of Progress Exposition in 1933. Some versions said she danced, but was no competition for the younger performers at The Streets of Paris. Others said she only appeared at intervals, while another stated she simply talked to customers.

She had herself authenticated by former Mayor Carter Harrison II and Edward Artekema, president of an organization of people who attended the 1893 fair.

On the other hand, Congressman Sol Bloom, chairman of the House Committee on Foreign Affairs, repeatedly denied there was a "Little Egypt" at the World's Columbian Exposition—and he had been manager of the American Midway at the fair in 1893.

We like the letter that appeared in the *Chicago Tribune*'s Lin-O-Type column about the controversy headlined: "There Were Dozens of Little Egypt."

> To cast the light of reason upon the "Little Egypt"
> controversy: "There Were Dozens of Little Egypt."
> This name started as a general designation for

"Muscle" or "hootchy-kootchy" dancers in Oriental shows on the Midway of 1893, particularly in the large concession called "The Streets of Cairo." I can remember seeing a couple of dozen of such so-called dancers, all doing ballyhoos in front of their booths at the same time. The spielers would call them Fatima, Little Egypt, the Sultan's Favorite, or by any other name that happened to strike their fancy at the moment.

I saw Fahreda Mahzar, who claimed to be the first "Little Egypt," both at the fair and later on South State Street. In both places other "Little Egypts" were being advertised in the same block at the same time.

A.E.E.

Adolph Luetgert
(1845–1910)

Adolph Luetgert was a broad-shouldered bear of a man, six feet tall, 200 pounds, with huge beefy fists and rolls of fat on the back of his thick neck to testify to his voracious appetite for food and drink.

His claim to a place in Chicago's history depends on that which he did, or did not, one day slip into his sausage machine.

A tanner by trade, Luetgert came to the city from his native Germany shortly before the Chicago Fire of 1871. He liked to boast, in later years, that he arrived with only three cents in his pocket.

That Luetgert was a man to be reckoned with became apparent in 1879 when an obscure loafer named Hugh McGowan was found dead in the alley behind Luetgert's saloon and grocery at Clybourn and Webster Avenues.

The evidence indicated that McGowan had been beaten and tossed bodily out the back door of the saloon, but what killed him was a thick plug of chewing tobacco that had been crammed down his throat.

Police questioned Luetgert at length, but made no arrest. What they suspected, but couldn't prove, was that Luetgert had warned the uncouth Irishman: "You spit on my floor . . . and I'll ram that chaw of tobacco right down your throat!"

Two years later Luetgert's wife died unexpectedly while in confinement awaiting childbirth. There were rumors about that death, too, but nothing ever came of them.

As for the grieving husband, he shut down the saloon, opened a sausage factory, and married 26-year-old Louisa Bicknese, a comely, blonde servant girl who had been working for a family in the Fox River Valley.

On their wedding day Luetgert, who was 10 years older than Louisa, gave her an unusual 14-carat gold ring, three times the thickness of an ordinary wedding band. On the inside the sausage maker had engraved the bride's new initials, "L.L."

Business prospered, and Luetgert's sausages became widely known for their quality. In 1894, with visions of becoming "Sausage King of the World," he built a new $141,000 plant at Hermitage Avenue and Diversey Parkway. Next door to the factory on Hermitage he built a great three-story home for Louisa and their two young sons, Louis and Elmer.

Neighbors said that Luetgert, a man of violent temper, quarreled often with his wife and at times drove her from their home. Eventually he packed his clothes and moved into the factory, where he converted an ante-room to his office into living quarters.

Mary Simerling, the Luetgerts' young servant girl, began spending her evenings with the Master in his office-bedroom. A wealthy widow, Catherine Feldt, also visited him in the dark of night, as well as did other women, according to neighbors.

In the spring of 1897 Luetgert closed down the sausage works for renovation. During the last week of March he had 375 pounds of crude potash delivered to the closed factory, along with 50 pounds of arsenic. Late in April he had his workmen break up the mixture and toss it into one of three large sausage vats in the basement.

On the evening of May 1, after the servant girl had gone for the night, Luetgert turned on the steam to the vat and melted down the potash and arsenic mixture. He then picked up his lantern and went next door to visit his 42-year-old wife.

Louisa, a slightly-built woman, barely 5 feet tall and weighing just 117 pounds, was in the kitchen, reading.

Twelve-year-old Louis had just come home from the circus to find his mother sitting by the stove, huddled in a brown flannel wrapper and gray shawl.

"Well, was the circus worth the 10 cents?" she asked the excited youngster.

Louis was about to tell her all about it when his father came in through the door, lantern in hand, and said sternly, "It's after 10 o'clock. You go to bed now."

"Yes, Pa," the boy answered obediently, and went up to his room. Some time later, before drifting off to sleep, he heard his mother and father go out.

The next morning the two boys were surprised to find their father rummaging around the kitchen when they came down for breakfast.

"Your mother has gone to visit your aunt," he told them.

But Louisa never returned home, and six days later—after the boys had made pests of themselves asking neighbors if anyone had seen their mother—Luetgert hitched up his wagon and drove over to the East Chicago Avenue police station to report his wife missing.

Police Captain Herman Schuettler put his best men on the case. It did not take them long to confirm the couple's domestic spats. Furthermore, Mrs. Luetgert's sister, Wilhelmine Mueller, said Louisa had not been to visit her as Luetgert had claimed.

Several neighbors reported seeing Louisa and Adolph going into the sausage works together on the night she disappeared. Frank Bialk, the plant watchman, said Luetgert had sent him away on an errand, and then gave him the rest of the night off.

When Bialk returned the next morning he found Luetgert asleep in his office with his feet propped up on his desk. The fuming vat in the basement was overflowing, and there was a greasy substance on the floor, he told detectives. A chair was placed next to the vat, as though someone had sat vigil during the long night.

Schuettler's men drained the vat and detectives poked through its gooey residue with sticks. Policeman

Walter Dean found a small piece of bone, a cheap ring guard, and a wide gold wedding band engraved with the initials "L.L." in the sediment.

Luetgert was arrested and tried for murder. His defense lawyers argued that it was not uncommon to find bone fragments in a sausage plant—and, as for the steaming cauldron in the basement, Luetgert had simply been making soap!

Prosecutor Charles Deneen (who would later become governor) offered evidence that steam turned on in a vat of potash and arsenic would produce a seething, searing, caustic brew capable of consuming a human body in about two hours.

Medical experts testified that the tiny bone fragment found in the residue from the vat was a human sesamoid, from the tendon under the big toe.

Relatives of the missing woman identified the "L.L." wedding ring as Louisa's. Defense lawyers claimed police had "planted" the ring in the vat, but they could not account for how police had obtained it if, indeed, Louisa was still missing.

After two trials Luetgert was found guilty, despite the absence of a corpus delecti.

"She'll come back! Then you'll see what fools you've been," he shouted as he was led off to Joliet prison, where he died, still protesting his innocence.

The "Boiling Cauldron Murder" case, as it was known, had a marked effect on the eating habits of Chicagoans for a long time to come. With Luetgert's arrest rumor spread throughout the city that his missing wife had been made up into sausage. Never mind that the plant was closed at the time, it was too gruesome a story not to pass on, and people stopped eating sausage, just thinking about it.

The prospect of having Mrs. Luetgert over for dinner was one thing, but as the main course—well, that was something else.

Neighborhood youngsters even put together a clumsy verse, which they chanted while jumping rope on warm summer nights:

Old man Luetgert made sausage out of his wife.

He turned on the steam,

His wife began to scream,

"There'll be a hot time in the old town tonight!"

Charles T. Yerkes
(1839–1905)

In the 1890s, Charles T. Yerkes was the man whom Chicagoans loved to rant against. Streetcar and cablecar riders criticized him for delays, overcrowding and breakdowns. Reformers blamed him for bribing the City Council to get exclusive track franchises on the city's streets.

One hundred years have passed. The delays and the poor condition of the moving stock have been forgiven; the corruption, forgotten. Still, people mumble the name Yerkes in ire in Chicago today when informed that it was he who girded the Loop with the atrociously ugly structure of elevated tracks.

Criticism never bothered Yerkes. He was more interested in making money than kowtowing to critics.

His economic credo reportedly included such dicta as: "Buy old junk, fix it up a little, unload it on the other fellow" and his response to running more cars on a line was, "Why should I? It's the strapholders who pay the dividends."

Twenty-five years after his death, enmity was still so strong against Yerkes in Chicago that Lloyd Lewis and Henry Justin Smith wrote in 1929: "For years the name of Yerkes had been pronounced with suspicion, with that facetious tolerance which has saved Chicagoans so much strain and concealed so many skeletons."

Despite all this, the city was fascinated by its traction mogul, and even proud of him in a perverse way.

In his native Philadelphia, he had been a financial whiz kid who handled the sale of municipal bonds and who had done so successfully for a decade. He raised funds for the city and made a fortune for himself. In early 1872, however, a Depression hit the East Coast, partially triggered by the economic losses resulting from the Chicago Fire. Yerkes was overextended and could not cover his technique of buying bonds to keep the value high. He, as a result, went to jail.

After he was released, he recouped his losses and paid off his creditors.

Theodore Dreiser later wrote a novel, *The Financier*, based on Yerkes' experiences in Philadelphia. He followed it with a book on his machinations in Chicago, called *The Titan*.

Chicago was very ripe for a would-be traction czar. The city had installed its first cablecars in the early 1880s. It would add "L" trains, at first pulled by locomotives and later electrified, in the 1890s. The rapid expansion of the city brought almost unlimited traction opportunities.

Chicago's population doubled in the 1870s, again in the 1880s and once more in the 1890s. It almost tripled in area with annexations in the late 1880s. All this meant new streets on which to run transit lines. The City Council needed to approve a lease for any extension,

exacting bribes to do so. Ultimately, Yerkes wanted his franchises on the city streets to be more permanent and pushed for what critics called an "eternal monopoly."

His representative on the City Council was Alderman Johnny "de Pow" Powers, who handled the boodle for the other council members. A partially-reformed City Council led by Mayor Carter Harrison II took Yerkes on and battled him ferociously. The swing votes against him came from Bathhouse John Coughlin and Hinky Dink Kenna, the deeply corrupt aldermen of the First Ward. Yerkes had offered too much money to the pair, who believed in "Sticking to the small thing."

As the fight ensued, a large reform element pushed for municipal ownership of the transit system. Still, Yerkes knew how to play the public. He rehabilitated and put back into use two tunnels under the Chicago River and donated to the city double bridges at Lake, Clark and Wells Streets.

Even more dramatically, he contributed a million dollars to the University of Chicago to buy a telescope. It is now at Williams Bay on Lake Geneva, Wis., and bears his name.

He used the very well-promoted donation to give the impression of his financial solidity and kick up the price when he sold his traction holdings in Chicago.

Yerkes moved to New York and London, where he helped develop the subway or "tube" system. Some Chicagoans believed he should have wound up in jail instead, where escape tunnels could have been his main occupation.

1900s

"Bathhouse" John Coughlin
(1860–1938)

Michael "Hinky Dink" Kenna
(1858–1946)

John Joseph Coughlin and Michael Kenna were both products of Chicago's lusty First Ward. They grew up to become known as its two most unsophisticated and unrepentant rapscallions.

The two of them, working in tandem, would dominate the First Ward and its utterly lawless Levee district for decades.

Coughlin was known as "Bathhouse" or the "Bath," because he once worked as a rubber in a Turkish bath. Kenna was called "Hinky Dink" because of his small stature. The two of them would go down in history as the "Lords of the Levee."

Coughlin, a powerfully built man, 6 feet tall, with broad shoulders and a neck like a bull, was noted for his good nature.

He started rubbing backs in a Clark Street spa, and worked his way up to head rubber in the Palmer House baths, where senators, congressmen, politicians and businessmen were among his treasured customers. He soon saved enough to open a saloon, buy his own bathhouse on east Madison Street, and then another in the Brevoort Hotel in the heart of the Loop.

An ardent Democrat, he once explained, "A Republican is a man who wants you t' go t' church every Sunday. A Democrat says if a man wants t' have a glass of beer on Sunday, he can have it."

A garish dresser who sported orange vests, green trousers and lavender tail coats, the Bath made a fortune in politics and lost it all on the horses.

Kenna, a quiet man, discontinued his formal education at the age of 10 and got a job hawking newspapers. He also sold food at the race track, and made extra money running errands for saloonkeepers. By the time he was 24 he had saved enough to open a saloon of his own.

Coughlin's place was called the Silver Dollar, and had large silver dollars painted on the ceiling. Kenna owned the Workingmen's Exchange on Clark Street.

Both got their starts in politics as precinct workers. While Coughlin was a back-slapper and glad-hander, Kenna was known as the glummest little man in the Democratic organization.

"Coughlin was all sound and fury; Kenna was silence and action," wrote Herman Kogan and Lloyd Wendt in their *Lords of the Levee.*

66

It was Kenna who, in one of his longest speeches of record, told Coughlin, "Let's stick together and we'll rule the roost some day."

In the late 1800s every ward had two aldermen, elected in alternate years to two-year terms. Coughlin was elected to the City Council in 1893, and Kenna took his seat beside him in 1897.

Together they built an organization of saloonkeepers, gamblers, pimps, pickpockets and brothel owners who would help them, term after term, hold their seats in City Hall through both Democratic and Republican administrations.

The City Council was a notorious band of boodlers, whose opportunities for corruption and graft knew no bounds.

Bathhouse and Hinky Dink had their own limits, however.

When transit magnate Charles T. Yerkes offered them $150,000 for a favorable vote on a matter of interest to him pending in City Council, they turned him down and told Mayor Carter Harrison II of the bribe offer.

Explaining their stand to Harrison, they said they practiced a credo of "keep clear of th' big stuff, it's dangerous. Stick to th' small stuff; there's little risk and in th' long run it pays a damned sight more."

The indignant Bathhouse asserted, "I ain't going to be unethicult for nobody."

On another occasion when Harrison complained to Kenna about a corrupt police captain, Kenna defended the lawman saying, "He's one of our best captains. I can always count on him. He's a good conscientious son of a bitch, even if he does run a whorehouse."

Coughlin and Kenna were best known throughout the city—and the United States—for their First Ward Ball, a bacchanal of epic proportions, staged in the Armory, through which the two ward leaders enriched their coffers by about $50,000 a year—a lot of money, especially at the turn of the century.

The annual event featured a grotesque masquerade of pimps, pickpockets and prostitutes, safecrackers and sadists, gamblers and every known character of the underworld, parading with the city's leading politicians.

The grand march would be led by the Hink and the Bath, each with one of Chicago's most notorious madams on his arm.

Waiters paid $5 apiece for the privilege of working the affair because of the lavish tips they would collect from the drunken revelers.

So successful did the First Ward Ball become that it had to be moved to the Coliseum, which had more space.

Nevertheless, the shoulder-to-shoulder crowds were so dense that one newspaper reporter wrote, "Those already drunk were forced to stand erect."

The Bath, who fancied himself a poet (although it was rumored that mischievous newspaper reporters fed him his lines), started off one annual ball by declaring:

On with the dance
Let the orgy be perfectly proper
Don't drink, smoke or spit on the floor
and say keep your eye on the copper.

The *Chicago Tribune* wrote, "If a great disaster had

befallen the Coliseum, there would not have been a second story worker, a dip or plug ugly, porch climber, dope fiend or scarlet woman remaining in Chicago."

The balls inevitably degenerated into riots, which prompted the normally introverted Hink to observe, "Chicago ain't no sissy town."

Public outcry forced Mayor Fred Busse to finally lower the curtain on the annual orgies in 1909, but the sponsors retained their seats of power in the City Council for years to come.

Coughlin once accused a Civic Federation leader of libeling him after a particularly damaging report denouncing him as a grafter and crook. The charges of corruption and boodling were not what bothered him, however.

"You said I was born in Waukegan. That ain't true and I demand a retraction," he insisted, with Kenna at his side.

One of their protégés was Big Jim Colosimo, who started out as a bagman for the aldermen before he advanced to head the city's underworld empire. After Colosimo was murdered, Bathhouse knelt at his bier and recited the Catholic prayer for the dead.

With Colosimo's death, the aldermen's awesome power waned. In 1923, when legislation reduced the number of aldermen from each ward to one, Kenna stepped aside and let Coughlin keep the seat, which he held until his death in 1938, operating out of Capone's old Lexington Hotel. Thanks to his affection for the ponies, he died $56,000 in debt.

Kenna remained a powerful ward committeeman, and died a wealthy man in 1946.

Coughlin's most memorable legislation was a law requiring 12-foot walls around cemeteries.

A curious Mayor Harrison once pulled Kenna aside and said, "Tell me, Mike, do you think John is crazy or just full of dope?"

Kenna answered, "No, John isn't dotty and he ain't full of dope. To tell you th' God's truth, Mr. Mayor, they ain't found a name for it yet."

Cap'n George Wellington Streeter
(1837–1921)

George Wellington Streeter, a squatter and former ship captain, was Chicago's Don Quixote. He saw himself as the last of the explorers and pioneers, claiming and settling vacant land as he battled the windmills of the city's establishment.

Chicago refused him the land to which he laid title, but for his being so quaint, it named a section of the city for him.

He did not wear armor as Don Quixote did, but rather donned an image to help achieve his goal. His projection was that of a colorful, gun-toting, self-sufficient rebel unaware that a large powerful city out there saw him as a gnat on its hide.

In actual fact, he was a fairly sophisticated entrepreneur and hustler, a man who had spent years entertaining crowds as a menagerie and theater owner before taking on his highly publicized and ultimately unsuccessful venture to claim a section of the city's lakefront.

Chicago Daily News reporter Bob Casey described Capt. Streeter's appearance in the late 1890s:

> The man was tall and gaunt and old and dusty. He had sharp blue eyes, a face that looked like wrinkled leather and an incredible scraggly mustache stained with tobacco juice.

Capt. Streeter lived or rather squatted in a former steamboat that had been beached on the sand several thousand yards east of Pine Street (now, north Michigan Avenue) and one third of a mile north of the Chicago River. The area appeared on no maps of the city, state or country because it was ignored shoreline that the lake was filling in by piling up with ridges of sand.

Today, that same area bordered by the river, Michigan Avenue, and Lake Shore Drive on the east and on the north, is worth billions of dollars, even without the improvements on it. Then, it was unused and unclaimed.

Capt. Streeter, after his steamboat, *The Reutan*, beached there in 1886, was the first to settle on the land and claim it. The city establishment would try eventually to remove him. Several attempts would lead to armed battles for the land and decades of litigation. He claimed the land was not part of Chicago, since it was not on the map or in the legal documents. Rather, he said, it was "The District of Lake Michigan."

He irritated the powerful men of Chicago further not only by living on this land whose future was starting to become clear, but also by running it as a wide-open area in violation of the city's gambling and liquor laws. In the meantime, he sold title to plots of the area and allowed people to build shacks and shanties on them.

The city followed his adventures and efforts in the newspapers, reading interviews with him that philosophized:

> This is a frontier town, and its got to go through its red-blooded youth. A church and a WCTU [Woman's Christian Temperance Union] never growed a big town yet.

Capt. Streeter knew the press and he knew how to play it. He had been a captain in the Civil War and became the owner of a menagerie of animals with which he toured the Midwest. These included such wild creatures as a bear, deer and a wolverine. Also, he had an enormous white pig that he billed as a "white elephant." He moved to Chicago, where he then purchased an interest in the Apollo Theater, later selling it at a substantial profit to the boss of Chicago politics and crime, Mike McDonald.

After 20 years of such entrepreneuring efforts, Capt. Streeter built *The Reutan* to ply the Great Lakes.

He took a shipload of people on an excursion to Milwaukee in 1886, but they did not consider it a seaworthy enough vessel to make the return trip with him. They were right. It beached on Chicago's shoreline.

He and Mary "Ma" Streeter decided to leave the ship there and live in it. They made it their home and claimed the land. The millionaires who lived north of Division Street along the lakefront had no claim to the land, and realized they would have to get rid of the Streeters if they wanted to make one. They hired detectives and strong-arm goons to provoke and dislodge them and then have them hauled into court for disturbing the peace.

Streeter defended his land, however, with a rifle and good marksmanship, refusing to be arrested when the police came to serve warrants. The public of Chicago took the Streeters' side, and the police refrained from supporting the private hirelings sent to dislodge him and his growing community.

In one of these battles, a man was shot and killed. Capt. Streeter was charged with and convicted of murder. He had not fired a shot and the conviction, he argued, was the result of poor legal counsel. He secured a black attorney by the name of Anderson, who eventually got Judge Edward Dunne, a future mayor of Chicago and governor of Illinois, to release him.

The court battle over ownership of his property was not settled so easily or favorably, however. His wife had died while he was in jail. He married again, and his second wife continued his legal fight after he died in 1921. His heirs and the people to whom he sold land rights in his District of Lake Michigan eventually lost all claims to it in the 1940s.

Today, if you look on the buses heading into the area, you will see that the heirs of the winners of the battle have nodded in deference to the one-time squatter and have called the extremely valuable high-rise area, "Streeterville."

The Everleigh Sisters

Ada
(1876–????)

& Minna
(1878–????)

Chicagoans, looking back over their city's history, are fascinated by four phenomena or events: The Chicago Fire, the Fort Dearborn Massacre, Al Capone, and the

73

Everleigh Club, not necessarily in that order. People—including many high school students who do not know what the Fort Dearborn Massacre was or when the Chicago Fire occurred—can tell you about the Everleigh Club and its owners.

The two sisters ran the Everleigh Club, the most expensive whorehouse in Chicago, from 1900 to 1911. Its prices were $10, $25 and $50. The $10 fee was little more than an entrance charge. If a customer, in the course of the evening, did not spend $50, he was requested not to come back. It is difficult to translate that into current dollars, but it would certainly amount to $500 today.

So what did a man get for such an extravagant outlay of cash?

First, there was the ambiance.

The first floor of the brothel at 2131-3 S. Dearborn St., in the city's Levee district, included: a music room, a library, a grand ballroom lit by cut-glass chandeliers and an art gallery, furnished with some very good paintings. Also there was a dining area for large parties; a Pullman Buffet, made from part of a railroad dining car; and several parlors where "boarders" could entertain gentlemen customers.

Leading to the second floor were two mahogany staircases, flanked by potted palms and statues of goddesses. The parlors these led to included ones labeled and decorated in: Moorish, Gold, Silver, Copper, Red, Rose, Green, Blue, Oriental, Japanese, Egyptian and Chinese. Each contained—in addition to cushions, a drum and plush rugs—a gold-plated spittoon and a fountain that sprayed perfume.

What else did the club offer besides ambiance?

Minna indicated the "how" if not exactly the "what" in a speech she made to her courtesans the first night the club was open. Her talk was reconstructed in *Come Into My Parlor*, the sisters' biography, by Charles Washburn.

"Be polite, patient and forget what you are here for," Minna had said in her final instructions. "Gentlemen are only gentlemen when properly introduced. We shall see that each girl is properly presented to each guest. No lining up for selection as in other houses. There shall be no cry, 'In the parlor, girls,' when visitors arrive. Be patient is all I ask. And remember that the Everleigh Club has no time for the rough element, the clerk on a holiday or a man without a check-book.

"It's going to be difficult, at first, I know. It means, briefly, that your language will have to be lady-like and that you will forego the entreaties you have used in the past. You have the whole night before you and one $50 client is more desirable than five $10 ones. Less wear and tear. You will thank me for this advice in later years. Your youth and beauty are all you have. Preserve it. Stay respectable by all means.

"We know men better than you do. Don't rush 'em or roll 'em. We will permit no monkeyshines, no knockout drops, no robberies, no crimes of any description. We'll supply the clients; you amuse them in a way they've never been amused before. Give, but give interestingly and with mystery. I want you girls to be proud that you are in the Everleigh Club. That is all. Now spruce up and look your best."

The two sisters, who grew up in a village near Louisville, Ky., had a grandmother who signed her letters, "Everly Yours." In looking for a pseudonym that buried their past as respectable young wives who both abandoned abusive husbands, they adopted the word "Everly" as their last name, changing the spelling.

Although never involved directly or indirectly in prostitution, they opened a high-ticket brothel in Omaha and saw it fail for lack of wealthy customers.

They then surveyed Washington, New York, New Orleans and San Francisco for possible opportunities, and chose Chicago. Their grand opening was Jan. 1, 1900, a date that many people throughout the world were strongly convinced would be the end of the universe.

The Everleigh Club prospered, despite attacks on it by reformers and the 1911 Vice Commission Report, which singled it out but refused to name the club.

Minna, commenting some 20 years later, said:

[The crusaders] not only filled us with embarrassment and shame, but they made fools of themselves . . .

We gave little resistance to the rebels. Truthfully, we were open to offers. We believed we could have adjusted an age-old problem if given half the chance to supervise its operations. We weren't consulted.

The boarders did well. None is ever known to have left to "go straight." They made up to $100 a week, more than ten times what they might have earned in the sweatshops which were the personal hell of young women of the day.

The sisters did even better. After a brochure they thought restrained and dignified fell into the hands of Mayor Carter H. Harrison II, the word went out to them to close up shop. They did, leaving with over $1 million in cash, considerable jewelry and I.O.U.s amounting to $25,000.

The Everleigh sisters left the business as madames and never returned to it.

Courtesy of the University of Chicago.

Mary E. McDowell
(1854–1936)

Mary E. McDowell, founder of the University of Chicago Settlement House, was the Jane Addams who stayed home. Rather than win the Nobel Peace Prize, as her mentor did, Miss McDowell earned such titles as: "Fighting Mary," "The Garbage Lady" and "The Duchess of Bubbly Creek." Although from 1923 to 1927 she headed the city's public aid system, her neighborhood, the Back of the Yards, was what consumed her interest and her efforts until the day of her death.

Her extraction was Irish, and it showed in her quick humor, charm, determination and practical humanitarianism.

Jane Addams said of her:

> For some of the social hopes, such as better race relations, she exhibited that unresting energy which one of her own ancestors might have called "God-driven." With that phrase so applicable to her, may we rest our case!

She was a native of Cincinnati and moved with her family to Evanston. There, in 1871, she helped minister to the refugees from the Chicago Fire.

She joined Jane Addams and the women of Hull House in the world-famous settlement house in the early 1890s. It was through the strong recommendation of Addams that she was selected by the then new University of Chicago to head its settlement house in the Back of the Yards.

The school was beginning to formulate the basic research ideas of the social science that came to be known as sociology. The Back of the Yards, adjacent to the Union Stockyards & Transit Co. on the city's Southwest Side, was described by her biographer Howard Wilson in *Mary McDowell: Neighbor.*

"Packingtown" . . . was like a frontier town—crude, ugly, dirty, and separated from the rest of Chicago by the square mile of packing plants and stockyards which dominated its whole existence. After leaving the lakeshore districts one bumped along on a horse-drawn street car across some forty unelevated railroad tracks and through miles of drab prairies populated chiefly with squat factories and grimy smokestacks until the conductor shouted "END OF THE LINE!" at the corner of Ashland Avenue and Forty-seventh Street, the heart of Packingtown. In 1890 the community situated out there, known as "back of the yards," was bounded on the north by the backwater in a long, dead arm of the Chicago River where carbonic acid gas continually broke through the thick scum on the water's surface and lent some semblance of descriptive truth to its name of "Bubbly Creek." On the west were the city garbage dumps, vast open pits into which was thrown uncovered, day after day, the garbage which open, horse-drawn wagons carted from other sections of the city. On the east were the "yards" and the vacant land near them used as "Hair Fields" where the hair thrown out from the slaughtering houses as useless putrefied in the process of drying. On the south the community gave away to open but bedraggled prairie.

She opened the settlement house in November 1894, in a four room flat above a feed store. Eventually, the settlement house became an oasis in the neighborhood. It would possess—in addition to "the settlement house lady"—gymnasiums, community centers, playgrounds and classrooms.

Living and working conditions in Chicago's Packingtown have been dramatically described in *The Jungle* by Upton Sinclair, published in 1906. It delineates the packer's efforts to find the cheapest labor possible as well as the deeds of the many others who exploited the immigrant packinghouse workers.

Fighting Mary sought to soften their conditions not only with kindness and neighborliness but also by standing up for them.

"I've fought and won a few battles in my day," she told reporter Frances Farmer,

> . . . and one of them, the longest and most bitterly contested of all, had a good deal [to do] with the subject of garbage.

The city contracted $475,000 a year to a company to dump Chicago's garbage from wagons into an enormous hole just west of the Back of the Yards neighborhood. The company made a fortune taking the clay out of the hole. Meanwhile, the garbage sat there and rotted, spreading disease and stench throughout the area.

McDowell fought the issue for 19 years. The morning after women got the vote, she led representatives of all the women's organizations in Chicago to a meeting with the mayor. They immediately got the agreement that sanitary garbage disposal methods would be installed.

Her battle for cleaning up Bubbly Creek was no less resourceful. Bubbly Creek was a small branch of the Chicago River that wound southward along Ashland Avenue into the stockyards. It served as a sewer for the slaughterhouses and got its name from the putrid bubbles that arose to try to break through the often-encrusted surface.

On a hot day, it seemed to liquify the air with its horrible stench. The Duchess of Bubbly Creek lobbied everyone she could find to fill in the creek. Everyone had an excuse or postponed her. Finally, she figured she could get the federal government to help clean it up. All she had to do was prove it was a navigable waterway. But how? She did it by rowing a boat down the middle of it, no little feat. She was successful, however, and Mary McDowell had made another contribution to the Back of the Yards, her home.

1910s

Resurrection Mary
(????–????)

Resurrection Mary is the ghost-myth of Chicago's Southwest Side.

Mary's story has been told and repeated now by several generations of Chicagoans. All who hear it know her name comes from Resurrection Cemetery, 7500 south on Archer Avenue.

According to the tale, some time ago, two young men were attending a neighborhood dance when they spotted a girl whom they had never seen before. One of them approached her and asked her to dance. She accepted the invitation.

The young woman was attractive and an excellent dancer. She moved effortlessly and lightly across the floor, but there was also something cold and distant about her. She spoke little, responding only to direct questions.

Both young men danced with her and later agreed on their description of her manner. Nevertheless, they were fascinated and continued dancing with her late into the evening.

At the end of the dance, the pair offered to take her home. She gave them directions, which led to Resurrection Cemetery. There, she got out of the vehicle and promptly disappeared.

The young woman, who gave her name as "Mary," had told them a home address. They looked at it more carefully and saw it was in the Back of the Yards neighborhood.

(Resurrection Mary portrayed by Jenna Harvey)

They went there the next day and knocked on the door of the house whose address she had given. An older woman, whose face showed lines of grief, answered the door. They inquired after the young woman and were told the lady lived there by herself. She had, she said, a daughter named Mary, but she was dead for 10 years.

The woman asked them to wait a moment and went into the house. She returned with a picture, which she showed them. It was her daughter, she said, and was a picture of the young woman with whom they had danced the evening before.

One of the young men asked, "Would you tell me, where is she buried?"

"Resurrection Cemetery," the woman answered.

The story has been repeated for a long time in Chicago and is similar to ghost stories in other cities. It is always Resurrection Cemetery with which the stories are associated.

There have been many other reports of the appearance of Resurrection Mary. Often she has been reported as hitchhiking on Archer Avenue along the cemetery. People have allegedly given her a ride only to have her disappear.

Another popular Resurrection Mary story is that she was seen standing next to the gates of Resurrection Cemetery; her handprints were found burned into the iron fence and remained there for many years, until the gate was removed by the cemetery.

There are those who have claimed to have found her grave in the cemetery, only to return and be unable to locate it.

Resurrection Mary is only one of many ghosts associated with Chicago, but she certainly remains the most popular and the most romantic.

Billy Sunday
(1863–1935)

Billy Sunday is remembered in a popular song as a fire-and-brimstone evangelist. Even he, according to the lyrics, "couldn't shut down" Chicago.

But there is something else you should know about him: Billy Sunday stole things!

As a major league ball player, Sunday—"the fastest man in baseball"—stole a record 95 bases in one season. It was a record that would stand until the immortal Ty Cobb came along.

It was baseball, in fact, that brought Sunday to Chicago in the first place.

He was born Nov. 19, 1863, in Ames, Ia. His father died in the Civil War within a week of Billy's birth; his mother died shortly thereafter, and Billy grew up an orphan.

As a youngster, he possessed amazing speed. He would win prizes at the volunteer firemen's carnivals by outrunning a fire department horse.

Sunday was playing center field for the Marshalltown, Ia., ball club when Adrian "Cap" Anson, player-manager of the Chicago White Stockings, spotted him during a visit to his hometown in 1883.

Anson brought the 20-year-old back to Chicago, put him into a White Stockings uniform, and welcomed him to the major leagues. Although not much of a hitter, Sunday became one of the best runners ever to wear the Chicago colors. As a center fielder, he was said to cover more ground than anyone else on the team.

The story is told that, while sitting in a saloon with teammate Mike "King" Kelly in 1891, Sunday was so taken by the hymns wafting in through the window from a nearby revival meeting that he became, as we say today, "born again."

As a preacher, the Rev. William Ashley Sunday became one of the most effective evangelists in this country's history. Converting millions to his form of Christianity, he also became a major force in converting America to Prohibition. His down-to-earth style, with its analogies from baseball, and his shirt-sleeve wrestling with the devil, captured the masses and earned the one-time White Stocking cheerful tolerance even from his opponents.

While Sunday wrestled with the devil in his "biting, blasting condemnation of sin," he became the closest thing to perpetual motion, on the go every moment he was on stage.

Sunday's biography describes his "acrobatic preaching":

> Some of the platform activities of Sunday make specta-tors gasp. He races to and fro on the platform. Like a jack knife, he fairly doubles up in emphasis. One hand smites the other . . . No posture is too extreme for this restless gymnast . . . In a dramatic description of the marathon he pictures the athlete falling prostrate at the goal and—thud!—there lies the evangelist prone on the platform. Only a skilled baseball player, with a long drill in sliding to bases, could thus fling himself to [its] floor without serious injury. On many occasions he strips off his coat and talks in his shirt sleeves. It seems almost impossible for him to stand up behind the pulpit and talk only with his mouth.

And while converting the masses, Sunday was also

successful in prodding many states into voting "dry," with their legislatures supporting the 19th Amendment.

Sunday's success in influencing the little people, unfortunately, was used by causes other than religion and Prohibition. *Harper's Weekly,* on June 19, 1915, asserted that, in addition to faith and fervor, Sunday displayed:

> . . . the ignorance of everything pertaining to democracy, industry, economics and politics. Special Privilege reached for him. Special Privilege used him.

In Ludlow, Colo., 24,000 men, women, and children huddled cold and hungry in tents on a mountainside to protest low wages, broken laws and unbearable working conditions in the coal mines. The mining interests imported Sunday to preach to the protesters.

Ignoring the bloodshed and brutality fostered by the company, Sunday scolded the workers, preaching that the cause of their poverty and distress was godlessness and booze.

He helped make Prohibition the overriding issue in Colorado's upcoming gubernatorial election, and a "coal company man" running as a "dry" Republican snuck into office.

Harper's soundly excoriated Sunday for similar actions—or distractions—he performed during a coal strike in West Virginia, and at a locomotive manufacturing strike in Philadelphia.

As one-time *Daily News* reporter Ben Hecht wrote in his autobiography, *A Child of the Century:*

> . . . the Stockyards' owners imported Billy Sunday to divert their underpaid hunkies from going on strike by shouting them dizzy with God.

Shoeless Joe Jackson
(1888–1951)

Sports writer Grantland Rice asked three ballplayers who was the greatest natural batter who had ever played. The three were Ty Cobb, Babe Ruth and Tris

Speaker. Without a moment's hesitation, each answered, "Joe Jackson."

It was, however, to Shoeless Joe that a little boy at a hearing on the Black Sox scandal addressed the challenge, "Say it ain't so, Joe."

Alas, it was so. He was implicated with other White Sox players in the throwing of the 1919 World Series to the Cincinnati Reds. He played very well, but he had accepted the fix.

What a ballplayer he had been and what a character he was.

Jackson played for 14 seasons and batted .356, including a .408 season in 1911. Shoeless Joe also stole 202 bases. Even in the thrown series, he batted .375.

It was not mere statistics that made Joe the idol and character of his day. It was a unique style. Born in Greenville, S.C., he made his baseball debut with the Greenville team in 1908. He acquired the nickname "Shoeless Joe" when playing baseball barefooted because his spikes gave him blisters. The outfield, however, was full of glass and rocks. About the fifth inning, he complained of the condition of the field, not because it cut his feet, but because, "It's fuzzing up the ball and I can't throw it."

Joe could not read or write and probably did not understand the nickname, "The Carolina Crashsmith," that a reporter tried to tag him with. He returned home after his first major league game because his teammates ribbed him unmercifully about his illiteracy. Chicago acquired him in 1915 from Cleveland for $30,000 and three players. To fans in both cities, he would always be "Shoeless Joe." It was probably his insecurity and sense of inferiority, rather than the money, that impelled him to go along in agreeing to accept payoff money for the 1919 series against the Cincinnati Reds.

When Shoeless Joe realized he was caught up in the vortex of the payoff, he told the team he didn't want to play in the 1919 series, but did not give a reason.

"You play," he was told.

He, and especially fellow White Sox teammate Buck Weaver, had the aura of two kids playing the game of baseball. Neither was emotionally or intellectually

84

mature enough to handle the situation of the World Series conspiracy, but they had to take their punishment as though they were. Many in society saw them as both innocent and guilty. Judge Kenesaw Mountain Landis, not noted for his flexibility or understanding, found them only guilty, and banished all eight players from baseball for life.

But a small part of Shoeless Joe stayed on in baseball, making not only the Hall of Fame but its pinnacle. His batting style had a student whose name was Babe Ruth. When Babe Ruth went from star pitcher to full-time heavy hitter, he looked around baseball for the best batting technique to imitate.

Grantland Rice in a 1932 article in *Collier's* magazine explained:

> Standing over six feet and loose-jointed without the slightest touch of tension, he [Jackson] had a free, smooth lash that was hard to forget. A left-handed hitter, he stood with his right foot slightly advanced, the left foot a trifle back, in perfect position to step into the ball and l..t against his right leg. This was the batting method that Babe Ruth took for his model when the Babe went in for hitting in a serious way.
>
> "I wanted to improve my batting," the Babe says, "so I decided [to follow] the best hitter I could find. Naturally, Ty Cobb was a great hitter, but I wanted to take a fuller swing at the ball and not choke up the bat. After looking them all over I decided Joe Jackson was at the top of the class. The only change I made in following his style was to get my right foot farther advanced, with my left foot farther back so that I almost had my back to the pitcher. You are already partly turned in this way and you have more leverage.
>
> "Jackson had finally arrived at this method in a natural way, for no one ever taught him how to hit and I know he never tried to copy any other style."

Three years after Jackson was banned, Rice found him playing semi-pro ball for an Americus, Ga., team and batting more than .500.

He died Dec. 5, 1951, in Greenville, S.C., according to his obit, "a popular and respected figure in the area."

Mary Garden
(1877–1967)

Mary Garden gave Chicago a wonderful time both as an opera singer and as a genuine character.

Between 1910 and 1931, she was the boast of the Windy City's culture as she sang such roles as *Thais, Louise* and *Salomé*. And, for a year—1921-2—she directed the Chicago Grand Opera Company.

While Chicago loved Mary Garden, she also had her critics. These included: the chief of police, reformer Billy Sunday, multi-millionaire Andrew Carnegie, her patroness Edith Rockefeller McCormick and a would-be assassin, who thought she talked too much.

Police Chief Leroy T. Seward was not pleased, at least not publicly. He compared her Dance of the Seven Veils in *Salomé* to "a cat wallowing in catnip."

Arthur Farwell, president of the Law and Order League, did not go to see Mary Garden. "I am a normal man," he said, "but I would not trust myself to see *Salomé*."

Billy Sunday preached fervently against both her and her "sinful opera." In response, she went to the tent where he was performing. When she introduced herself, he was speechless. Eventually, he acknowledged, "I guess I've been hearing a lot of lies about you." The two ended up having a drink together, albeit the kind served at a nearby soda fountain.

Mary Garden also attempted to affect the aloof Carnegie, the very wealthy steel manufacturer who considered himself an arbiter of culture and mores for other rich Americans.

"*Louise*," he told her, "is a bad, bad story." He huffed about the plot and "that girl and her young man" in it. She did not manage to convince him otherwise.

Her difficulty with the even more arbitrary Mrs. McCormick came only after Edith had sat through three consecutive performances of *Salomé*. The imperious financier of the company had power to stop an opera from being performed and she used it. She ordered Mary to cancel the scheduled fourth performance of the opera.

"Why?" Miss Garden asked.

"Miss Garden, the truth came to me in a flash when I went home after your third performance."

"And just what do you mean by the *truth?*" Mary asked.

"I said to myself, 'Edith, your vibrations are all wrong.'"

The opera star later commented: "And Miss McCormick crossed her hands over her breast and I saw there was no use talking anymore."

Once, in order to promote a charitable opera in Chicago, Mary went to the Stock Exchange to address the stock brokers and to try to sell boxes for the performance. Her pitch was interrupted when the police wrestled to the floor a man with long grey hair and shabby clothes, who had a gun.

The police tried to get an explanation as to why he wanted to kill the opera star.

All he would say was, "She talks too much."

Mary Garden had the reputation as a pretty good singer and a very good actress.

She also had the verve and self-confidence of an outstanding diva and something else, an enviable figure.

Miss Garden was five feet, four inches tall, weighed 112 pounds and was known as "Mary of the divine form."

Of her shape, she wrote in retrospect:

> I have nothing to say about my body except that it is the way God made it and the way I kept it. You see, I never allowed fat to get on it. I was very fussy about weighing myself every Sunday morning of my life, and I even do it now. I get on the scales once a week, and if I see a fraction of weight more, that fraction is gone the following Sunday. So many women come to me and say, "Miss Garden, how do you keep your figure?" I don't think they know what a scale is. I never walked or did exercise of any kind while I was singing. I never took a step I didn't have to take. I just looked at my scales. But when I went for my vacations, in Monte Carlo and Corsica, I never did anything but exercise—swimming, golf, tennis—never walking; I hate it.
>
> My body didn't begin to develop till seven years after my debut, and the change became noticeable in the opera *Aphrodite*. I had never had any breasts, and suddenly I began to grow there, and then I had a bosom, with a tiny waist, but no thighs, and no hips. My chest developed with singing.

Chicago loved her, her singing, and her shape.

St. Frances Xavier Cabrini
(1850–1917)

Back in 1915, a cub reporter for the *Chicago American* named Harry Reutlinger was sent to Columbus Hospital to snatch a wedding photo from a patient who had just

Courtesy Columbus-Cabrini Medical Center

killed his wife and turned the gun on himself. As Reutlinger sneaked down the hall, his way was barred by an elderly nun mopping the floor. "Mother Cabrini sent me," he lied. The nun's response was a wet mop across the startled reporter's face. Then they both burst out laughing. Reutlinger had not expected to meet the world-famous nun who founded the hospital mopping floors.

Reutlinger never got the picture, but he and Mother Cabrini became fast friends.

The nun, who would become America's first saint, was born Francesca Maria Cabrini, two months premature, in a small village on the Lombard Plain of Italy in 1850. At the age of 7 she became interested in the idea of becoming a missionary in China, and play-acted the role as she grew into adulthood.

Frail health prevented her becoming a nun, however, until she founded her own order in an orphanage where she was teaching at the age of 30. In the next seven years, through her Institute of the Missionary Sisters of the Sacred Heart, she founded seven convents.

In 1888 the shy, quiet nun, then 38, obtained an audience with Pope Leo XIII in the Vatican. She told him she had taken Saverio as a middle name in honor of St. Francis Xavier, the Jesuit missionary, and expressed her desire to go to China.

The Pope granted her permission to open an orphanage, but not in the Far East. He instructed her to go to America, where every month thousands of Italian immigrants were arriving, homeless and with no one to guide them. Over the next 10 years, by literally begging on the streets, she succeeded in establishing schools, hospitals and convents in New York, Brooklyn, New Orleans, Spain, France, Nicaragua and Argentina.

Mother Cabrini, who had become an American citizen, arrived in Chicago in 1899, and opened a school in the Old Assumption Church, 313 W. Illinois St. Then she was off to do more good in the world, returning to Chicago in 1903 to found Columbus Hospital in what had been the North Shore Hotel at Deming Place and Lake View Avenue. Eight years later she established Mother Cabrini Hospital at 1200 W. Cabrini St.

Meanwhile, she continued her work throughout the world, making 24 ocean voyages during the last 30 years of her life, founding some 70 hospitals, schools and orphanages, and inducting more than 4,000 women into her Missionary Sisters of the Sacred Heart.

Her last home was in Chicago at Columbus Hospital, which she named for the Italian explorer, rather than a saint, so anti-clerical elements of the community would not consider it a religious institution.

On Friday, Dec. 21, 1917, though suffering from malaria contracted on one of her do-good expeditions, she spent the wintery day packing candy and toys for the impoverished children in her beloved "Little Italy" on the city's West Side, so that they would have some sort of Christmas.

Shortly before noon the next day, while seated in a dark green wicker armchair in her first floor room at the hospital, she rang the bell that summoned the hospital's nuns, her "daughters," to her side. She gazed fondly upon them one last time, and then quietly died at the age of 67.

A placard placed above the chair in later years read: "From this chair the soul of St. Frances Xavier Cabrini took flight to Heaven."

Only 29 years after her death Pope Pius XII proclaimed her canonization, making her the first American citizen ever to be elevated to sainthood.

The city of Chicago later gave her name to a public housing project, and a life-size statue of Mother Cabrini was placed on an altar in the room at Columbus Hospital in which she died.

The statue of the saint holds an open book inscribed in Latin with her motto, a quotation from St. Paul: "I can do all things in Him Who is my strength."

Chicago May
(1876–1929)

She was born Beatrice Desmond just outside Dublin, Ireland, in 1876—or was she?

There are so many stories about "Chicago May" that one hardly knows what to believe.

Turn-of-the-century police called her "The world's cleverest woman crook."

And *Chicago Tribune* reporter Genevieve Forbes Herrick wrote in 1928: "Chicago May was the source book for the girls who today get their names scratched across the police blotters."

May, herself, once boasted, "I was a prize graduate of the Chicago school of crime." Of that there can be no doubt.

Early newspaper clippings say she was born Mary Vechs, the blue eyed, golden haired daughter of a German baker on the East Side of New York.

However, in her own life story, *Chicago May—The Queen of Crooks*, by May Churchill Sharpe, she claims the Dublin origin, and says she adopted the name May Churchill to spare her family the shame of letting the world know that "Chicago May" was their daughter.

According to her own story, she came to America in 1889 after stealing £60 from her father's money box, arriving at the age of 13.

She passed through Chicago the first time, took up with Albert "Dal" Churchill, whom she described as a member of the Dalton gang, and married him at 14. He was lynched after a bank job out West, and she returned to Chicago, a 15-year-old widow.

She soon changed her name to May Vivienne, choosing Latimer as her favorite last name, although she was also known as May Fletcher, Katie Fitzgerald, Mary Guerin and Mary Miller. But "Chicago May" was the moniker that stuck.

May was hailed at the World's Columbian Exposition of 1893 as the country's first shoplifter. She wore voluminous skirts with inside pockets, and a very beguiling smile.

An innovative entrepreneur, May would take a "john" to bed while a girlfriend went through his pants pockets. She later originated the trick of throwing a customer's trousers out the window as soon as he took them off, and then running down to claim their contents while the pants-less party was unable to give chase.

"During the construction of the World's Fair in 1892 we nicked the builders," she revealed. "When the fair opened we nicked the customers."

A pioneer of women's rights in the world of crime, May originated the "fainting fit," in which she would deftly steal the gold watches and diamond stickpins of chivalrous men who were trying to help revive her.

While in the loving arms of a man in the back seat of a horse-drawn cab, with her head nestled on her lover's shoulder, May perfected the art of snitching the gent's diamond scarf pin with her teeth.

She was also credited with introducing the camera to the art of blackmail, in which a confederate snapped pictures from a place of concealment while the soon-to-be victim thought he was enjoying May's intimate company in private.

After perfecting her talents in Chicago she moved on to New York, where she was able to test them on a larger market.

In 1899 she married James Montgomery Sharpe, after he got her out of jail when she was pinched for robbing a Lutheran minister. Both were 23. Sharpe is said to have committed suicide, although May maintained he simply disappeared.

From New York she sailed to London, where she rented a house in Montagu and began to mystify Scotland Yard. Her blackmail victims are said to have included one earl, a knight, half a dozen canny barristers and a number of wealthy clubmen—many of whom were too embarrassed to report it.

In the spring of 1901, at a gathering in the Horse Shoe tavern after a thief's funeral, she hooked up with Chicago's famed "Cockney Eddie" Guerin.

The bankrobber son of a respectable Chicago family, Guerin had fled after he thought he killed a detective in a fight over a woman. Although May and Guerin had worked Chicago at the same time, they never met until the London funeral.

The two of them went to Paris, where Guerin pulled off the $50,000 robbery of an American Express Co. office, while May stood lookout. He was sentenced to life on Devil's Island, the penal colony in French

Guiana, and she got five years in Montpelier prison as his accomplice. As May was being led away she kissed her hand to the judge who sentenced her.

After serving three years May sailed for Brazil, where a British nobleman fell in love with her but killed himself when he discovered her true identity.

May returned to England, where she took up with 25-year-old Charles Smith. Guerin, meanwhile, had escaped from Devil's Island, made his way to Chicago, and then returned to London. There, in an encounter with May and her new lover, Smith shot Guerin in the foot, depriving him of two of his toes.

This time she got 15 years in the women's jail at Aylesbury, and Smith was sent off to Dartmoor Prison for even longer.

When May got out 10 years later, in 1917, she was deported. She spent the next decade writing her "confessions" and getting paid for telling about her life of crime. In 1928, at the age of 52, May announced her engagement to marry 26-year-old Netley Lucas, a British author and criminologist, whom she met while he was researching a book called *Ladies of the Underworld*.

Alas, May died the following year, at the age of 53.

Her epitaph was written by the three-toed Guerin, who penned in his memoirs, "Oh, woman, woman! You have much to answer for . . . Ah, if I had never known Chicago May."

1920S

Louis Armstrong
(1900–1971)

In the summer of 1922, Louis "Satchmo" Armstrong came up the river (the Mississippi) to play trumpet with Joe "King" Oliver's band in Chicago. Jazz was then spelled with two s's instead of two z's. The young musician was so obviously a competitor for the band leader that historians have never figured out how or why exactly Papa Joe invited Armstrong to Chicago and the big time, but the two made unbelievable music together as a two-trumpet team.

Oliver was the king; Armstrong, the prince. The band leader was described as a "great gut-bucket man, full of jokes and riotous ideas." Satchmo's musical style was called a "markedly individual compound of kidding, creative paraphrasing, showmanship, blues inflections and unerring swing." The words try to tell what he was like, but they fall short because, more than anything, he was an original.

The Lincoln Gardens on Chicago's South Side could hold a thousand people. The front six rows were reserved for visiting musicians, almost always white, who regularly came to hear Louis Armstrong and the King Oliver band help create and define the new music that was giving its name to the era.

Jazz appealed to youth, and it was an age of youth as World War I had damned the world of old people. Their age's rules were there to be broken: Jazz music symbolized the end of those rules and the beginning of an era in which creativity, sincerity and feeling became the guides.

"When you play jazz, you don't lie," Satchmo once said. "You play from your heart."

What Armstrong and jazz offered Chicago and the country was just such a validation of feelings, good feelings.

His wife, Lucille, once told him, "It's against the law of averages for you to be so happy all the time."

And it was after his death Americans learned that, like many other musicians of the era, Armstrong used marijuana to keep his mood elevated.

But freedom was another element of the jazz credo, and smoking marijuana helped exemplify it, as did the

breaking down of racial and sexual barriers.

At his best, Armstrong's jazz was joyous and at times nonsensical, as he played songs such as "Ding Dong Daddy from Dumas" and made up some of the sounds and adlibbed many of the words.

Louis Armstrong, who had spent his early life in poverty and in a reform school, became the ambassador of the carefree and happy life and its music.

Armstrong spent much of his life on tour. First it was on Mississippi riverboats, even before coming to Chicago. A year after his arrival in Chicago, he was on tour in Illinois, Ohio and Indiana. By 1924, he was heading East and playing in New York. He spent much of the 1920s in Chicago, but also played up and down the East Coast. Next, he toured coast to coast, and was conquering Europe in the early 1930s, opening at the London Palladium in 1932. He was off to Australia and the Far East in both 1954 and 1956, South America in 1957. In the early 1960s, his itineraries included Iceland, India, Scandinavia, Eastern Europe and Africa.

He played before the King of England and came up with his famous line, "This one's for you, Rex." In Africa, he found places that knew one word in English, "Satchmo."

Armstrong became popular as an ambassador of good will and good feelings for the United States in his 50 years of traveling and touring.

He helped create a new sound, a new era and a new freedom that ultimately served not only the 1920s but also the next 40 years with all their changes.

Satchmo remained through his 71 years a warm-hearted, unaffected person whom the world found little trouble loving.

He fortunately lived when even some of his early Chicago music could be recorded. In addition, he had parts in more than 40 films, so he played not only for three generations of the world but for posterity.

His time gave him the highest accolade it could to a musician. It called Louis "Satchmo" Armstrong, "The Greatest."

Ben Hecht
(1894–1964)
Charles MacArthur
(1896–1956)

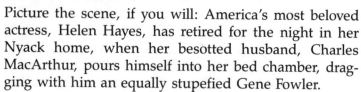

Picture the scene, if you will: America's most beloved actress, Helen Hayes, has retired for the night in her Nyack home, when her besotted husband, Charles MacArthur, pours himself into her bed chamber, dragging with him an equally stupefied Gene Fowler.

MacArthur proudly presents Fowler to the half-asleep queen of the stage. Fowler graciously bends forward to kiss her hand, loses his equilibrium, and flops onto the floor.

"See! Didn't I tell you? He's wonderful," bubbles MacArthur. "And he knows all about Egyptology!"

Fowler picks himself up off the carpet and apologizes, "Madam, I beg your pardon. I grew dizzy for a moment, thinking I was five thousand feet above the canyon, in a high wind."

Helen Hayes glares suspiciously at the Denver newsman-turned-screenwriter.

Deducing that the welcome mat is not exactly out, Fowler mumbles, "I am overdue at the home of my old friend, Ben Hecht. Would you be so kind as to point the way to his house?"

"I'll do better than that," obliges Miss Hayes. She picks up the phone, routs Hecht out of his warm bed and commands, "Come and get him. He belongs to you."

The story is told by the late Fowler's long-time friend, H. Allen Smith, in *Life and Legend of Gene Fowler*.

Hecht, MacArthur and Fowler were all journalistic legends in those lusty-gusty days around the Roaring Twenties, when it was a much rowdier profession than it is allowed to be today.

They first met face-to-face in Chicago, where Hecht wrote for the *Daily News* and MacArthur for the *Examiner*. While idly going over police reports MacArthur discovered that the famous Fowler was in the Central District police lockup. He turned to his competitor friend, Hecht, and suggested, "Let's go down and bail him out."

Fowler had been on his way to New York. Rather than pay his own train fare, however, he had polled Denver funeral parlors until he found a body that was destined to be shipped East. He volunteered to accompany it, since dead people were not permitted by law to travel alone, and the grateful undertaker bought his ticket.

Fowler's scheming colleagues on the *Denver Post*, meanwhile, contacted Chicago police and informed them that he was transporting a female across state lines for immoral purposes, a clear violation of the Mann Act. So when the train pulled into Chicago, the cops grabbed Fowler—who was not exactly sober—and locked him up.

MacArthur and Hecht posted his bail, gleefully introduced themselves, and took their new-found friend on an extended tour of the Loop's more fashionable saloons. The trio had been pals ever since.

Hecht had come to Chicago from Racine, Wis., about 1911, and MacArthur arrived in town a year later after serving as a private in the conflict with Mexico.

He worked briefly for *Oak Leaves*, and then the City News Bureau before landing a spot on the *Tribune*. After a break to serve with the artillery in World War I, he returned and went to work for Walter Howey on the *Examiner*.

After a night of drinking in a downtown saloon called Quincy Number 9, MacArthur liked to clear his head while barreling down the Michigan Avenue sidewalk in a flivver, with North Side bootlegger Dion O'Banion at the wheel, as pedestrians dived for cover.

For six years MacArthur was married to Caryl Frink, an *Examiner* reporter who had been hired during the wartime manpower shortage and was good enough to hold her job after the doughboys returned. The knot was tied by MacArthur's father, the Rev. William Telford MacArthur, who performed the ceremony for free. When they were divorced in 1926, after six years of marriage, Caryl sued Helen Hayes for alienation of affection.

MacArthur met Miss Hayes at a party in New York

in 1924, where he dropped several peanuts into her hand and said, "I wish they were emeralds." He squired her home in a Central Park carriage, and when he dropped her off at her apartment he asked, "What's your phone number?" The actress smiled and said, "I'm in the book."

They were married as soon as MacArthur's divorce from Caryl became final. It was a union that lasted until his death 36 years later, and would give them a son, James MacArthur, who became a movie star in his own right.

Both MacArthur and Hecht left their Chicago jobs in the mid-1920s and went to New York to try their hands as playwrights. It was there, in 1927, that they collaborated on *The Front Page*, a play about newspaper life in Chicago, that was later made into a movie.

MacArthur was variously known as a ribald rascal, a rogue, a wit and a charmer. F. Scott Fitzgerald once told Helen Hayes, "Some men do not have to create something to prove they are artists. Charlie is one of them."

MacArthur's endless escapades were chronicled by Hecht, who was his companion on most of them. Some of the stories are undoubtedly true, although Hecht was widely known as a storyteller who never let the facts stand in the way of a good yarn.

MacArthur, by all accounts, was a thoughtful writer.

His consummate abuse of alcohol took its toll on his body in later years, and shortly before his death, he wrote, "I don't think God is interested in us after puberty. He is interested only in our births, for this requires His magic. Our dying requires only His indifference."

Carl Wanderer
(1895–1921)

Carl Wanderer was twice respected as a hero—first as the homecoming soldier with lieutenant's bars on his shoulders, and second when he told how he won a blazing gun duel with a ragged stranger who had accosted him and his pregnant wife in the lobby of their Northwest Side apartment building.

Wanderer, 25, a quiet church man who never smoked, nor drank, nor swore, had worked as a butcher since the end of World War I. At 9 o'clock on the night of June 21, 1920, he and his wife, Ruth, 23, were returning home from a movie, *The Sea Wolf*, at the Pershing Theater. As they entered the vestibule of their apartment at 4732 N. Campbell Ave., a voice from the darkness ordered, "Don't turn on the light! Throw up your hands."

A series of shots rang out in the night. When a neighbor turned on the lights he saw Wanderer on his knees, raining blows with his army revolver on the head of a poorly dressed man who already lay dead from three bullet wounds. A second gun, with two shots fired, lay near the body.

Lying nearby in a pool of blood was Wanderer's young wife, moaning, "My baby is dead. Mama, mama, mama . . ." She, too, was dead by the time help arrived.

The city's heart went out to the melancholy butcher who had fought so bravely to save the life of his bride of less than nine months—his childhood sweetheart and the only girl he ever had.

The slain gunman carried no identification, nor were his fingerprints on file. Though dressed like a tramp, police theorized he could have pawned the gun he carried for $75 if he needed money. In an effort to identify the dead man, Sgt. John Norton ordered a check of the weapon, a Colt bearing serial number 2282.

The Colt was traced to a Chicago gun shop, which had sold it to a Peter Hoffman in 1914. After checking scores of Hoffmans, police found the man, who told them he had sold the weapon to Fred W. Wanderer. Fred Wanderer said he loaned the gun to his cousin, Carl, the day before the slaying.

Police intensified their investigation of the would-be hero, and learned that Ruth Wanderer had withdrawn $1,500 from her savings account the afternoon before she was slain. They also learned that Carl, the "model husband," had been exchanging love letters with

16-year-old Julia Schmitt, a pretty, plump typist.

Confronted with the results of the police investigation, Wanderer confessed. "I was sick of marriage—yes, even after only nine months. I wanted out, but I loved Ruth too much to let another man have her."

Wanderer said he sought out a skid row derelict at Madison and Halsted streets to set up the perfect crime.

"I told him I wanted to stage a robbery in the vestibule of my home. I'll impress my young wife with my courage, and no one will get hurt. I gave him a dollar to buy his supper and told him to be in the hall between 9 and half past. He didn't need a gun. He could pretend he had one in his pocket, and I would chase him away. I didn't know him. He was just a bum."

When the hired thespian ordered "Throw up your hands," in accordance with the script, Wanderer blasted away with a gun in each hand, killing his wife with one and the unknown bum with the other.

Wanderer was tried and found guilty of both murders. He was sentenced to 25 years in prison for the death of his wife, and sentenced to death for the murder of John Doe.

All efforts to identify the "ragged stranger" failed, and he was buried in Glen Oak Cemetery at Roosevelt and Manheim Roads.

On Sept. 30, 1921, Carl Wanderer went to the gallows in the old county jail at Dearborn and Hubbard Streets.

For his final comment before the trap was sprung, according to reporters Ben Hecht and Charlie Mac-Arthur, they had arranged for Wanderer to read a note denouncing their city editors at the *Daily News* and *Examiner.* At the last moment, however, Wanderer realized he would be unable to refer to the typewritten text because his hands were strapped at his sides. He would have to improvise.

As he stood on the trap door with his arms and legs bound, the death cap in place and the noose fixed, the sheriff asked if he had any last words before the sentence was carried out.

In a strident baritone voice that filled the execution chamber he began to sing:

"Old Gal, old pal,

"You left me all alone—

"Old gal, old pal,

"I'm just a rolling stone—

"Old pal, why don't you

"Answer me. . . ."

The trapdoor dropped. Wanderer's body plummeted into space, and stopped with a jerk at the end of the rope!

Terrible Tommy O'Connor
(1890–????)

Terrible Tommy O'Connor has been an embarrassment to the City of Chicago and County of Cook ever since Dec. 11, 1921, when he went over the wall at the old county jail, leaving the official hangman holding an empty noose.

To this day he is ranked with the baddest of the bad, a vicious cop-killer with three known homicides on his record, including that of his closest friend.

If, miraculously, O'Connor is still alive out there, still thumbing his nose at the cops, he would be at least 100 years old.

Born in Ireland 10 years before the turn of the century, he was brought to Chicago by his parents at the age of 2. The family settled at 13th and Paulina Streets, in the old Maxwell police district—"Bloody Maxwell" it was called.

"The wickedest police district in the world," the *Chicago Tribune* declared in an editorial. "Murderers, robbers and thieves of the worst kind are here born, reared, and grow to maturity in numbers that far exceed the record of any similar district anywhere on the face of the globe."

This is where Tommy spent his formative years,

with burglars, holdup men and neighborhood thugs as his teachers.

O'Connor made his first kill of record on Feb. 1, 1918. He and three of his pals were robbing the Illinois Central railway station at Michigan Avenue and Randolph Street when they encountered Dennis E. Tierney, a retired policeman who was working as a railroad security officer.

O'Connor, who could have easily gotten away from the old man, pumped two bullets into Tierney's chest at close range, killing him on the spot.

"Why in the hell did you have to shoot?" asked O'Connor's accomplice, Harold Emerson, as the bandits sped away in their getaway car. "Because I felt like it," O'Connor snarled, thrusting his revolver into Emerson's ribs. "If you don't like it, I'll give you some of it too."

The wanton murder so unnerved Emerson that he admitted his role in the robbery, fingered O'Connor as the killer, and was packed off to prison.

O'Connor, who was now a fugitive, was so enraged that Emerson had squealed on him that he concocted a plan for his boyhood friend, Jimmy Cherin, to visit Emerson at Joliet penitentiary and kill him.

After Cherin reneged, his bullet-riddled body was found in an abandoned car in suburban Stickney. O'Connor's lifelong friend had been shot five times. Police found an eye-witness to the Cherin killing, and O'Connor was indicted for his second murder.

"Terrible Tommy," as he was now being called, was arrested when members of a massive police dragnet found him hiding under his father's bed. He was tried for the Illinois Central murder but acquitted, despite Emerson's eye-witness testimony.

A description of O'Connor at the time was given by Dr. Francis McNamara, medical director of the Cook County Jail:

> "He was a coward, I am sure. He only fought when cornered. He always looked as if he were frightened, and I believe he was, most of the time. His hair stood up from his forehead and crown as if he had just seen a ghost. His high arched eyebrows gave him a constantly startled expression. There were lines of nervous strain on his lean checks."

Before O'Connor could be tried for Jimmy Cherin's murder, however, Louis Miller, an eye-witness to the killing, disappeared. Without their star witness, prosecutors had to drop charges and O'Connor went free.

There were now actually four deaths hanging over O'Connor's head, although he was directly responsible for only two. After Cherin was killed, his young wife committed suicide and took her and Jimmy's baby with her.

Miller, the missing witness, was located a year later where he had been in hiding since being abducted by three members of O'Connor's gang. He agreed to testify, under police protection, and a new warrant was issued for O'Connor's arrest.

As a squad of five detectives led by Sgt. Patrick O'Neill approached O'Connor's brother-in-law's house on South Washtenaw to check out a report that he was holed up there, O'Connor opened fire, fatally wounding O'Neill in the chest.

For the next two months, O'Connor was the most hunted man in the country. The trail ended in St. Paul in July of 1921 when he was cornered in the railroad yards. Returned to Chicago to face trial, he boasted, "I've had so much publicity since shooting O'Neill that I'll have no trouble getting a job as a screen star."

O'Connor was tried and found guilty of O'Neill's murder, and sentenced to "hang by your neck until dead."

That was in the days before appeals and years of languishing on "death row." Judgment day was scheduled for Dec. 15, 1921, and that was it.

Ten men had gone to the gallows in the old county jail at Hubbard and Dearborn Streets that year, and O'Connor was supposed to have been number eleven.

But history would not have it that way. It was rumored in those days that you could smuggle the world's tallest building into the Cook County Jail. That wasn't necessary, however. All somebody had to slip O'Connor was a gun.

Accompanied by three fellow inmates, he calmly marched out of the jail, leaving four guards tied up behind. After scaling the 20-foot high wall, O'Connor jumped onto the running board of a passing car, pointed the gun in the driver's face and said, "Drive like hell, you son of a bitch. I'm Terrible Tommy O'Connor!"

Harry J. Busch, a young law student who was behind the wheel of his father's Mitchell touring car, recognized O'Connor from his photographs and stammered, "I know that." Following the gunman's frantically shouted directions, Busch drove north on Clark Street and made a series of turns until he skidded into a factory wall. O'Connor jumped off the running board and dashed to a waiting car.

When police came to investigate the crash, Busch excitedly told them, "Tommy O'Connor has escaped!" Police called the jail and were assured, however, that O'Connor was safe in his cell on death row. It was another hour before someone actually looked into the cell and reported O'Connor missing, and with that convenient lead time he was long gone.

For all anyone knows, he's still running.

The last legal hanging before Cook County switched to the electric chair was in 1927. But the law said O'Connor must hang. So when the old jail was torn down the gallows was dismantled and placed in the basement of the new jail at 26th Street and California Avenue to await Tommy's return.

Fifty years later, when a custodian discovered the pile of rope and lumber gathering dust in the boiler room, Chief Judge Richard J. Fitzgerald of Criminal Court ruled they could be thrown out.

"Heck, under present laws we couldn't execute the guy even if he surrendered tomorrow," Fitzgerald said. "But just out of curiosity, I'd like to see what the old gallows looks like. I think in view of the fact that it's a somewhat historic piece of the past, we should reconstruct it one more time before we destroy it."

And so the old six-man gallows, which had claimed the lives of 96 convicted murderers since it was built in the 1870s, was set up one last time, noose and all. A painter lettered a sign: "Tired of Waiting, Tommy." If O'Connor couldn't be there in person, he was at least there in spirit.

Then the gallows was disassembled to be carted off

to the junk heap—but not quite yet.

Larry Donley, owner of the Seven Acres Museum in Union, about 50 miles northwest of Chicago, drove into the city and saved the gallows from destruction. He and his son, Michael, spent hours carrying the old timbers out and loading them aboard a truck.

The gallows was hauled out to the museum in Union where it was reassembled, just the way it stood that wintery Sunday in December 1921, when Terrible Tommy O'Connor broke his date with death and went over the wall.

"As a boy I had heard about the gallows waiting for Tommy," said Donley. "They did away with the wall from the St. Valentine's Day Massacre, and I just couldn't let that happen to this piece of Chicago history."

After all, with O'Connor gone, that's all we have left.

Colleen Moore
(1902–1987)

She was born Kathleen Morrison in Port Huron, Mich., but spent most of her childhood in the South. Her immediate Chicago connection was the fact that Walter Howey, the zany Front Page era city editor of the Hearst *Examiner,* was her uncle.

When Kathleen was 15, Howey got D.W. Griffith to give her a six month contract in Hollywood, in exchange for Howey's help in getting Griffith's "The Birth of a Nation" past the censors.

Howey also gave her the name Colleen Moore, explaining that 12 letters was the limit on a movie marquee. He and Edward Scott Beck of the *Tribune* dreamed it up over a few beers one night, when they decided the movies needed an Irish starlet.

When Howey put his young niece aboard the Santa Fe Chief for California he handed her a letter:

"Dear Baby. Hollywood, where you will now be living, is inhabited by a race of people called Press Agents. The studios pay them a lot of money to think up stories about the players under contract to persuade editors like me to print their stories. So the moral of this letter is, never believe one damned word you ever read about yourself."

She soon knew why Uncle Walter had written the note. She no sooner arrived on the West Coast when she read a story that Howey, himself, had concocted to further her career.

Howey claimed that "Colleen" was masquerading in a maid's uniform while visiting him in Chicago, when Griffith came by the house for dinner. Unaware that the beautiful young maid was the Howeys' niece, Griffith told Howey's wife, Lib, "Mrs. Howey, you've just lost a maid, and I've gained a new movie star."

The six-month "payoff" lasted 17 years, with Colleen Moore rising to become one of the highest-paid stars of the silent era. At the peak of her career she commanded a million-dollar salary, and helped start a fashion craze when she cut her dark hair in a Dutch Boy bob during the Roaring Twenties.

She appeared in 100 films, including half a dozen talkies, ending with *The Power and the Glory,* co-starring Spencer Tracy.

In 1936 she returned to Chicago, where she married stockbroker Homer Hargrave.

The first night they went out together Hargrave took her to a North Side nightclub, where she stared in awe as he pointed out several henchmen of gangster Al Capone. In reality, the "gangsters" were the impish Hargrave's business partners at Merrill Lynch, Pierce, Fenner & Beane.

After Hargrave's death 28 years later, she turned her attention to promoting an elaborate doll house, called the Fairy Castle, that she had created in the 1920s at a cost of $470,000.

Miss Moore's interest in doll houses started when her father, an engineer, gave her a 1-inch square dictionary for her seventh birthday. She gradually built a small world around it.

Much of the work on her Fairy Castle was done by her father and Horace Jackson, who designed her movie sets.

The house featured electricity, running water, a radio and cathedral organ, and readable music by Rachmaninoff on a rosewood piano that could be played.

During the 1930s and '40s Miss Moore sent the castle around the country for displays in department stores to help raise money for handicapped children. It has been on permanent display at the Museum of Science and Industry since 1949—her gift to Chicago.

Meanwhile, Miss Moore, as Mrs. Homer Hargrave, became a prominent member of Chicago society. She was a founding member of the Chicago International Film Festival in the 1960s, and was a longtime member of the Woman's Board of Northwestern Memorial Hospital.

She died in 1988 at the age of 85, but her memory

lives on in her Fairy Castle, which draws as many as 4 million people a year at the museum. At the push of a button they can hear her own voice describe each little room.

© Copyrighted, Chicago Tribune Company, all rights reserved, used with permission.

Samuel "Nails" Morton
(1894–1923)

"Nails" Morton, a Jewish lieutenant in Dion O'Banion's North Side Irish bootleg mob, will be remembered more for the way he went out of this world than what he accomplished while he was in it.

Born Samuel J. Markcovitz in the Maxwell Street ghetto, he earned the nickname of "Kid Nails" because as a youth he was good with his fists. He joined the Army in 1917 and went off to France with the famous "Rainbow Division."

Morton rose quickly through the ranks to sergeant, and won the *Croix de Guerre*, France's highest decoration for bravery, for hand-to-hand combat in the trenches during which he he took a bullet wound to the arm and shrapnel in his leg. After being wounded a third time he was given a battlefield commission to first lieutenant, and returned home to Maxwell Street with a chest full of ribbons.

Shortly thereafter he linked up with O'Banion, a former altar boy who conducted his bootlegging and bloodshed business out of a flower shop across from Holy Name Cathedral.

As in the military, Morton quickly rose through the ranks. Along with Earl "Hymie" Weiss, Vincent "Schemer" Drucci and Louie "Three-Gun" Alterie, he became one of O'Banion's trusted confidants. It was said that Morton, who appreciated the finer things in life, taught O'Banion to wear a dinner jacket and use the proper fork when he ate.

It was also said that Morton had six notches in his imported pearl-handled weapon.

In 1922 Morton and Hirschie Miller, an ex-deputy Municipal Court bailiff, were acquitted of charges of murdering Detective Sergeants William Hennessy and James Mulcahy during a row in the Beaux Arts Club, a cabaret at 2702 S. State St.

The *Daily News* used the word "fix" in reporting that two witnesses had been paid to alter their testimony. Both witnesses admitted receiving money from Morton, but said it had nothing to do with their telling the truth during his trial.

"If the detectives had been sober instead of crazy drunk this thing would never have taken place," Morton explained.

In another bar brawl, a combatant accused Morton of taking his hat and watch. Witnesses said Morton pulled a roll of $1,000 bills out of his pocket and scoffed, "There's $20,000 there—do you think I want to hook a punk timepiece?"

Morton developed an interest in horse flesh as a frequent guest of Alterie, who owned a ranch in Colorado. He eventually purchased a bay, which he stabled at a North Clark Street riding academy.

On Sunday, May 13, 1923, Morton, tastefully attired in a green sport coat, cream colored jodhpurs and riding boots, saddled his horse and headed for the Lincoln Park bridle path, where he was to be joined by the O'Banions for a morning canter.

As they approached the park the mount reared up out of control. Morton stood up in the saddle to get a firmer hold on the reins, but a stirrup broke and he was thrown to the ground. The horse plunged wildly and kicked the fallen rider in the head.

When Policeman John Keys, who saw the incident and ran to the hoodlum's aid, bent over the dying man he gasped in surprise, "Why, it's Nails Morton. He was my lieutenant in France." Morton, who had survived the World War, the gang wars and two murder trials, died without regaining consciousness.

After his funeral the *Daily News* reported, "Five thousand Jews turned out to pay tribute to Nails Morton, the man who made the West Side safe for his race." The funeral cortege stretched two miles long, and it took six limousines to carry the flowers. At the cemetery, Morton's friends laid on his grave a $1,600 floral piece of red carnations in the shape of a nail.

After Morton was buried with full military honors, O'Banion reportedly flew into a rage and bellowed, "Someone's going to pay for this."

Alterie took it upon himself to avenge his friend's untimely death. Accompanied by two of his henchmen, Alterie visited the riding stable and asked for Morton's horse. When the stable owner refused to produce the animal, Alterie pressed a gun to the man's ear and explained that he wasn't kidding.

The mount was saddled up and led to the spot in Lincoln Park where Morton had died. There each man ceremoniously emptied his weapon into the condemned horse's head.

After the deed was done, it was reported, Alterie called the stableman and told him where he could pick up the saddle.

Johnny Torrio
(1882–1957)

Johnny Torrio, to whom we are indebted for Al Capone, was one of the few underworld chieftains ever to live out a normal lifespan—but one day he almost didn't make it.

A vicious member of New York's Five Points Gang, Torrio was the nephew of Big Jim Colosimo, Chicago's first organized crime boss, who imported him to act as his bodyguard.

Torrio tended to the nuts-and-bolts operation of his uncle's saloon, gambling, whorehouse and labor racketeering empire, but he envisioned millions more to be made in bootleg hooch. The 49-year-old Colosimo, however, was more interested in Dale Winter, a church choir singer half his age.

On May 11, 1920, after Torrio arranged for Colosimo to be in the lobby of his restaurant at precisely 4 o'clock to receive a liquor shipment, somebody put a bullet into the gang chief's head.

The consensus was that the fatal shot was fired either by Frankie Yale or by young Al Capone, a scarfaced gunsel that Torrio, himself, had brought in from

New York a year earlier for $75 a week. Once Colosimo was out of the way Torrio took over the rackets, with Capone acting as enforcer.

Aside from the fact that he was a cold blooded killer, the slightly-built Torrio was practically a virtuous man—a devoted husband who did not smoke, drink or use bad language, and who thoroughly enjoyed the opera. Furthermore, he was the godfather to Capone's only child.

A most astute businessman, it was Torrio who discovered Jake "Greasy Thumb" Guzik, a brothel handyman who was good at figures, and promoted him to head bookkeeper for the mob.

Torrio set up headquarters in the Four Deuces, a saloon and brothel at 2222 S. Wabash Ave., where he patiently groomed his protege, Capone, on the fine points of the business. In 1923 alone the pair shared a profit of $7 million.

In a marriage of North and South Side bootlegging, Torrio and Dion O'Banion became partners in Sieben's brewery, one of the biggest in Chicago. After Torrio bought his partner out, O'Banion set Torrio up for an arrest, letting him get caught with 13 truckloads of beer, and had a good laugh afterwards.

Torrio was sentenced to nine months in jail, and he wasn't laughing. Shortly thereafter, while Torrio was free on bond, O'Banion was shot to death in his flower shop across the street from Holy Name Cathedral. Torrio and Capone both sent wreaths to his funeral.

On January 24, 1925, two months after O'Banion's murder, Torrio and his wife, Ann, were walking up to the front door of their apartment at 7011 S. Clyde Ave. after a Loop shopping spree.

As Torrio walked behind his wife with an armful of packages, two men got out of a black Cadillac across the street and opened fire. Torrio fell to the ground with bullet wounds in his chest, right arm and groin, and and a load of buckshot in the jaw.

As his wife watched in horror, one of the men bent over the bleeding Torrio and pressed his automatic against the gang chief's temple to administer the *coup de grace*. His gun was empty, however, and the would-be assassin had to flee before he could reload.

Torrio was rushed to Jackson Park Hospital where he hovered between life and death, while guarded by both police and members of his own mob.

Bugs Moran, a North Side bootlegger who had been a pall bearer at O'Banion's funeral, was identified as one of the shooters, but Torrio, as soon as he was well enough to talk, refused to press charges.

"I know who they were. It's my business," he told police. "I've got nothing to tell you."

One close call was enough, however, and wily Torrio decided to opt for early retirement. He turned his whole gangland empire over to Capone, and the rest is history.

Torrio cautiously left the hospital by way of the fire escape, dropped his appeal from the brewery arrest, and went off to serve his nine months in the comparative safety of the Lake County jail in Waukegan.

A bullet-proof screen was installed across the bars at Torrio's expense, and three deputy sheriffs hired by him served as special guards while he slept on his own brass bed.

After getting out of jail, Torrio quietly boarded a steamboat for his native Naples, where he stayed until things cooled down. Upon his return to the States he went into the rum-running business on the East Coast, never daring to return to Chicago.

Treasury agents arrested him in 1935 on a liquor fraud charge, and he spent two and a half years in jail for income tax evasion.

Torrio led a quiet life thereafter, until he suffered a fatal heart attack in a Brooklyn barber chair in 1957—at the ripe old age of 75.

Bessie Coleman
(1893–1926)

Long before anyone ever heard of Martin Luther King, Bessie Coleman "had a dream" of her own. She wanted to fly like a bird. The trouble was, there was no room for blackbirds in the sky over America in the pioneer days of aviation.

And Bessie was black. Her mother was "colored," as they said down Texas way where she was born in 1893. Her daddy was Cherokee.

The one thing Coleman had going for her was a world of ambition, which she brought with her when she came to Chicago shortly before World War I, in search of a better life.

She worked as a manicurist in the Comiskey Park barber shop while managing a chili parlor on the side, hoping to set aside enough money for college.

But the sky was where she wanted to be. Eddie Rickenbacker, Baron Manfred von Richthofen and other wartime aviators had kindled the world's interest in flying, and Coleman was no different than anyone else. Women had been soaring aloft for years, first in balloons and then airplanes. But, sorry, if you were black the field was closed. No one was even willing to take you on as a student.

In the years immediately following the War to End All Wars, the French Federation Aeronautique Internationale (International Aeronautical Federation) took the lead in aviation. It was the only country where one could earn a pilot's license, after passing FAI examinations.

"Why don't you learn French?" one of Coleman's friends, the publisher of a black weekly newspaper, suggested, pointing out the new careers opening in the field of aviation. "Then go to France and learn to fly."

It was, she agreed, the only solution. She withdrew her college savings and sailed for France, where she earned her pilot's license on June 21, 1921, at a flying school outside Paris. She returned home aboard the steamship Manchuria the following September, holding the only such license ever issued to a black, male or female.

The *U.S. Air Service News Letter* reported the fact that Bessie Coleman was the only black licensed pilot in the United States in its issue of Nov. 1, 1921.

With the remainder of her savings she purchased three Army surplus Curtiss bi-planes, which she hoped would earn her enough money to open a flying school. Several black man, impressed by the young woman's accomplishment, had already asked her to teach them to fly.

After picking up the excess aircraft at Rockwell Field, Calif., she embarked on a barnstorming tour—stunt flying, wing walking and parachuting—high over any crowd that would pay the price of admission. It was a game played by many returning airmen, giving small town residents across the country their first close-up look at the flimsy, fabric-covered "flying machines."

An *Air Service News Letter* of 1922 noted that Coleman made her debut as an air gypsy on Labor Day at Curtiss Field near New York City, clad in her aviator's uniform of "O.D. breeches, leather leggins, Sam Browne belt, and coat cut on the lines of the Canadian officers."

Though her family objected to her new daredevil vocation, Coleman told them she knew what she was doing. She was, in fact, a double drawing card. Large crowds turned out, not only to "ooh" and "ahhh" at the fancy stunt flying, but also to get a look at the only black woman who could do it.

Her first of many Chicago appearances came the following October at Checkerboard Field near Maywood, where thousands craned their necks as she looped and dived, flew figure eights and performed other daring stunts.

She became known as "Brave Bessie" after another woman, billed to make a parachute jump before a waiting crowd, got a last-minute case of the jitters. Rather than send the crowd home disappointed, Coleman strapped on the harness and bailed out in the other woman's place.

In 1924, thrill-seekers, hoping to see a crash, were rewarded when Coleman's bi-plane cracked up in California. She suffered face cuts, a broken leg and three fractured ribs. As soon as she was well enough she was back in the cockpit, thrilling crowds from coast to coast.

By the end of summer in 1926 she had amassed almost enough funds to open her own flying school, and she banked on a Labor Day air show, sponsored by the Negro Welfare League in Jacksonville, Fla., to put her over the top.

It would never be, however.

Early that morning Coleman took off with her mechanic for a test flight to make sure everything was in order for the holiday performance. Clipping along at 110 miles an hour at an altitude of 3,500 feet, the young pilot put the plane into a dive from which it never recovered. At about 2,000 feet the craft did a flip-flop and Coleman, who was neither strapped in nor wearing a parachute, was thrown out and plunged to her death. The plane continued its pilotless dive to earth, killing the mechanic, Willie Wills.

Brave Bessie was only 32, but she had made her mark. Her accomplishments have earned her a place of honor in the Smithsonian Institution's National Air and Space Museum exhibit, "Black Wings: The American Black in Aviation."

Clarence Darrow
(1857–1938)

The twentieth century's greatest criminal lawyer, Clarence Darrow, was also its most famous agnostic, cynic and pessimist; but he could be outright funny about it.

"This world is all a big bughouse," he said. "I'll be glad to leave it."

"Life," he argued in many debates, "is not worth living."

In his 80s, he wrote a friend:

> I've seen this play of life well into its fifth act. I'm pretty
> well tired and disgusted with it. I want to lie down and
> go to sleep.

Darrow, remembered today for his courtroom successes, was also known in his day for his debates, his against-the-grain philosophy and his challenge to the public to think and feel.

The Chicago lawyer, bitterly opposed to the death penalty, represented 220 men who faced it and saved every one of them from the gallows or electric chair. The only client he lost to the gallows was an individual whose appeal, rather than trial, he handled.

His summaries to the jury were long, often lasting eight and a half hours, usually without benefit of any notes. His speeches were full of history, drama, pathos, self-depreciation, humor and, above all charm. Darrow regularly challenged jurors to think differently than they ever had before sitting in the jury box.

His most famous defense was not before a jury, but before a judge. His clients, he acknowledged, were guilty and they had confessed. Nathan Leopold and Richard Loeb admitted that they had murdered young Bobby Franks in a thrill-seeking effort to commit the "perfect crime." In his argument, he begged:

I am pleading that we overcome cruelty with kindness,

and hatred with love. I know the future is on my side. Your Honor stands between the past and the future. You may hang these boys by the neck until they are dead; but in doing it you will turn your face to the past.

Judge John R. Caverly sentenced them to life plus 99 years. Loeb was murdered in prison, but Leopold spent a useful life there, and after being freed, made personal sacrifices for medical science.

Another of the cases that brought him international attention was the so-called "Scopes Monkey Trial" in Dayton, Tenn., in 1925. Young John Scopes was indicted for teaching evolution in the public school there. Tennessee law specifically forbade defending such theory in the classroom.

Darrow's opponent was former Presidential candidate and fundamentalist, William Jennings Bryan. The court was opened each morning with a prayer, and a courtroom sign said, "Read your Bible daily."

Darrow lost the case; but struck a tremendous blow for free thought, intelligent questioning and ultimately thinking, as the public daily followed his arguments.

He defended communists, anarchists, the insane, the very wealthy, the very poor, gangsters and especially, the unpopular. One writer described him as:

. . . a sort of human Rock of Ages for the unadjusted and underprivileged.

Darrow came to Chicago in 1887. He was a close friend to the idealistic Governor John P. Altgeld. He had read a booklet on the criminal and penal system that the future governor of Illinois had written and was profoundly moved by it. The young lawyer also initiated a friendship with First Ward Alderman Michael "Hinky Dink" Kenna, who was never accused of being idealistic. Through him, Darrow received an appointment as assistant corporation counsel of Chicago.

While serving in the Illinois State legislature, he very reluctantly voted against a special pension for the widow of Altgeld, a man whom he considered a father to him.

Was his life worth living?

We have his own words in a 1925 debate against Professor Frederick Starr:

> To one life is of little value. I don't mean to me individually, but as I see life. The great senseless, wasteful, cruel spawning of life upon the earth. I see not only its pain, but its pleasures, and its joys annoy me more than its sorrows, for I don't want to lose them. I love my friends; I love people; I love life; but its everlasting uncertainty; its manifest futility; its unavoidable troubles and its tragic end appall me.

Earl "Little Hymie" Weiss
(1898–1926)

Earl "Little Hymie" Weiss, according to his mother, Mary, began life as a good boy. He went to work at age 13 as a newsboy and always gave her all his earnings. He progressed to driving a newspaper delivery wagon. He was in World War I and left the service with a good record.

Hymie ended his life full of machine-gun bullets on the steps of Holy Name Cathedral at Superior and State streets. The Catholic Church refused him burial and a good many people said, "Good riddance"; but none as enthusiastically as Al Capone, who had had him rubbed out.

Weiss, second generation Polish, changed his name from Wajciechowski. On the police blotter he was Earl, but in gangdom he was known as "Hymie," "Little Hymie," and "Hymie the Polack."

An article at the time of his death called him "the only man Al Capone ever really feared." And Capone's reaction was for good reason. Hymie was angry at Al and attempted to have him killed three times. The most sensational effort was in Cicero on Sept. 20, 1926, when Weiss and ten carloads of his North Side gang members drove past Capone's headquarters at the Hawthorne Inn and sprayed the windows with machine gun fire. Capone's associate, Frank Rio, pulled Al down on the floor at the sound of the first shot and they stayed there until it was over.

Weiss' anger stemmed not so much from territorial fights between the two aggressive gangsters, but from the fact that Capone's men had killed Dion O'Banion, Weiss' boss, whom he also worshipped.

Dion O'Banion and Hymie Weiss were also united by a religious piety. O'Bannion had been an altar boy and operated a flower shop across the street from Holy Name Cathedral. Two of Capone's men gunned him down in his shop Nov. 10, 1924. Weiss was noted for always fingering his rosary beads.

He was nicknamed in earlier days, "The Perfume Bandit," although no one remembered exactly why. Weiss, however, was not a cute character. He was considered an ugly human being. He was a suspected jewel robber, safe-cracker, election terrorist, murderer, and a convicted hijacker. He was both brainy and brutish. Weiss is credited with inventing the phrase "take him for a ride." When a gang suspected a member of treachery, the man was "taken for a ride," with the individual sitting in the front seat with his head in a ready position for a gunman in the back seat.

Weiss took over O'Banion's North Side empire, but his greater interest was in avenging Dion's death. Capone tried to negotiate, but Weiss was not interested. Weiss had shot up and almost killed Capone's boss, Johnny Torrio. Capone, who took over after Torrio retired, had retaliated twice. He sent his men to shoot Weiss in the Loop in broad daylight. It didn't eliminate Weiss, but helped to hurt the city's image something awful.

Capone focused his efforts. Two of his men rented a room at Superior and State streets and waited several days to get clear and final shots at Weiss as he entered or exited his headquarters above O'Banion's old flower shop.

On Oct. 11, 1926, from their rented room, Capone's gunmen killed Weiss and his driver Sam Peller, wounded three other Weiss gang members and destroyed the date and half the words on the cornerstone of the cathedral.

Ironically, the assassination brought a peace pact ten days later. It was worked out by rival gangs at the Hotel Sherman, a strange memorial to the battling Little Hymie Weiss.

Al Capone
(1899–1947)

Throughout the world, the word "gangster" is synonymous with "Al Capone"; and, in many places, so is Chicago.

In 1929, in writing their book, *Chicago, the History of Its Reputation*, Lloyd Lewis and Henry Justin Smith explained, as it was happening, the phenomenon of Al Capone:

> He [Capone] was in a high place in gangdom when crime became a box office and circulation hit, when it became "sure fire" before the footlights and magazine editors frenziedly offered authors $1 a word to write about Chicago gangs. Capone, without being much of an actor or hero in fact (indeed, some say he was only a "front" for a brainy committee), became celebrated from Spokane to Miami, and even as far as London and Berlin.

They wrote this before the St. Valentine's Day Massacre, Feb. 14, 1929. On that day, in a garage at 2122 N. Clark St., seven members, or associates, of the Bugs Moran gang were killed with machine guns by Capone's hoodlums dressed as policemen.

Moran, who happened not to be there, later said, "Only Capone kills like that."

The mass slaying focused on the ruthlessness of the bootlegging and gang wars, at the center of which the world saw Capone.

It was not simply cheap pulp writers and sensational magazines that carried the message of Al Capone to the far-flung corners of the world. The *New York Times* mentioned him more than 300 times in one year alone.

The more one researches Capone, the more evident is the fact that one act of his created the tremendous need to know about him around the world. It was his use of the Thompson submachine gun or Tommy Gun. He was not the first gangster to shoot one, but he perfected its use.

The machine gun had been developed as a "trench broom" as World War I ended. It was then advertised as the weapon of choice to protect one's estate or ranch. The bootleggers' troops easily purchased them at their local hardware stores, but had problems, as the gun's kick sprayed bullets in every direction except that of their intended victims.

Capone was cold and calculating enough to know you had to practice holding the gun steady for future possible use. That ability to plan made Capone an international phenomenon. It changed the balance of power in the Beer Wars of Chicago and tipped the monopoly of crime in his direction.

This course of history made Capone rich, powerful and infamous. Those without money, power and fame were mesmerized by how quickly and simply he had acquired all three. They practiced with fantasized guns, making the sound, "ratatatat" and dreamed of doing in those who were keeping them from their dreams.

Capone's dream ended Oct. 24, 1931, when he was sentenced to 11 years in the penitentiary for income tax evasion and immediately incarcerated in Cook County.

Lewis and Smith, in an addendum to a subsequent edition of their book published in 1933, described Capone's downfall:

> Capone in prison. Yes. The rotund hoodlum king, convicted before Judge Wilkinson of income tax fraud, protesting to the last that he was not as bad as painted, hustled off to Atlanta [Penitentiary] handcuffed to an auto thief, silenced.

He, however, despite a blatant attempt on his life, did all right in Atlanta as he garnered a favored life. He did not do well in the prison where he was subsequently moved, Alcatraz. His world caved in and so did he. Capone talked and gave valuable information to federal investigators. He also developed tertiary syphilis and broke down mentally.

A very sick man, he was released from prison on Nov. 16, 1939. His associate Jake Guzik described him as "nuttier than a fruitcake."

Al Capone died Jan. 25, 1947, in his Palm Island, Fla., home, of pneumonia.

Rio Burke
(1903–   )

As she drifts gracefully into her twilight years, 87-year-old Rio Burke pulls her calico shawl comfortably about her soft shoulders and recalls fond memories of rat-a-tat romance, patent leather shoes, diamonds, furs and bootleg booze.

"I'm a pretty tough old bird," she smiles, looking back on her not-so-halcyon days as the wife of a top Prohibition Era mobster.

Rio Burke, nee Ray Rucker of Richmond, Ky., was married to dapper Dominick Roberto, alias Dan Roberts, a Capone lieutenant in south suburban Chicago Heights.

"Dominick would come home late at night and take me in his arms," she says wistfully. "He wouldn't tell me where he'd been. Gangsters don't tell their wives *anything. Nothing!* The wife is for the nursery, the kitchen and the bed. The mistresses, *they* knew what was going on.

"Now it was not uncommon for Capone's lieutenants to come home in the early morning hours bringing six or seven of their pals with them. The wives were expected to get up and make them dinner or breakfast, depending on what the men wanted. I wasn't one of those Italian wives and refused to cook like that.

"Only once did Dominick hit me, and I hit him right back. He never raised a hand to me again."

Though her once-dark hair is streaked with gray, Burke's features, notably her flashing brown eyes, still reflect the beauty of the sultry, fur-coated brunette pictured in the scrapbook of her glory years.

An avid reader of paperbacks, which line her small North Side apartment, she speaks eloquently of those days when women were women, and gin was made in bathtubs.

Born in Kentucky in 1903, Ray Rucker studied music as a child and learned to play the piano and violin. A cousin, who was a Follies girl, helped her to land her first singing job at Big Jim Colosimo's cafe on South Wabash Avenue at the age of 19.

She met Roberto a year later during a three-week gig at a nightclub he owned with fellow mobster Jimmy Amaratti in Chicago Heights.

"Dominick fell in love with me and we were married on April 14, 1924, in a little Indiana town on the Ohio River," she relates. She was 21 and Roberto, an immigrant former railroad worker, was 10 years her senior.

"I knew he was a racketeer because he was loaded down with diamonds and money, and that was a big deal for me at that age," she explains. "But I didn't know what a racketeer was. I didn't know that it included killing or anything like that. I knew he made money fast and had plenty of it. Fur coats and diamonds went to my head."

The lovebirds settled in a rented home on Chicago Road in "the Heights." Roberto chose the furnishings and hired a maid and gardener. "All I had to do was look pretty," she laughs.

"One day the maid found a gunny sack in a closet off the front room. We opened up the sack and it was full of guns—sawed-off shotguns, revolvers. When I asked Dominick about them he said, 'Oh, a bunch of the boys are going hunting.'

"Then, in his bureau drawers, I began to find these things that looked like fountain pens. Dominick told me they were guns. He never went to bed without one of those pistol pens under his pillow. Never!"

On the night of April 27, 1925, Assistant State's Atty. William McSwiggin, the "hanging prosecutor," was cut down by machine gun fire outside the Pony Inn in Cicero. Capone, himself, wielded the Tommy Gun, according to State's Atty. Robert Crowe, but police were unable to find him for questioning.

"That's because he was at our house," Burke reveals. "Capone came to our house in the Heights and stayed for eight days. He never went outside. He didn't expect anything special. He ate spaghetti and whatever anybody else ate."

Whenever Capone visited the Roberto residence he was a "perfect gentleman" Burke related. "We women spoke to him, of course, but we stayed in the background."

After the heat died down Capone returned to his seven-room suite in the Metropole Hotel.

"Capone liked to receive gifts, and he was also generous, if you were on his side," she says.

"When Al moved into the Metropole, Dominick

and Jimmy Amaratti gave him a special, hand-carved chair. The back of the chair was bullet-proof. It came up over Al's head. Dominick often talked of how expensive that chair was. I wonder where it is today."

Capone, in turn, rewarded Roberto with an extravagant diamond-studded belt buckle. Big Al had 30 of the gold buckles engraved with the initials of his dearest friends. They cost $273 apiece, and Capone paid the jeweler in cash.

Alfred "Jake" Lingle, the $65-a-week *Tribune* reporter who was on Capone's payroll, owned one such diamond belt when he was shot to death in 1930.

"Dominick would never wear his because he said it was gaudy," Burke says. "He had it made into a diamond cluster ring for me."

Capone moved from the Metropole to the Lexington Hotel in 1928, the same year she and Roberto were divorced. They remained intimate friends, however, and she visited him in the federal penitentiary at Leavenworth, Kan., where he was serving time for perjury.

"In Kansas City I was given instructions to see a certain priest, who got me into Leavenworth after the night count of inmates," she says. "Dominick and I spent hours together in the warden's office. That's what money can do."

In 1933, two weeks after he was paroled, Roberto was deported to Italy. Burke went on the road as a big band singer and nightclub entertainer. She met her second husband, Jack Burke, later a Hollywood florist for movie stars, in Kansas City.

In later years she was a popular singer on radio station WLW in Cincinnati, with Enrique Madriguera's band. It was during that period that she changed her name to Rio. "Ray sounds too boyish," her producer argued.

Her second marriage also ended in divorce. For half a century she lived alone on Chicago's North Side, a sweet little old lady with a past that nobody knew.

Finding herself a stranger in a changing neighborhood, Rio Burke moved to South Bend to be close to a friend her own age. Small town life did not befit her, however, and she quietly moved back to Chicago.

After her divorce from Burke she never remarried. If the truth were known, she still carries a torch for the dapper Capone gangster who once showered her with diamonds and furs.

"On Dominick's last night in Chicago before he was deported I had dinner with him. He still loved me, and before he left he gave me $1,000. Then he sailed for Europe on the *Ile de France* and was gone." She never heard from him again.

Mayor William Hale "Big Bill" Thompson
(1867–1944)

Once upon a time there really was a Big Bill Thompson. And he was the tumultuous mayor of the city of Chicago in wild and incredible years.

Thus, Herman Kogan and Lloyd Wendt began their book, *Big Bill of Chicago.* They continued:

In the beginning he was a fearless hero, by chance a champion of reform, and he strutted and shouted his way into the city's heart.

Then the two authors eloquently describe the two very divergent views of the man who served as mayor from 1915 to 1923 and from 1927 to 1931:

Big Bill Thompson? They called him a charlatan and a genius, a knave and a saint, a P.T. Barnum and a George Washington, a churl and a gallant, a petulant child and a canny thinker. "Bill Thompson's the man for me," some sang and others answered "He has the carcass of a rhinoceros and the brain of a baboon!" Some cried, "Big Bill's heart is as big as all outdoors!" and others replied, "The people have grown tired of this blubbering jungle hippopotamus!"

The authors of those words left us a sense of how difficult it is for future generations to grasp that Big Bill not only lived in Chicago, but was three times chosen its number one citizen.

Another writer, Philip Kinsley, explained:

Thompson was a master of mass psychology and a figure representative of certain tendencies of his period. He is to be explained by the forces that pushed him upward as well as by his own reactions to the problems of the day. He was both cause and effect . . . He lived in action, not introspection, and he had the color of the frontier and the western plains, the indomitable onward march of democracy.

Writing in 1937, Kinsley predicted that there would be writing about Big Bill and his phenomenon "a hundred years hence." He continued:

His genius for the spectacular made him an international figure. He might induce dismay and ridicule, but he was a force to be reckoned with. "Cowboy Bill," "Big Bill the Builder," he was always on the front seat of the great American bandwagon.

Dismay and ridicule were, indeed, the responses of many Chicagoans to the man and his antics. Those reactions heavily taint any historical assessment of Thompson. He is associated with Capone, whose thugs helped him get re-elected in 1927. People chuckled over his threat to punch the King of England in the nose. And, today, we know exactly how indulgently corrupt he was. At his death, two safe deposit boxes he rented at American National Bank and Trust Company were found to be stuffed with $1,466,250 in cash.

He lost his last campaign for mayor in 1931 and his supporters, for the most part, have died off; but history has to acknowledge there was an army of Chicagoans who did not see him as a buffoon and "blubbering jungle hippopotamus" or who voted for him anyway.

Big Bill was born in Boston in 1867 and brought to Chicago as a nine-day-old child. His father was in real estate. Instead of going to college, Bill traveled with his mother in Europe and then went to Texas to work as a cowboy. He helped drive a herd of longhorns up the overland trail to the short grass country and ranched in New Mexico. Thompson returned to Chicago after his father died in 1892 and took over his real estate business.

He captained the Chicago Athletic Club's football team to a national championship, helping to project him as the town's number one dandy and jock.

It was a time for reform, which in 1900 in Chicago meant the sons of the superwealthy, such as the Palmers and the McCormicks, were elected to offices traditionally held by tavern owners. It didn't get the garbage picked up or other city services provided, but it helped keep them off the streets. And so Big Bill became alderman of the old Second Ward in 1901.

He arrived there as an ally of the Blond Boss of Cook County, William Lorimer, who was later to be expelled from the U.S. Senate for having purchased the office. In one of the most calculated political operations in the city's history, a group of supporters spent two years creating a successful pledge card campaign to make Thompson mayor of Chicago in 1915.

He hired 10,000 temporary payrollers and assessed city drivers and inspectors $3 a month to build a fund to help groom him for president of the United States. He was given the nickname "Kaiser Bill," for his hesitancy to become enthusiastic about World War I.

Big Bill, full of bombast and showmanship, won re-election in 1919, but by a far narrower margin than in his election in 1915. On the other hand, he knew the power of images and vitality. He used his cowboy hat to symbolize himself and exaggerated, colorful language to describe his enemies. He called himself, "Big Bill the Builder" to take credit for the new buildings going up in Chicago. His enemies, the reformers, he referred to as: "Liars! Hypocrites! and Fourflushers."

The corruption trials of many of his appointees, closest friends and advisors doomed his popularity. Pledge cards in behalf of his re-election were sent out, but few came back signed, and he did not run for re-election in 1923. Instead, he kept his name in the news by leading a tree-climbing fish expedition to the South Seas. He launched a yawl paid for by the cypress wood industry on the Chicago River at Riverview amusement park. Somehow, the would-be scientist and his buddies did not make it all the way down the Mississippi, much less to the South Seas.

Had not Big Bill run again, he would have been remembered simply as an incompetent but flashy mayor who wore out his welcome in office.

But in 1927, he made an unbelievable political comeback. The extent to which Al Capone and his fellow gangsters not only helped, but also made it possible, has been the subject of newspaper stories, biographies of both men, history books and movies.

Thompson had consistently boasted of ridding Chicago of crime. He had pledged at the beginning of his first days in office to get every crook out of the city in 60 days. His police chief, who led the crusade, was subsequently indicted for taking bribes and saved from jail only by the legal acumen of Clarence Darrow. The reformers, he constantly argued, were the real crooks. Apparently, they were the ones he would liked to have gotten out of town.

The year 1927 represented a whole new scenario and opportunity for crime and corruption. Capone, who had controlled Cicero through its mayor, realized Chicago was possible.

Big Bill used perhaps the strangest central campaign issue in the history of American mayoral politics: the King of England.

Hugging American flags at political rallies, he cried:

> "This is the issue! What was good enough for George Washington is good enough for Bill Thompson . . . I want the King of England to keep his snoot out of America first, and last, and always! . . . If you want to keep that old American flag from bowing down before King George of England, I'm your man. If you want to invite King George and help his friends, I'm not . . . America First!"

He attacked school and library books in Chicago as being pro-British and tried to have them burned.

John Kobler, in his biography of Capone, called Capone's Hotel Metropole suite a covert annex to the Thompson campaign headquarters.

"Capone," Kobler described during the campaign as:

> . . . hunched over a mahogany conference table behind a battery of nine telephones, a cigar in his mouth, issuing orders to his forces scattered throughout the city, to triggermen, sluggers, kidnappers, bombers . . .

His first act in 1915 had been to have a "Prosperity Parade" in honor of himself and the good times Chicago was enjoying.

Thompson's last term would include: the "Pineapple Primary" of April 10, 1928, so called for the many bombs, "pineapples," used to intimidate politicians; the St. Valentine's Day Massacre and what Kogan and Wendt call Thompson's "Jonah years."

He ended his final term with the city in a Depression and depressed with its mayor.

Urbine J. "Sport" Herrmann
(1872–1938)

In 1924, Mayor Big Bill Thompson was temporarily out of office. In a bizarre publicity venture, he took along some cronies and headed off down the Mississippi River on an expedition to catch tree-climbing fish in the South Seas. The most outlandish member of this inane crew was Urbine J. "Sport" Herrmann. In *Big Bill of Chicago*, Herman Kogan and Lloyd Wendt describe his participation in the Thompson fiasco:

> Strangest of the passengers was Urbine J. "Sport" Herrmann, owner of the Court Theater and an irrepressible playboy. He wore a yachting cap, tennis shoes and an athletic supporter. When Captain A. J. Aiken Duken, Big Bill's skipper, touched port, Herrmann was stowed out of sight and Thompson put on more presentable clothes to speak on the need for a waterway that would compete with railroads along the route.

Sport was the same individual whom Thompson would appoint president of the Chicago Public Library board and who would lead the campaign to censor and burn any pro-British books in the library.

He was a jovial, pleased-to-meet-you man. He loved three things: sports (especially yachting), fist fighting, and Big Bill Thompson. His nickname came from his fanatical interest in sports. He was a part owner of the Boston Red Sox, had been a commodore of the

Columbia Yacht Club, and rarely missed a boxing match.

Herrmann, who was only mildly interested in politics, worshiped Thompson, with whom he often sailed in races and for pleasure. A close Thompson-Herrmann alliance had the mayoral candidate often using the Court Theater for some of his more zany political appearances.

On April 6, 1926, he appeared on the stage of Herrmann's theater with two caged rats, whom Big Bill told the crowd represented his political enemies, but former appointees, Dr. John Dill Robertson and Fred Lundin. "Doc" Robertson, whom Thompson in an earlier administration had appointed health commissioner, he now excoriated as not having "had a bath in twenty years."

The "rat" speech was the talk of the city for the next year and was a bizarre but effective way of Thompson admitting mistakes in his earlier terms in office.

The son of the lighthouse keeper at Sac Harbor, Delta County, Wis., Herrmann acquired the Court Theater in Chicago in 1909. He also owned other businesses. His obituary commented:

> Besides attracting attention by his business career, Herrmann also became known as a ready fighter with his fists.
>
> In 1910 he was arraigned before Judge Bruggermeyer on a charge of assaulting A. L. Baker, manager of the Columbia Yacht Club. Baker said the Assault took place on Sept. 31. "Impossible," replied Herrmann, who was acting as his own lawyer. "Remember the old adage, judge?—'Thirty days hath September, April, June and November—?" The judge remembered. He dismissed the case.
>
> In 1917 he had a fight with a man in the Hotel Sherman. In 1919 he fought two patrons who criticized the location of their seats in his theater. In 1923 he wrecked a ticket scalping office in Randolph Street because cut rate tickets for the Court were offered. He wrecked it again two weeks later. In the same year he battled three policemen and still another time battled four. In 1926 he had a set to with a park official. That closed his pugilistic career.

In 1927, Sport accepted the appointment to the library board with the explicit promise that he would not have to read a book. Thompson had campaigned to get elected on an anti-British and, more specifically, an anti-King of England platform. He argued that many books in both Chicago schools and public libraries were pro-British, and, therefore, anti-American. Big Bill chose Herrmann as his point man to get rid of them.

Sport actually did line up four books on his desk and touched a match to one of them as a sort of experiment. But, by that time, even Thompson realized he had made a mistake and an injunction that prohibited the book burning was not unwelcome.

In 1930, when the library was a victim of the Depression and without funds, Sport Herrmann and a business associate would partially atone for the days of his book-burning crusade by contributing $250,000 to buy books.

Herrmann was killed in 1938 in an automobile accident on his way to his yacht. Had he survived, he would have had to change the ship's name. He called it *The Swastika.*

Flagpole Joe Powers
(1906–   )

Probably no one in Chicago in the late 1920s and early '30s lived higher on the town than Joe Powers. He was a flagpole sitter.

In July of 1927 Joe perched atop the flagpole high above the Morrison Hotel for nearly 17 days. At one point a violent summer storm lashed him so fiercely that seven teeth were knocked out, but he held his airspace. A pair of enterprising dentists repaired the damage, aided by an impression taken 637 feet in the air.

The Morrison Hotel caper, in which he spent exactly 16 days, 2 hours and 45 minutes atop the flagpole, eclipsed the records of "Spider" Haines and "Shipwreck" Kelly, and a bearded, unkempt Powers came down a local hero.

While celebrating his first day down with a dinner at the Morrison's swank Terrace Garden, Powers related,

"I've been soaked by rain, blistered by sun and blown around like a toy balloon. In one electrical storm flashes came out of my toes and fingers. I felt like Franklin's kite."

Joining him for his victory dinner—after hotel officials had treated him to a shave, haircut and bath, of course—was Josephine Kilroy, the daughter of Joe's boarding house landlady, Agnes Kilroy.

When he left the hotel an admiring taxi driver bubbled, "You didn't go as far as Lindbergh, but Joe, you sure did stay longer."

In 1930 he celebrated his 24th birthday atop a flagpole at 2800 Milwaukee Ave., where he spent several

weeks enjoying a bird's eye view of the Northwest Side and Lake Michigan to the east.

In 1934 Joe tried to repeat his 1927 feat, secretly shinnying up the Morrison's pole to his old room with a view—north, east, west and south—but the annoyed hotel people called the police who coaxed him down before another storm could knock out the rest of his teeth.

Undaunted and ungrounded, Powers, sometimes known as "Roosting Joe," made his way to the top of the flagpole on the ten-story Flatiron Building at West Madison Street and Ashland Boulevard. It was one of the lowest stunts he had ever pulled, and flagpole fans said they could get a clear view of him for the first time without a telescope.

As one admirer said, "He used to look like a dot. Now I can see his arms and legs."

Unfortunately, with the end of the Depression, flagpole sitting went out of style and Flagpole Joe Powers faded into obscurity. But he sure lived high on the "hog butcher to the world" while he was up there.

Hack Wilson
(1900–1948)

Lewis Robert "Hack" Wilson was one of the greatest baseball players of the Prohibition Era. But more important than that, he was a Chicago Cub. He roosted on the ball diamond during the same years that Al Capone ruled the underworld.

Purchased from the New York Giants for $5,000 in 1926, the five foot, six inch outfielder quickly grew on his new hometown, and became one of Chicago's most colorful figures.

During his six seasons with the Cubs, from 1926 to 1931, Wilson slammed 190 home runs. In 1929 he hit six home runs in four days. His best season was 1930, when he socked 56 homers for a National League record. He also set a major league record of 190 runs batted-in that same year. In all, during his six years with the Cubs, he drove in 768 runs.

He was originally known as Lew Wilson, but his squat, powerful figure so resembled that of a Russian wrestler named George Hackenschmidt that a *New York Times* sportswriter hung the name Hack on him, and it stuck.

A true showman, Hack liked to hike up to the batter's box, scoop up two handfuls of dirt, and rub them all over his clean uniform and the back of his bulging, red, sweaty neck before hunching over the plate and glowering at the pitcher.

Westbrook Pegler, then a sportswriter, dubbed him "Hack Wilson, that porous party of perspiration."

Wilson's teammates were as colorful as he was—Kiki Cuyler, Gabby Hartnett, Guy Bush, Charlie Grimm, Rogers Hornsby—many of them castoffs from other ball clubs.

Wilson was also a notorious brawler, especially if anyone dared call him a "bastard," since he was sensitive about the fact that his father, Robert Wilson, and his mother, 16-year-old Jennie Caldwell, never married. Reds' pitcher Pete Donohue called him that once and ended up with a mouthful of blood.

Unfortunately, Wilson was also a night-owl and a boozer, and his performance occasionally suffered from his carousing the night before.

Cubs trainer Andy Lotshaw at times had to sober Wilson up by placing him in a tub of water with a 50-pound cake of ice before he could go out on the field.

"I've never played drunk," Wilson once explained to a skeptical fan. "Hung over, yes, but never drunk."

The team's manager, Joe McCarthy, once tried to discourage Wilson by bringing a bottle of gin into the locker room and dropping a worm into it. As the worm slowly stopped wiggling McCarthy asked, "What does this prove, Hack?"

Wilson, eying the deceased worm, responded, "It proves that if you drink, you won't get worms."

The besotted Wilson's glory days with the Cubs ended with the close of the 1931 season.

He gradually faded away from major league baseball and returned to Martinsburg, W. Va., the place that he called home, where he did odd jobs until sclerosis of the liver claimed him.

Authors Robert S. Boone and Gerald Grunska, in their book, *Hack,* said, "With his style of play and personality, he was made for Chicago in the 1920s. And he was made for no place else."

Sally Rand
(1904–1979)

Sally Rand burst upon the Chicago scene undressed as

Lady Godiva astride a white stallion. It was enough to get her a job at the A Century of Progress Exposition in 1933, and the rest is history.

Actually, she had quietly introduced her famous fan dance a year earlier in a Huron Street speakeasy, after arriving in town as an unemployed silent film actress at the age of 28.

The way she told the story, she was in a costume shop looking for something to wear when she spotted a pile of old ostrich plumes on the floor. They evoked memories of "white herons flying through the moonlight" over her grandfather's farm in Missouri, and she decided to get herself some.

With $200 borrowed from friends, she ordered a pair of "white, double willowed, 21 stem" ostrich fans from New York. They arrived on the day of her debut as a dancer in the North Side speak.

"I had planned to use my chiffon nightgown as a sort of Grecian tunic for the act," she explained. "At the time I was too dumb to know that the last girl hired—me—was the first girl on. I heard my music and there I was, with only my slippers and fans."

It was a moment of decision. There was no time to dress, so on stage she went, one fan in each hand, wearing "not even paint or heavy cold cream."

A short time later Rand met a Chicago politician who promised her a job at the about-to-open World's Fair. All she had to do, he suggested, was play Lady Godiva at a $100-a-plate benefit for the fair's Streets of Paris exhibit on the evening before it opened. She rented a horse for $75, added some false tresses to her long, blonde hair, and played Godiva on the lakefront.

It was only a step from the back of the horse to back of the fans, and Sally Rand was on her way to becoming the biggest name in local show biz.

Her fan dance in the Streets of Paris was broken up by police as often as four times a day, with each arrest giving her more publicity than the last. By the end of summer she was earning $3,000 a week, and the scientific theme which was intended to dominate the fair was all but forgotten.

Sally Rand was born Helen Gould Beck, the daughter of an army officer, on April 3, 1904, in Hickory County, Mo.

She came to Chicago at the age of 15 to study ballet, paying for her courses by modeling nude for anatomy classes at the Art Institute. A year later she appeared in a Ziegfeld-type revue at the old Marigold Gardens. From there it was on to Hollywood, under contract to Cecil B. DeMille, for a fling at silent films.

"I had changed my name from Helen to Billy Beck, but Mr. DeMille didn't like it," she said. "So I chose Sally. It's short, and that's good for theater marquees—and he was looking at an atlas and chose Rand, for Rand McNally & Co."

At the height of her career she was giving an incredible 16 performances a day. She was doing seven shows at the Streets of Paris, seven at a Loop theater, and two fan dances in a North Side nightclub.

Each act was the same, dancing deftly behind the feathered fans to Debussy's "Clare de Lune" and Chopin's "Waltz in C Sharp Minor" for six suggestive minutes under a blue light.

She commuted between jobs by speedboat, which whisked her from the fair at Northerly Island (the site of today's Meigs Field) to the Wrigley Building, where she would transfer to a taxi.

In the early morning hours of Aug. 14, 1933, after her last show at the Streets of Paris, Sally was cruising back downtown for her engagement at the Near North bistro when she stood up in the boat for a breath of air and toppled backward into the water.

"The speedboat was one of those big mahogany things, and she just flew off the back end of it," recalled Coastguardsman George Piotrowski, then 21, who was on duty at the Coast Guard station at the mouth of the Chicago River.

Piotrowski launched a boat as fellow Coastguardsman George Arnold, 26, dived into the water and swam 100 feet to the screaming woman.

"We didn't realize until we got her out of the water that it was Sally Rand," said Piotrowski, now retired in Kenosha, Wis.

The "rescue" made page one of all the papers. It

was not until later that Rand confessed to her press agent, the late Luther "Mike" Meredith, that she had planned the whole publicity stunt.

The city tried without success to close down the

Streets of Paris, on grounds that Sally's fan dance was "lewd and lascivious," but Judge Joseph B. David refused to issue an injunction.

"Some people would like to put pants on horses," he declared. "This court holds no brief for the prurient or ignorant. Let them walk out if they wish. If you ask me, they are just a lot of boobs come to see a woman wiggle with a fan or without fig leaves. But we have the boobs and we have a right to cater to them."

After the world's fair closed, the curvy blonde offered her seven-pound ostrich feather fans to the Chicago Historical Society, but the red-faced board of directors refused the donation.

So Sally, who was 5 feet tall, 110 pounds, and measured 35-25-35, took her show on the road, performing at nightclubs and in carnivals throughout the country, wearing a skin-tight transparent gauze costume in communities where nudity was a no-no.

She earned enough to put six brothers through college, and at the age of 52, entered the University of California, despite the fact that she never finished high school. She earned a diploma with a 95 point average.

In 1966 the Chicago Historical Society relented and accepted a set of her fans—unfortunately not the ones she hid behind at the A Century of Progress, which had long since worn out. She continued doing her act well into her 70s, explaining, "God knows, I like doing this. It's better than doing needle point on the patio."

Chicago, where she really got her start, remained one of her favorite towns. She played a number of return engagements at Mangam's Chateau and other clubs during the 1960s and 1970s, and sometimes stopped off just to visit when passing through.

On her last visit to Chicago, shortly before her death in 1979 at the age of 75, Sally did what she liked to do best. She got a group of oldtime news reporters together for lunch at the Tavern Club and talked about the good old days. She was still 35-25-35.

Joseph "Yellow Kid" Weil
(1875–1976)

He lies in everlasting peace in Rosehill Cemetery along with such notables as A. Montgomery Ward, Julius Rosenwald, Richard Sears, John G. Shedd, Morris B. Sachs and no less than 13 Chicago mayors. He was the biggest of them all—depending on how one measures greatness. Joseph "Yellow Kid" Weil was the greatest flim-flam man this country ever produced, a native son of whom all Chicago can be proud.

In the heyday of his colorful career, which ran from the turn of the century into the early 1940s, Weil gleefully conned greedy investors out of millions upon millions of dollars.

In the end, as he approached the sunset of his days—crochety, partly senile, but saber-tongued as ever—Weil himself was conned into reminiscing about those sinful days for the price of a 30-cent can of beer.

It was Saturday afternoon, June 30, 1973, and a reporter from one of the downtown papers had gone to visit Weil in a North Side nursing home on his 98th birthday, in hopes of prying a story out of him.

"He don't wanna talk to ya," an attendant said, slowly closing the door.

"Wait a minute," the reporter begged, stuffing several $1 bills into the attendant's shirt pocket. "If I wanted to get the old guy something he couldn't get here, what would I bring him?"

"Well," the attendant mused, fingering the singles. "He likes ice cream. And he likes beer . . ."

A half hour later the reporter walked unannounced into Weil's room, handed him an ice cream bar on a stick, and set a six-pack of Miller High Life on the table in front of him.

"What the hell do you want?" the old man barked.

"Just stopped by to wish you a happy birthday."

"Umph," he replied, chomping off the top third of the ice cream bar in one gigantic munch.

"They say you conned people out of more than $10

million . . . ."

"Hell no!" he interrupted. "I made $13 million in one deal alone. That was my biggest killing. Phony stocks."

Wiping a smear of chocolate off his chin, he looked wistfully into space and dreamed aloud of kings and queens and million dollar schemes.

"The most fun was horses, though. I owned two race horses, Black Fonzo and Mutineer. I could win with them or lose with them, depending on how the bets were going. You feed them in the morning and they're no good in the afternoon."

Flipping back through his card-file mind, The Kid recalled how he was credited with being the first con man ever to fleece his victims by phone, back in 1907 when such devices were still considered new fangled.

"We set up elaborate brokerage offices in the Loop and phoned likely prospects for orders. We'd buy up worthless mines for a few dollars and incorporate them for a million times their worth. We also published a financial paper, in which we planted phony items extolling our stocks. The customers came by the thousands," he explained.

"Unfortunately, postal inspectors thought our mail was too heavy and my lawyer, Clarence Darrow, advised me to close up shop."

At times like this he was apt to weigh anchor on his 95-foot yacht and chart a course for points unknown until things simmered down a bit. Weil cut a dashing figure in those days, attired in patent calf-leather shoes, buff colored spats, Scotch tweed suits, pearl beaver hats, black silk ties with three-carat diamond stick pins and pince-nez tortoise shell glasses.

In later years he grew a luxurious beard that gave him the appearance of an Old Testament prophet.

Now, shorn of his whiskers and unceremoniously clad in a woolen bathrobe, T-shirt, pajamas and slippers, he looked back on a life still rich in memories.

"If I had my life to live over again, I'd do the same damned thing," he said, popping the tab on a can of beer to wash down the ice cream. "It was an exciting, splendid way to live."

Weil was born at Clark and Harrison Streets, just south of the Loop, in 1875. A whiz at arithmetic, with visions of becoming an actor, he quit school and hired on as a police reporter for the City Press Association. This led to a job on the old *Chronicle.*

His newspaper career ended after he penned a touching story about a woman in the morgue, and how a Bible, opened to an appropriate passage, had been found in her room. Unfortunately, it turned out that she could not speak English, much less read it.

Weil earned the "Yellow Kid" sobriquet while hanging around in Alderman "Bathhouse John" Coughlin's First Ward saloon. The bartender lost $16 betting a customer he couldn't stand an egg on end on the bar.

"You just moisten your hand and put a little salt on it. Then you rub the egg in the salt, and it'll stand up," Weil related.

"Bathhouse John suspected I had shown the man how to do it. I forget whether I did or not. Anyway, Bathhouse John ran me out, and he called me 'Yellow Kid,' out of a character in a comic strip, and the name stuck."

Around World War I Weil entered into a spectacular triumvirate with Fred "The Deacon" Buckminster, a Chicago detective, and a smooth-talker named James "Gentleman Jimmy" Head. Posing as unschooled agents for European capitalists looking for American investments, they sold vast German holdings about to be seized as enemy property.

In the swindle, as carefully rehearsed as a Broadway play, Weil played the title role of "Dr. Henri Reuel," a wealthy German. He even had 200 fake copies of a Washington newspaper printed, with a front page story devoted to his quest for funds.

Weil subsequently became known and admired by police on five continents as the man who originated the "setup." This was a delightfully elaborate scheme in which he convinced crafty enterprisers into thinking they were taking advantage of his lack of business acumen.

Weil would pose as an inept nightclub operator, hoping to get out from under. After lining up a sucker he would outfit a hall with rented furniture and equipment, converting it into a lavish casino or speak-easy. He would hire a host of actors to pose as customers, bartenders, cigarette girls and entertainers for a one-night stand, while he showed off the establishment to the crafty would-be buyer.

When the sucker, who invariably thought he had taken Weil to the cleaners, returned the next night to oversee his newly-purchased operation he found an empty hall.

"And you know what? I never found a man I couldn't take, and any con man knows you can't cheat an honest man," Weil smiled, draining the last drop of beer from the can.

Asked whether he had any advice for future generations, Weil nodded sharply and said, "Damn right! If you expect to get something for nothing, you'll always end up on your ass!"

A year later, on Weil's 99th birthday, he said, "I don't want many more. I have been hearing about Heaven all my life, and I want to find out what that place is like."

Joseph Rene Weil lived to be 100, and went off to find out about Heaven on Feb. 26, 1976. Before leaving, he made sure he had spent every cent he ever stole.

For a while officials at Rosehill Cemetery were reluctant to believe that the man who died penniless could have been the same person for whom an empty plot awaited beside the graves of Weil's wife, Anna, and his daughter, Josephine.

It took several calls from a newspaper reporter to convince cemetery officials that there was only one Joseph "Yellow Kid" Weil.

Eleanor Jarman
(1904–????)

If Terrible Tommy O'Connor was an embarrassment to the County of Cook for leaving the hangman holding an empty rope, Eleanor "The Blonde Tigress" Jarman was an embarrassment to the State of Illinois for going over the wall of the women's prison at Dwight.

The 29-year-old Depression Era gun moll's date with destiny began at 2:39 on the lazily warm afternoon of August 4, 1933, outside Gustav Hoeh's haberdashery at 5948 W. Division St.

The siesta-like atmosphere of the neighborhood was shattered with a crash as the front door of the men's clothing store burst open, and two men and a woman spilled out onto the sidewalk, locked in combat.

The 71-year-old Hoeh was struggling desperately with a dark-haired man much younger than himself, and a blonde woman, barely five feet, three inches tall. The blonde was throwing her entire 110 pounds into the fray, clawing, scratching and hammering her fists on the elderly shopkeeper until he fell to the pavement. Then shots rang out. The man and woman jumped into a waiting car and fled, leaving Hoeh dead in front of his shop.

Five days later Eleanor Jarman and her boyfriend, George Dale, were arrested for Hoeh's murder. They were also implicated in 48 holdups in which the "Blonde Tigress" used a blackjack on uncooperative victims while her partner held a gun on them. Witnesses to Hoeh's slaying said she struck him on the head before Dale pumped the fallen shopkeeper full of bullets.

After a speedy trial, just three weeks after their arrest, Dale was sentenced to death and Jarman to 199 years in prison. With time off for good behavior, she would be eligible for parole in 1999 at the age of 95.

Dale met his fate in the electric chair in the basement of the Cook County Jail at 26th and California on April 19, 1934. The Blonde Tigress was shipped off to the women's prison at Dwight—but life in a cage was not her style.

Shortly before noon on August 8, 1940, on the eve of the seventh anniversary of her arrest, Eleanor Jarman scaled a 10-foot fence topped with barbed wire, discarded her prison frock and pulled on a polka-dot dress she had stolen from staff headquarters while mopping floors, and disappeared.

The FBI launched one of the biggest woman-hunts in the nation's history, but she was never heard from again. All authorities know for sure is that the convicted murderess never again got into serious trouble, because if she had her fingerprints would have given her away.

If alive in 1990 Jarman would be 86 years old—still nine years shy of serving out her full prison term with time off for good behavior, which she is hardly likely to get.

At the time of her flight Chicago police called her "the Most Dangerous Woman Alive!" For all anyone knows, she still is.

Edith Rockefeller McCormick
(1872–1932)

Edith Rockefeller McCormick, the *avis rara* of Chicago's turn-of-the-century society, was so rich and haughty that her own children had to make appointments when they wanted to talk to her.

The daughter of John D. Rockefeller had everything that money could buy, except a husband who stayed at home. He had an opera singer.

She married Harold Fowler McCormick, scion to the McCormick reaper fortune, in 1895. To help sate her appetite for priceless jewelry he gave her a rope of pearls worth $2 million one year. The following year he presented her with a $1 million emerald necklace. Then he bestowed upon her a necklace made up of 1,657 diamonds, so exquisite that no price tag could be put upon it.

Mrs. McCormick, who believed she was the reincarnation of King Tut's mother, required the presence of four butlers at her breakfast table, whether she ate or not. And she spoke to her servants only in writing through her secretary.

She and her husband set up housekeeping in a turreted mansion at 1000 Lake Shore Drive, where they dined on golden plates that Napoleon had given his sister. Guests sat on chairs once owned by Bonaparte, and walked across a $185,000 carpet that a shah of Persia had once given to Peter the Great of Russia.

Her dinners, at which no drop of liquor was ever served, were so formal that it was said "she taught Chicago how to wear and to own a dress suit."

The couple built a regal 44-room Italian villa on 269 acres in Lake Forest in 1911, but never moved into it. The furniture was never unpacked, and Villa Turicum stood vacant until it was torn down in 1956, because it was too expensive to keep up.

Mrs. McCormick left for Switzerland in 1913 to study psychology with Carl Jung. Upon her return in 1921 she divorced her husband, who had taken up with Ganna Walska, a Polish opera singer of mediocre talent.

Her own souvenir of her stay in Europe was an architect, Edwin Krenn, whom she installed in the Drake Hotel, across the street from her home. He became her constant companion, and she put him in charge of her personal fortune.

With Krenn and his prep school classmate, Edward Dato, she envisioned a resort city for millionaires that would be the Saratoga of the Middle West. She purchased 1,500 acres, just over the Illinois-Wisconsin line on the shore of Lake Michigan, in Kenosha County. She named it Edithton Beach, in honor of herself.

She spent more than $4 million laying out an 18-hole golf course and building a yacht harbor. The town, designed by Krenn, was to have Spanish castle-like homes and its own railroad station on the Chicago & North Western's Chicago-Milwaukee line.

The dream crashed with the stock market in 1929. Edithton Beach was abandoned, the golf course was overgrown, and the clubhouse on the beach was subdivided into apartments. A Waukegan newspaper reporter who lived there liked to show guests his bathroom, with three shower stalls.

Today the vast expanse south of Kenosha, known as the Chiwaukee Prairie nature preserve, is still criss-crossed with narrow roads, and is an occasional dumping ground for Chicago murder victims.

After Edith's fortune evaporated in the stock market crash of 1929, her brother, John D. Rockefeller, Jr., set her up in the Drake with a $1,000-a-day allowance.

When she died in 1932 it was revealed that for years she had kept a room for her husband at 1000 Lake Shore Drive, in the hope that he might one day return to her.

Harold Fowler McCormick
(1872–1941)

Harold Fowler McCormick had a wife who was one of the richest women in the world, a girlfriend who was the worst opera singer in town, and a set of monkey (or were they human?) glands that didn't do what they were supposed to accomplish.

Whatever good the wealthy scion of the reaper family accomplished in Chicago, those are the three things for which he is most remembered, more's the pity.

McCormick, who was married to John D. Rockefeller's daughter, Edith, was president of International Harvester Co. He was one of the city's leading financiers, and was also a pioneer aviation enthusiast.

McCormick established the first airport in the Midwest, the Cicero Air Field at Cermak Road and Cicero Avenue, in 1910. A year later he sunk his own money and knowhow into bringing the first international aeronautical show to Chicago's lakefront landing field in Grant Park. Aviators were paid $2 for every minute they could keep their home-made planes aloft, and some were reported to have made as much as $8 or $9.

In 1913 McCormick made headlines when he flew to work, landing his "aeroyacht" in the lake off Grant Park.

That was the year his wife went to Switzerland, and stayed for eight years. Meanwhile McCormick, a patron of the opera, fell head over heels for Ganna Walska, a Polish diva, whose career he fostered.

Walska was so bad that an audience in Havana pelted the stage with rotten eggs and vegetables during her debut in 1917. But he thought the dark, heavyset singer was the greatest in the world, and he divorced his wife in 1921 in order to become Walska's fourth husband.

She apparently convinced him that he was not up to her sexual standards, however, and he set out to do something about that, too. He underwent a secret operation in Wesley Memorial Hospital by a controversial surgeon (some said crackpot) who claimed he could rejuvenate aging males by implanting glands from monkeys.

While the doctor refused to comment upon the exact nature of the operation, the press of the day speculated that Harold had been implanted with the glands of a young man. It was only a matter of time before Longfellow was being paraphrased wherever high society gathered:

> Under the spreading chestnut tree,
>
> The village smithy stands;
>
> The smith, a gloomy man is he;
>
> McCormick has his glands.

The operation apparently didn't do its stuff, since Walska divorced McCormick 10 years later at a reported cost to him of $6 million—one-fourth of his Harvester holdings.

After that McCormick took up whistling. In fact he became so proficient that he gave a recital over the radio. And his dear friend, Baroness Violet Beatrice von Wenner, accompanied him on the harp when he gave a concert.

And he continued to send his first wife, Edith, a single rose every year on her birthday until her death in 1932. He died nine years later in California, where he was living with his third wife.

George Cardinal Mundelein
(1872–1939)

The first Cardinal of the Roman Catholic Archdiocese of Chicago almost didn't make it. Except for the fact that he was counting calories at the moment, he might well have been poisoned at his first day on the job.

As it was, three people died and scores became ill at a dinner at the University Club held in honor of George William Mundelein's enthronement as Archbishop of Chicago on Feb. 10, 1916.

One of the cooks at the gala affair, an atheist named Jean Crones, had deliberately poisoned the soup.

While Mundelein passed up the entree because he was dieting, other guests fell violently ill and began to drop all around him. Andrew J. Graham, a banker, and two others died after sipping the lethal soup.

A frantic search of the kitchen revealed that Crones, an anarchist who held anti-religious beliefs, was missing.

The fact that more people did not die was attributed to the action of another cook, who did not like the looks of four other cans of poison stock Crones had prepared and poured them down the drain, thus diluting the fatal brew.

After fleeing for parts unknown, Crones wrote a letter explaining, "I am sorry that not at least 100 got killed." The would-be mass murderer was never captured.

Mundelein, a many-sided man who developed an almost fanatical interest in his fellow beings, was elevated to Cardinal eight years later, becoming the the first Cardinal west of the Alleghenies.

He was known from the start as a builder. During his reign in Chicago he founded more than 100 new parishes and erected hundreds of churches, convents, rectories, hospitals, schools and charitable institutions. His crowning achievement was the beautiful St. Mary of the Lake Seminary in the Lake County town of Area, which was renamed Mundelein in his honor. The seminary was acclaimed as a model of institutions for the study of the priesthood.

Mundelein, who was born to a poor German family in a Lower East Side tenement in New York, could trace his heritage to the early days of this country. His great-grandfather's father helped build the first German Catholic church in the United States in 1834, and his maternal grandfather fell in battle as a Union soldier in the Civil War.

As a 9-year-old child Mundelein had a "play altar" in his room, and would bring his playmates home from grade school to assist him in pretending to celebrate mass.

He was ordained in Rome in 1895, and later assigned as bishop of Brooklyn.

Following his reassignment to Chicago in 1916 a religious leader of the day declared, "It seemed that when Archbishop Mundelein arrived in Chicago he waved a magic wand over the entire church, and immediately every wheel began to move and everything began to take on life."

Mundelein, who was given the Cardinal's red hat by Pope Pius XI in 1924, became the first American prelate to preside at a beatification ceremony when he participated in the beatification of Mother Cabrini in 1938.

He also became the first Chicago Cardinal to participate in the election of a pope, when Pius XII was named in 1939.

A warm friend of President Franklin D. Roosevelt, and an outspoken anti-Nazi, despite his German ancestry, Mundelein caused a world furor in 1937 when he denounced Adolf Hitler as "an Austrian paperhanger, and a poor one at that." Der Fuhrer was so enraged that he threatened to break off diplomatic relations with the Vatican.

The most important event during Mundelein's administration was the 28th International Eucharistic Congress held in Chicago in 1926, attended by more than a million Catholics, including 12 Cardinals, 64 archbishops, 309 bishops, 500 monsignors and 8,000 priests.

Yet as important a man as Mundelein was, he was never too busy to play Santa Claus for the children in parishes at Christmas time.

After serving 24 years as the Catholic Archbishop of Chicago, he died in his sleep at the age of 67 at his country villa at St. Mary of the Lake. So many people walked by his body in a final, silent farewell in Holy Name Cathedral that they wore out the blue carpet in the nave where his body rested.

Mundelein was buried beneath the altar of Immaculate Conception Church at the St. Mary of the Lake Theological Seminary.

1940s

George Halas
(1895–1983)

Quick, which well-known Chicago sports figure played right field for the New York Yankees? No fair peeking at the name at the top of this chapter.

That's right. George Halas, whose name is synonymous with pro football, started out his own professional career batting baseballs for the 1919 Yanks. A hip injury suffered while sliding into third base ended his major league career.

Halas was an achiever at every sport he lit into.

As a high school student who grew up around 18th and Wood Streets, he went out for track and played football, basketball and baseball at Crane Tech. He went on to the University of Illinois, where he earned letters as a halfback and end on the Illini football team, as a guard on the basketball team, and as an outfielder on the baseball team.

At a banquet honoring the Illini at the end of Halas' senior year, football coach Bob Zuppke commented, "Why is it that just when you boys are beginning to know something about football, I lose you by graduation?"

That off-hand remark gave Halas the idea of keeping players together after college, providing super football for the public.

But first there was World War I to attend to. Halas was commissioned an ensign at Great Lakes Naval Training Station, where he played football with the Navy Bluejackets. In the only Rose Bowl game between service teams, the Navy beat the Mare Island Marines

17–0. And Halas, who caught a touchdown pass, was honored as the game's most valuable player.

From there Halas went to the Yankees. After the injury ended his baseball career he picked up on Zuppke's remarks and went to A.E. Staley, owner of a Decatur starch works, who sponsored a first-rate semi-pro baseball team. Halas pitched Staley to support a football team during the off-season.

Staley liked the idea. Halas got together a team, and Staley gave the players year-around jobs with two hours a day off for football practice. There were semi-pro teams in other cities, but no organized league in those days. In 1920 the Staley Starchmakers, under Halas' coaching, won 12 out of 13 games.

When the cost of maintaining the hard-hitting football team became too much for Staley's small operation, Halas moved the team to Wrigley Field in Chicago, in partnership with Edward "Dutch" Sternaman. Staley generously gave Halas $5,000 "seed money" to retain the team's name through 1921.

In 1922 Halas changed the team's name to the Chicago Bears, and the rest is history. As the team's young owner-coach, Halas became a founder of the National Football League, and retired as the league's winningest coach.

He was also an outstanding player, and in a 1923 rainstorm raced a record 98 yards with a fumble while being chased by the legendary Jim Thorpe, during a game with the Oorang Indians in Wrigley Field. Halas' record run was not duplicated in pro football until 1972.

"You never forget plays like that," he said.

The beginning was not easy, however. Halas and his partner lost $71.63 in their first season. In order to keep themselves going, Sternaman pumped gas and Halas sold cars on the side. In 1932, when the Bears lost $18,000, Halas paid many of his players in promissory notes in lieu of salaries. Halas eventually bought out his partner and sold stock in the team.

He learned early on that the secret of attracting large crowds was to use big name players. The first was halfback Red Grange, the "Galloping Ghost." Grange closed out his Illini career on Nov. 21, 1925, and was in a Bears uniform the following Thursday for a Thanksgiving Day game against the Chicago Cardinals that packed Wrigley Field to the rafters.

Grange was followed by the famed Bronko Nagurski, Sid Luckman, Bill Osmanski, Bulldog Turner, Joe Stydahar, Bill George, Dick Butkus, Gayle Sayers, and other drawing cards.

Halas fired himself as coach in 1930, but three years later he was back directing the team, which he did on and off throughout his long career. The Bears won NFL championships in 1932, 1933, 1940, 1941, 1943, 1946, and 1963.

Halas' most famous victory as a Bear coach was the

73–0 bashing of the Washington Redskins for the 1940 championship. He was unable to coach the winning 1943 team because he was back in the Navy as a lieutenant commander under Admiral Chester Nimitz in World War II.

During the lean years Halas was frequently urged to retire and let a younger man take over, but his answer was always the same: "I can't quit now, not while we're building."

When the Bears took the 1963 title, with Mike Ditka as a player, Halas said, "I think I can safely say Bears' fans went wild. I felt pretty good myself . . . If you live long enough, everything nice you want to happen, will happen."

It was Halas who brought Ditka back as head coach in 1982. Papa Bear died the following year, at the age of 88, two years shy of seeing Ditka take his beloved Bears on to a world championship.

It was through sheer luck that Halas lived long enough to start the Bears in the first place.

In 1915, while attending the University of Illinois, the 21-year-old Halas spent his summer vacation as an outfielder for the Western Electric Co. baseball team. On July 24 he was scheduled to join other Western Electric employees on a day-long outing to Michigan City, Ind., aboard the ill-fated excursion boat *Eastland*.

"When I finally reached the docks on the Chicago River near LaSalle Street, the great tragedy already had taken place—the *Eastland* had capsized, taking the lives of 812 persons. My name was printed in the newspapers as one of the casualties. A reporter had obtained a list of Western Electric employees assigned to the *Eastland* and assumed that I was on board," he related in later years.

"The next evening our front doorbell rang. Two of my fraternity brothers from Illinois, Walter Straub and Elmer Stumpf, had come to pay their condolences after reading of my demise. I'll never forget the shocked look on their faces when I opened the door."

Frank Knox
(1874–1944)

Colonel Frank Knox, a two-fisted newspaperman—literally—was just the kind of a leader Chicago needed during the Depression years of the 1930s.

He started out in the newspaper business by delivering them—two different papers—at the age of 11. He ended as publisher of the *Chicago Daily News*, which made him one of the most influential men in America.

Knox got his first peek at a newspaper office when he took a job as a carrier boy for the *Grand Rapids Democrat*, getting up at 3 a.m. to deliver the paper for $1.25 a week. After school he delivered the town's other paper, the *Grand Rapids Eagle*, for $1 a week. The morning paper paid an extra 25 cents because it was hard to find youngsters willing to get up so early.

Knox, who was born William F., but dropped his first name because it was the same as his father's, saved his dimes and put himself through Michigan's Alma College.

Though only five feet, nine and a half inches tall and weighing 165 pounds, he captained the school's football team, and played halfback.

When the Spanish American war broke out during his senior year, Knox pedaled his bicycle 60 miles to enlist in the state militia. He was sent to Florida, where he joined Teddy Roosevelt's Rough Riders and sailed with them for Cuba.

While charging up San Juan Hill, a bullet tore through Knox's cap, taking a tuft of his bright red hair with it.

Knox wrote such interesting letters home from Cuba that when he returned to Grand Rapids after the war he was promptly hired as a reporter on the *Herald* for $10 a week.

Knox quickly learned to cultivate politicians, and was soon made city editor at the grand weekly salary of $15, and then circulation manager, boosting his pay to $22 by 1900.

The first thing Knox did as circulation manager was go to Chicago to study circulation at the *Daily News*, which was even then his idea of a truly great newspaper.

Two years later, with a thorough knowledge of small-town newspaper operation, he purchased the *Lake Superior Journal* at Sault Ste. Marie for $3,000, and went into business for himself.

Knox developed a reputation as a crusading editor. He took an active role in Republican politics, and was named chairman of the Republican State Central Committee.

Not everyone admired the young crusader, however. A local saloonkeeper, furious over Knox's attacks on local vice, vowed to "get him" and marched down to the newspaper to do so.

The 26-year-old Knox met his opponent at the head of the stairs, drove his fist into the saloonkeeper's jaw, and sent him tumbling unconscious down the stairs. No one in Sault Ste. Marie ever doubted his sincerity again.

From Sault Ste. Marie, Knox, who had become a figure in national politics as an active backer of Theodore Roosevelt, went to New Hampshire as editor of the *Manchester Leader*.

He was 43 years old when the United States entered World War I. He enlisted as a private in the infantry. He was later commissioned a captain in the cavalry, went to France, and came home a colonel—a title he would carry for the rest of his life.

Returning to his post as editor of the Manchester paper, he caught the eye of William Randolph Hearst, who offered him a job as publisher of the *Boston American*. Knox didn't want the job, so he asked for the preposterous salary of $52,000 a year. Hearst gave it to him.

The "Chief's" assessment of young Knox proved right, and by 1927 Hearst was so pleased with his new acquisition that he promoted Knox to general manager of all Hearst newspapers, at $150,000 a year.

Knox resigned at the end of 1930, following a difference of opinion with Hearst, and was called to Chicago to take over the *Daily News*.

The two previous publishers had died, Victor Lawson in 1925 and Walter Strong in 1931. The board of directors wanted the best man available, and they convinced Knox he was the man for the job.

When Knox took over, a *Daily News* reporter, worried about his job because of the changes a new publisher traditionally makes, broached the subject to Knox head on.

"You tell the boys to sit back on their seats, take their hats off, and make a better newspaper than ever," the new boss told him. "And, while you are about it, take your own hat off."

Norman Beasley wrote in his biography of Knox, "It is still debatable in Chicago whether the Colonel 'took' Chicago or Chicago 'took' the Colonel, but it is agreed that publisher Knox became an integral part of Chicago's civic and business life with greater ease and celerity than any other newcomer ever seen there."

Within his first year Knox had become a trustee of the A Century of Progress Exposition, and the city's top businessmen had admitted him to their inner circles.

Although a Republican, he put his paper's support behind Tom Courtney, the Democratic candidate for state's attorney, because he sincerely believed Courtney was the best man for the job.

Nationally, however, he was frequently critical of President Franklin Delano Roosevelt, and was the first great editor in the nation to criticize FDR's New Deal.

So vociferous a foe of Roosevelt was he that in 1935 the Republicans suggested his name as a candidate for President. Knox did not want that, however. But after urging by party leaders he agreed to team up with Alf M. Landon as Landon's vice-presidential candidate, in an unsuccessful attempt to knock Roosevelt out of the White House in 1936.

Though political foes, the two men respected one another, and with the outbreak of war in Europe, Roosevelt looked around for a man who could get things done. He asked Republican Knox to come to Washington and serve as his Secretary of the Navy.

Knox had seen the war coming for years, and had preached preparedness in his *Daily News*.

As naval secretary he was a hands-on cabinet member. He flew to Pearl Harbor the day after the Japanese attack of December 7, 1941. He was later bombed while visiting naval installations at Guadalcanal and Espiritu Santo in the New Hebrides. In Italy he watched the fighting first-hand from the deck of a naval vessel at Naples.

Roosevelt lost a top cabinet member and Chicago lost one of its greatest newspapermen when Knox suffered a fatal heart attack in 1944 at the age of 70. John F. O'Keefe, vice president of the *Daily News,* was at his bedside in Washington when he died.

An 11-year-old newsboy who saved his dimes to go to college, a Rough Rider who followed Teddy Roosevelt up San Juan Hill, a crusading newspaper editor who cleaned up a tough border town at the age of 28, Knox was ever a gladiator, never a spectator.

He wrote in an early editorial, "For our part, in 1620 we would rather have been one of the Puritans who braved an unknown sea than one of the conformists who stayed at home."

Iva Ikuko Toguri d'Aquino
(1916–   )

From the jungles of New Guinea to the sands of Iwo Jima, and from the sweltering heat of Saipan to the bomb-pocked beaches of Leyte—she was our favorite enemy.

Iva Ikuko Toguri d'Aquino, an American-born Japanese, was known by another name during World War II in the Pacific. Call her Tokyo Rose!

Every night at 6 o'clock, Tokyo time, she would broadcast propaganda to the troops in the Pacific on her show called "Zero Hour." Her first broadcast aired on Nov. 13, 1943. She would continue for 21 months, until the war ended.

For many GIs sweating in the insect-infested jungles, the voice of Tokyo Rose would be the high point of their day.

She played popular dance records—Glenn Miller, Kay Kaiser, Woody Herman, Tommy Dorsey, Harry

James—interspersed with commentary prepared for her by American and Australian prisoners of war in Japan.

"Hello to all the boys of the 41st Division in Finschhafen, down in New Guinea," she might say. "While you boys are getting ready to board those ships that will take you to Hollandia, where you will be sunk by our bombs, do you know what your girlfriends are doing back in the States? They're going out on dates with the 4–Fs having a gay old time. They've forgotten all about you boys. Nobody in the States cares what happens to you.

"And now here's a blow to your morale, honorable boneheads—the Boston Pops."

It was almost as good as getting a letter from home.

Iva Toguri was born, ironically, on the 4th of July, in Los Angeles, and was an American citizen. She was an honors graduate of the University of California, with a degree in zoology.

Her personal nightmare began on July 15, 1941, just 10 days after her 25th birthday. Her mother's sister had become ill in Japan, and the family sent Iva to take care of her. When the Japanese bombed Pearl Harbor on Dec. 7, 1941, she was trapped in the land of her ancestors, where she barely knew the language.

After she ran out of money, she worked at several clerical jobs before finally taking the broadcasting assignment.

Sometimes she would twit the servicemen with off-beat comments such as, "Beware, this is vicious propaganda. I'm going to sneak up on you GIs on Saipan with my nail file and murder a whole battalion."

In October of 1944, on the day after an American armada sent most of the Japanese fleet to the bottom at the battle of Leyte in the Philippines, she reported from her Broadcasting Corporation of Japan studio:

"Orphans of the Pacific, you are really orphans now. How will you get home, now that all your ships are sunk?"

She would say later that the broadcasts were made under duress, and her comments were tongue-in-cheek. At Leyte, for example, virtually the entire Japanese navy had been destroyed, so the U.S. servicemen could hardly be "orphans" without ships. It was the Japanese who had no more ships.

By war's end the name of Tokyo Rose was as well known as those of Emperor Hirohito and Prime Minister Tojo.

In the wake of heavy pressure from Walter Winchell, who had branded her "a notorious traitor," she was arrested, returned to America and convicted of treason. She was fined $10,000, and served six and a half years of a 10-year sentence in a federal women's prison in West Virginia.

She left behind her husband, Felipe d'Aquino, a linotype operator and Portuguese citizen of Japanese descent, whom she married several months before the war ended.

There were other "Tokyo Roses" in addition to Iva, several of whom pinch-hit for her on her days off, or when she insisted on celebrating U.S. holidays.

But when the war ended, she was the only one who could be prosecuted for treason, because throughout the years she spent in Japan she had refused to renounce her American citizenship.

"The proudest moment of my life was when I returned to the United States—for trial—and my father saw me and said: 'Girl, we're proud of your stripes. A tiger can't change his stripes, but a person can do so easily. You didn't,'" she said.

The *Wall Street Journal* would later declare, "The trial, charging her with eight overt acts of treason, opened in July, 1949, lasted almost 13 weeks, totalled almost one million words, cost some $750,000 and involved 71 witnesses plus depositions from 19 witnesses in Japan. It was the longest treason trial in U.S. history, and it was hardly a proceeding of which the U.S. can be proud."

After her release in 1956 she came to Chicago, where her father had made a new home. She took an apartment on Belmont Avenue and helped operate a family-owned Oriental import shop on the North Side.

Though she never saw her husband again, they never divorced because of their Roman Catholic faith.

Mrs. d'Aquino, a small woman with jet-black hair

in two long braids, usually clad in a flowered blouse, slacks and saddle shoes, kept a low profile during her years in Chicago.

Only her closest associates were aware that the aging woman who spent most of her days behind a "No Admittance" sign leading to a workroom in the gift shop was the celebrated Tokyo Rose.

She refused to dwell on painful memories, or her years behind bars, except to say, "I didn't let time do me—I did the time. I did a lot of reading. I still do."

In January of 1977, on his last day in office, President Gerald Ford—upon recommendation of the Justice Department—granted her a full pardon.

"I hope now that the whole thing is really over and that I can go back to my simple life and work," she said. "The difference now is, however, that I have regained my American citizenship, a right and a privilege I have always cherished."

Andy Frain
(1904–1964)

Nobody in the history of Chicago—perhaps even the world—ever told more people to take a seat than Andy Frain. But how many know how the celebrated crowd control expert played a key role in Harry Truman taking his seat in the White House?

Call it Chicago shenanigans, if you will—because that's what it was.

Turn back the clock to 1944, and the Democratic National Convention at the International Amphitheatre on South Halsted Street. Frain, as usual, was in charge of seeing that everyone was properly seated.

Franklin D. Roosevelt was his party's clear choice for a fourth term, but Vice President Henry A. Wallace was not in his plans. Roosevelt favored a different running mate every election, and word was out that FDR intended to dump Wallace in favor of the senator from Missouri.

The Wallace faction got wind of this, and wasn't

about to see their hero cast aside without a fight. They decided to pack the convention galleries. Recalling Wendell Willkie's GOP nomination in Philadelphia four years earlier, they figured on creating such a furor in the galleries that their man would be placed on the ticket.

They descended upon Chicago as a well-organized group, some even carrying fake credentials to get them into the Amphitheatre. Chicago's Mayor Edward J. Kelly learned of the move at the last minute, and wanted to head it off.

Enter Andrew Thomas Frain.

A seasoned vet at handling crowds of any size, Frain juggled the seating arrangements so that Wallace tickets were scattered throughout the large arena instead of in one large block.

"Honest, some were so far apart they had to signal each other with flashlights," recalled Jack Brickhouse, who was broadcasting the convention.

Frain had divided and conquered, giving Mayor Kelly time to pack the house with Truman followers.

When Roosevelt died in office on April 12, 1945, Truman succeeded him as President. Had it not been for Andy Frain, it might have been Wallace.

A native of Canaryville, where he was one of 17 children born into a household without indoor plumbing, Frain obviously got an early start on crowd control.

"The last kid out of bed in the morning wouldn't find any clothes to wear," he said.

Young Andy began his career at the age of 12, renting seat cushions at Comiskey Park. He got his ushering organization off the ground when William Wrigley, Jr., owner of the Cubs baseball team, loaned him $5,000 to buy uniforms.

Frain's blue-and-gold clad ushers first directed baseball fans to their seats in Wrigley Field in 1924. Comiskey Park was next. His first big indoor ushering job was at the Tommy Loughran-Mickey Walker light-heavyweight boxing match, which opened the Chicago Stadium in 1929.

Then came other sporting events, horse races, concerts at Ravinia, trade shows and even the opening of model homes. Frain achieved national recognition when Andy's Army was hired for the Kentucky Derby.

He got the job by sneaking in and introducing himself to Colonel Matt Winn, who operated Churchill Downs. When Winn ordered the interloper thrown out, Frain crashed the gate again and appeared at Winn's private box chirping, "I'm back!"

He finally convinced Winn that trained Andy Frain ushers could save him thousands of dollars by keeping out gate-crashers.

From there it took only a phone call to take over crowd control at the national political conventions.

Through his work Frain became known as "Andy" to four United States Presidents, and Prince Rainier of Monaco.

On a single day as many as 7,500 Andy Frain ushers and usherettes might be on duty in the 26 cities where he had offices.

Frain offered financial aid to many of the young people who worked for him, and Andy Frain ushers went on to become priests, lawyers, FBI agents, public officials, doctors, dentists, business executives, newspaper reporters, magazine writers and even a Supreme Court chief justice.

Frain was the first honorary member of the Chicago Newspaper Reporters Association, which honored him in 1960 for his "friendship to all members of the newspaper profession."

Frain was always amused when people, claiming to be old college classmates, would ask him to get tickets for them to sold-out events. The closest Frain ever got to college was providing ushers for football games.

When one man tried to muscle his way into the Ingemar Johansson-Floyd Patterson heavyweight championship fight in 1961 by claiming to have been Frain's classmate at Vassar, Frain laughed and told him: "If I'd gone to Vassar, you can be sure I never would have forgotten it, Mister. I'm sorry I don't have a ticket to pass you in—you're the first good-natured phony I've met tonight."

By the time of his death in 1964 at the age of 60, Andy Frain had become Usher King of the World.

Sophonisba P. Breckinridge
(1866–1948)

Sophonisba P. Breckinridge, it was said, could be as formidable as her name. She was a lawyer, author, professor, field worker and delegate from the United States to international conferences an social, industrial and economic problems. And she was feisty. In the late 1920s and early 1930s, she did what few others had the courage to do—she flew just about everywhere she went.

The name, Sophonisba P. Breckinridge, never became a household word. She founded the School of Social Works Administration at the University of Chicago but received little attention even for that. Society writer Sarah Brown Boyden explained why:

> The chief reason that Miss Sophonisba Preston Breckinridge has not achieved bundles of newspaper stories is that she won't have them. Few people venture to rouse gentle Miss Breckinridge's ire if they can help it.
>
> So, to date, she has managed to confine public opinion to occasional limp paragraphs announcing that she was the first woman to represent the United States at a congress of the Pan American Union, or that she volunteered her services for field work in the Selective Service medical survey.

The writer then added a "number of facts on the busy life of a great lady." Those included that she was the first woman to be admitted to the bar in the State of Kentucky. This was particularly amazing in light of the fact that she was a member of one of Kentucky's oldest, most prominent families (that included governors, senators and a vice president). She was the first woman to receive a doctor of jurisprudence degree from the University of Chicago, doing so with honors. She had a long association with Hull House and, along with the other women there, was responsible for much of the advanced social legislation in Illinois.

Boyden's comments about her continued:

> Miss Breckinridge, wide-eyed and determinedly chinned,

Courtesy of the University of Chicago.

is quite fragile in appearance. She has a fiery temper, with which she has "wrestled and struggled" all her life. This combination produces piquant results in her frequent and still active battles for the general improvement of the human race. She usually winds up by demolishing her unwary opponent and then seeking him out for a heartfelt apology afterward, if she said anything to hurt his feelings.

Her great accomplishment was that as a professor

and author of works on social work she helped raise it to a profession. Her books included such subjects as child delinquency, truancy, housing and public welfare.

One writer described her as always seeming to have a "cloistered aura" around her.

So, one must ask, was she completely formidable? No. For one thing, her family and friends stripped her of her intimidating name and called her "Nisba." Her brother, who owned race horses, named one of them for her, "Naughty Nisba."

And her students loved the little woman who was so tiny, they said, that they feared a strong Southeaster would one day blow her off the campus.

Martin H. Kennelly
(1887–1961)

When former Mayor Martin H. Kennelly died in 1961 at the age of 74, Chicago humanist, 'fred Stein, wrote a poem to be read at his wake. It began:

> From Marshall Field Stock-boy
> to leading our city!
> To lose Mayor Kennelly
> is truly a pity.

> With honor and courtesy
> for one and all,
> Martin Kennelly
> put City Hall "On the Ball."

Kennelly was born in the Back of the Yards neighborhood in 1887. His father died when he was 2, and at the age of 13 he went to work for Marshall Field & Co. as a stockboy for $2 a week. When he left to attend De La Salle Institute his employer gave him a letter of recommendation which read:

> To whom it may concern:
> This is to certify that the bearer, Martin H. Kennelly, has been in the employ of Marshall Field & Co. in the packing and shipping room from July 19, 1901 to Sept. 6, 1902. He did his work very well and we found him honest. He left on his own accord.

After returning from World War I as a captain in the Army Quartermaster Corps, Kennelly formed a storage warehousing firm, and used the old letter to win one of his first contracts, from Stanley Field, to haul exhibits from the old Field Museum in Jackson Park to the new Natural History Museum in Grant Park.

By 1923 his operation was one of the largest movers and storage houses in the Midwest, and by the middle 1940s he had become one of Chicago's most respected business and civic leaders.

In 1947 the Democrats, realizing they could no longer win with the scandal-ridden Kelly-Nash machine, prevailed upon Kennelly to run for mayor.

To their way of thinking he was tailor-made for the job, a handsome Irish Catholic with silver-white hair, a ruddy complexion and an easy smile. He was 59, with a spotless reputation and a "poor-boy-who-made-good" background.

Kennelly agreed to run, after extracting a promise that he be given a free hand. The machine politicians agreed, not realizing that he meant it.

The wealthy Kennelly had little need for the mayoral salary of $18,000 a year, and ran the city like he had run his businesses. He pushed through a centralized city purchasing department that saved millions of dollars over the years, and he backed the Civil Service Commission against party bosses, putting nearly 95 percent of city employees under civil service protection.

During his administration great strides were made in public works programs, including the West Side subway, Congress Street and the Northwest and Southwest expressways, the remodeling of Wacker Drive, new streetlights, parking lots and street paving.

Every top ranking police officer who was in when he took office either quit, was fired or demoted.

Kennelly became the darling of the press, which called him "Marvelous Martin," but to the old-line ward bosses he was anything but. Alderman Mathias "Paddy" Bauler, the 43rd Ward saloonkeeper, derisively dubbed him "Fartin' Martin," and other council members called him worse than that.

By the time he was midway through his second

term, Kennelly was able to control everything but the political machine that had put him in, and by then the ward heelers couldn't work hard enough to put him out.

When he began his second term in 1951 he was sworn in by County Clerk Richard J. Daley. But when he sought a third term in 1955, the machine put up Daley to run against him, and Kennelly suffered a crushing defeat.

As he watched the sad returns come in on the night of his primary defeat he shook his head and muttered, "They're unbeatable, just unbeatable, aren't they?"

Declaring, "All I have in the word is my reputation, and I don't propose to have it dirtied up in politics," he quietly returned to his warehouse business. When a friend met him on the street he scrupulously avoided talking politics, particularly steering clear of any comment on the Daley administration that succeeded him.

Kennelly's private life was always his own. He never married, and few of his friends or business associates ever saw the inside of his apartment at 5555 Sheridan Rd., where he lived with his sister, Ella, until her death in 1956.

Kennelly remained ever proud of his rise from a $2-a-week stockboy to successful businessman and civic leader.

He liked to say, "I've eaten regularly, and I haven't hurt anybody getting where I am."

1950s

Mathias "Paddy" Bauler
(1890–1977)

Alderman Mathias "Paddy" Bauler once claimed there were but two honest men on the Chicago City Council, Alderman Robert Merriam and himself, for having the integrity to admit he was a crook.

Known as "The Clown Prince of City Council," it was he who, on the night in 1955 that Richard J. Daley knocked Mayor Martin H. Kennelly out of the box in the Democratic primary, uttered those immortal words, "Chicago ain't ready for reform."

One of 13 children, he was literally born into politics. His German immigrant father, a saloonkeeper, was a Democratic precinct captain. Two of Bauler's brothers, Herman, also a saloonkeeper, and John, a gambler, preceded him in the City Council before he took over as alderman of the North Side 43rd Ward in 1933.

Known as "Paddy" from his cradle days, Bauler said he never knew his name was Mathias until he was enrolled in St. Michael's parochial school at the age of 6.

A husky young prizefighter, Bauler packed a pistol and became a bodyguard for Mayor Carter H. Harrison II while still in his teens. He also worked as a singing waiter in his brother's saloon before opening his own Prohibition Era speakeasy at Willow and Howe Streets in 1920.

His speak became a gathering place for big names in the sporting world, politics, high society and show business. Considering his clientele, it was not strange that he was drawing a check as a timekeeper in the Cook County treasurer's office while at the same time minding his blind pig on the North Side.

Bauler held his seat on the City Council from 1933, with the exception of one term, until 1967.

As alderman he had 400 patronage jobs, and scores of old friends, including his bartenders, his brothers, his brother-in-law and his son ended up on city payrolls, although most of them never saw the inside of City Hall.

With the repeal of Prohibition in 1933 Bauler opened up a "legit" saloon in the old Immigrant National Bank Building at North Avenue and Sedgwick Street. Less than three weeks later he shot a police officer, Patrolman John J. Ahern, in a drunken brawl.

"I didn't know he was a cop," was Bauler's defense when he went on trial for assault with intent to kill. He was found not guilty, and Mayor Edward J. Kelly promptly endorsed him for reelection as Democratic committeeman crowing, "Paddy Bauler has always been a straight shooter."

In 1937 when Bauler was defeated by James B. Waller, a Gold Coast Republican, Mayor Kelly appointed him city collector at $6,420 a year—almost $1,500 more than he was earning as alderman.

"Kelly told me I could have the job but only if I'd stay in Florida for four years," Bauler told friends. "He said he didn't want me to get my hands on any of that money."

But apparently he did. A City Council investigation disclosed that during Bauler's brief tenure as collector 1,895 business establishments paid license fees for which they were not eligible—nor did they receive licenses.

When ordered to make refunds and submit a report, Bauler did neither. Instead he told the council, "What the hell! I ain't doing nothing that every politician in this town ain't done for 100 years. And I ain't apologizing for it, neither."

That was good enough for the voters of the 43rd

Ward, who threw the Gold-Coaster out after one term and put Bauler back in the City Council.

He lost his zest for politics after his only son, Harry, died in 1963. When Bauler came up for reelection in 1967 he announced, "What the hell, I've had it."

For years, until his death in 1977, Bauler was a *bon vivant* and world traveler, known to hotelmen of Hong Kong, Tokyo, Beirut, Munich and Vienna. He would take off for distant lands on the spur of the moment, and jet back to Chicago for council meetings. He once had a toothache in Paris, flew home to his Chicago dentist, and hopped the next plane back to France.

The last of the old-time saloonkeeper aldermen, he was always popular with news reporters who gathered in his saloon. He liked the press, too, and enjoyed telling them, "I'll talk about anything, as long as the statute of limitations has run out."

Richard J. Daley
(1902–1976)

In the blue-collar Bridgeport neighborhood on Chicago's South Side, the paunchy, red-faced man might come home after a hard day's work to his modest bungalow at 3536 S. Lowe Ave., kick off his shoes, plop down on the edge of his bed, loosen his pants and relax with a cold bottle of beer.

Like so many of his Irish neighbors in this enclave of workingmen's houses, churches and saloons, he lived his entire life within a block from the house in which he was born just after the turn of the century. He could have lived in a mansion if he wanted to, but Bridgeport was his home.

The son of a sheetmetal worker, he entered politics as a Democrat precinct captain at the age of 21, and door-knocked and elbowed his way to the top.

Richard Joseph Daley was the last of the old-time political bosses in America—"the Man on 5"—he served as mayor of Chicago longer than any other person in the city's history.

Daley earned his law degree from night school, working days at a clerical job in City Hall, but he never practiced anything but politics.

An opportunist from Day One, Daley—a staunch Democrat—first got himself elected to public office as a Republican in 1936, as a write-in candidate to replace a GOP state legislator who died. Two years later somebody else dropped dead, and Daley took his place in the Illinois Senate as a Democrat.

Unlike so many of his colleagues, Daley never yielded to the wine, women and graft of the Springfield social whirl. An amazed Senator Botchy Conners was moved to remark, "You can't give that guy a nickel, that's how honest he is."

It was that way throughout his political life. Surrounded by graft and corruption, and seeing some of his closest associates packed off to prison, Daley was never personally touched by scandal.

Whatever he knew about, he chose to ignore, because the thievery and chicanery were practiced by men who had the political patronage to keep him in office. Whenever anyone asked the mayor about the crime syndicate, which controlled nearly every illicit activity in the city, Daley would stare blankly and ask, "What crime syndicate?"

If a reporter got too inquisitive, Daley would turn purple with rage and bellow, "There are even crooked reporters, and I can spit on some of them from right here."

When faced with a colossal police scandal, in which babbling burglar Richard Morrison blew the whistle on uniformed cops who were burglarizing appliance stores while on duty and carting away the loot in their squad cars, he was able to turn it to his advantage by taking credit for revamping the police department in the scandal's wake.

Daley was both a builder and a destroyer.

The sprawling University of Illinois Chicago Circle Campus was built under his direction—never mind that thousands of old established homes in the Italian community had to be torn down and their occupants displaced to make room for it.

And he tried to erase mementoes of the city's bloody past by leveling the North Side garage where the St. Valentine's Day Massacre took place, and the South Side saloon that had been Al Capone's whorehouse and headquarters.

He put up such monuments as the Kennedy Expressway, the Dan Ryan and the Eisenhower, a convention hall on the lakefront and O'Hare International Airport, which he everlastingly called "O'Hara."

He was a master of the malaprop. "We have been boyhood friends all our lives," he explained in speaking of a long-time crony.

The press made fun of his malapropisms, but his

supporters thought he was great. Starting with 1955, when he knocked incumbent Democratic Mayor Martin Kennelly out of the box, he was elected to six straight terms.

A tyrannical mayor, he ruled the City Council with an iron hand, and the city with a giant patronage system that owed him everything. He personally went over the names of every city employee, present and hopeful, to see who they might be related to, and how many votes each was good for.

Fellow pols called him "the Man on 5" because his City Hall office was on the fifth floor. Reporters respect-fully called him, "The Great Buddha."

In the early days, newspaper reporters had easy access to Daley, who loved to lean back in his chair and talk baseball with them on slow news days. With the advent of television, and its reporters shrieking nonsen-sical questions while followed by cameramen who trailed electronic cables across the room, he was forced to resort to structured press conferences, and a lot of the fun went out of covering "dah mare," as he called himself.

When not at his desk in City Hall, or cutting ribbons at new civic projects, or attending political functions, he could be found at home with his beloved family. He rarely dined out in public because he was forever bothered by handshakers, job seekers or apple polishers.

An exception was the Chicago Press Club, where the unwritten law was that news types would let him eat in peace as long as he didn't bother them. The safest place to hide out from the press was in their very midst.

Daley was never afraid to debate on his own turf, however. When a black militant mumbled "Up your ass," at one of the mayor's news conferences, Daley bounced to his feet and declared, "And up yours too!"

For the most part, Daley tried to be the "fun mayor," staging circus-like events to keep unfavorable news off the front pages.

Unfortunately, it didn't always work. During the rioting, burning and looting in black neighborhoods following the assassination of the Rev. Martin Luther

King, the mayor made coast-to-coast headlines with his "shoot to kill" order to Chicago police.

He tried to counter that publicity by bringing the gala Democratic National Convention to Chicago in 1968, but it proved to be one of his darkest moments.

While young protesters battled with police in the city's parks and downtown streets, television viewers across the nation watched Daley's apoplectic face on the tube bellowing apparent obscenities at Senator Abraham Ribicoff.

But Daley survived to be reelected two more times. How great a mayor he was might never be known, because while he lived no one ever stood a chance of proving otherwise. As one of his tiny handful of political opponents, Alderman John J. Hoellen once said, "It's hard to be a Republican in Chicago." Daley made sure of that.

No matter who Daley crossed swords or rubbed shoulders with during the rest of the morning, afternoon and evening he started each day with the Lord.

The chauffeur-driven limo that picked him up to drive him to work every morning always stopped off at St. Peter's Church on Madison Street, on the way to City Hall, so he could attend mass.

As Mike Royko wrote in his book, *Boss*, "Regardless of what he may do in the afternoon, and to whom, he will always pray in the morning."

Paul Egan
(1899–1969)

Raspy voiced, jowly, bespectacled Paul Egan ran for mayor of Aurora in 1953 for one compelling reason. He needed a job. He was 54 years old, trying to support a wife and five kids on $27 a week unemployment compensation.

He shook no hands, rang no doorbells, and criticized Aurora's business and industrial leaders alike. He made only one public appearance, and left when the audience got angry at him.

Miraculously he was elected to the $8,000-a-year

job, and for the next eight years life in the western suburb of 64,000 was never dull, to say the least.

His term in office included:

• Lively fistfights with other elected officials.

• Invitations to Soviet Premier Nikita Khruschev and Cuban Premier Fidel Castro to visit Aurora.

• Mass firings that included City Council members, the entire Aurora Civil Service Commission, and nearly every police chief he hired.

• A declaration during a Palm Sunday City Council meeting that Lenin was "almost as great a man as Jesus Christ."

• Appointment of a parrot as chief of police.

As his very first act he fired both his police and fire chiefs, declaring that he would hold those jobs himself, in addition to being mayor, thus saving the taxpayers two salaries.

Discharged Police Chief Donald Curran, who had held office for 19 years, denounced the mayor as a "screwball" and got an injunction against him, which Egan totally ignored.

In all, Egan appointed eight police chiefs during his first four years in office, including a local minister and two men serving at once.

On one occasion Egan set up roadblocks banning interstate trucks from Aurora streets. This earned him a censure from the City Council and a Circuit Court order to cease and desist.

One of his actions so nettled Justice of the Peace John Chivari that he belted the mayor in the jaw, knocking him across his desk, after which Egan whacked the JP with a pair of scissors, slashing his forehead.

He also carried on a long-running, vociferous feud with his former secretary, Irene Davis, interspersed with lawsuits, after she charged he hit her on the head with his gavel when she harangued him for nine hours during a council meeting. Egan subsequently hired a 138-pound wrestler, Shirley Strimple, as a bodyguard to protect him from the 200-pound Davis, whom he referred to as "the fat lady."

Egan also made headlines on July 18, 1957, which

he described as "the worst day of my life."

He left City Hall in a hurry after landing a punch to the left eye of Commissioner W.B. "Scotty" Robertson, and was arrested for speeding in Forest Park. After posting his driver's license as bond, Egan drove to a gas station to meet an urgent need, and accidentally locked himself in the washroom. Upon his release a half hour later he got into his car and had a flat tire.

In explaining the fight that started it all he said, "Robertson was about to crack me, but I just happened to catch him first. After I clipped this guy on the kisser I lit out." That quote, of course, was highly sanitized, since Egan's everyday conversation was punctuated with obscenities.

There were only a few mild objections when the press called Egan "unquestionably the worst mayor in America." And those, it was said, came from folks who thought the denunciation covered insufficient ground.

At the end of his raucous term, when Egan announced he would seek reelection, political experts said "good riddance." During four short years, as the *Chicago Tribune* pointed out, "He had affronted just about everybody in Aurora, and had wounded local pride by making the city a national laughing stock. Churchgoers were aghast at his constant profanity. Local leaders, to a man, were against him, and so was the only newspaper."

In fact, everyone was against the bombastic Egan but the electorate, who returned the rotund, double-chinned street-brawler to office by a stunning 12,362 to 8,621 votes. The man he beat was a college graduate with a degree in business administration.

Egan kicked off his second term by kicking out the entire police force, and urging citizens to make their own arrests. He appointed a red-haired lady wrestler as chief of police, and when she resigned he gave the post to a 100-year-old parrot named Señor Carr.

"Hell, I didn't know Carr was a blankety-blank parrot," he confessed. "I understood he was a blankety-blank Spanish nobleman."

As criticism of his administration mounted, Egan petitioned President Eisenhower to send paratroopers to Aurora to quell the "rebellion." When that failed he placed a $72 phone call to the Kremlin to ask Khruschev to "send over 24 Russian Communists with guns" to put down his detractors.

Eventually his hijinks proved too much, even for those who had twice elected him to office. When Egan ran for a third term in 1961 the voters gave him the boot.

He got a job peddling vacuum cleaners door to door, and died in 1968 at the age of 69.

Chicago Magazine once described Egan as "an uninformed, self-seeking, bigoted, profane, impetuous, boisterous, bungling, unpredictable buffoon."

He was called a lot of other names, too, during his eight years in the spotlight—but nobody ever called Paul Egan a crook.

When the local painters' union offered to paint his house for free, because it was so shabby looking, he politely refused, saying that would amount to graft. He was a man of principle—to say nothing of pugilism and parrot police chiefs.

Hugh Hefner
(1926–   )

He was once referred to in print as "the playboy-till-ya-puke of the Western world."

When writer Tom Wolfe called Hugh Hefner "King of the Status Dropouts" because he ventured out of the fabled Playboy Mansion on Chicago's Near North Side only nine times in nearly three years, Hefner replied, "I don't need to leave here. Why should I? I've got more right here now inside this house than most people ever find in a lifetime!

"I'm in the center of the world."

Which is why every hot-blooded American stud in his right mind has envied him since that day in 1953 when he sat down at his kitchen table and produced the first *Playboy* magazine with $600 in borrowed money.

Hefner was working for *Esquire* for $60 a week, and quit when he was denied a $5 raise. Then he set out to put together the type of magazine he felt *Esquire* should have been. He called it *Stag Party*, but before the first edition came off the presses a magazine with a similar name complained, so Hefner wisely changed the name of his new product to *Playboy* and became a millionaire many times over.

While his magazine was an instant success, his marriage to Millie, the mother of his two children, ultimately failed.

So Hefner became a workaholic, often putting in 36 to 48 hours in a stretch on his magazine, while downing as many as 36 bottles of Pepsi per day.

In 1960 he purchased the 100-room mansion at 1340 N. State Parkway where he became noted for his Gatsby-style entertaining, often playing host to as many as 1,000 guests in a single evening.

Back when Dr. George S. Isham owned the Victorian home, overnight guests might have included Teddy Roosevelt or Admiral Peary. Once Hefner called it home, the guest list was more likely to include such names as Queen Elizabeth of England, Aristotle Onassis, Leonid Brezhnev, Dick Gregory, Lenny Bruce, Jesse Jackson, Linda Lovelace or Jack Mabley—plus any young nymph who measured 36–24–36.

He also had a television show, "Playboy's Penthouse," and soon opened a string of Playboy clubs, with the help of restaurateur Arnie Morton. Morton once called Hefner "the sweetest, most selfish man I've ever known."

In 1970 he bought a multi-million dollar castle near Hollywood, Playboy Mansion West, which became the setting for lavish parties, and a virtual nesting place for celebrities such as Frank, Sammy and the gang.

Hefner reportedly owns the largest collection of "blue" films in the world, which he can project onto the bedroom wall from his eight-and-a-half-foot round, rotating, vibrating bed.

"Visual stimulation, in a nonparticipating way, holds no interest for me," he said. "But as an additional stimulus while having sex—sure, I'm all for it."

Hef's "bunnies" were legendary—Janet Pilgrim (nee Charlaine Karalus), Karen Christy, Barbi Benton, Carrie Leigh, Shannon Tweed, Sondra Theodore. . .

Benton (real name Barbara Klein) was probably the best known, and rumors abounded that she and Hefner would eventually become Mr. and Mrs. Playboy.

It was not to be, however. America's best-known sex practitioner, who was rumored to have bedded down with more than 2,000 different women, according to his biographer, Frank Brady, finally found a playmate he liked well enough not to throw back. Kimberley Conrad became the second Mrs. Hefner.

They spend most of their time in Playboy Mansion West with their infant son, Marston (born on daddy's 64th birthday), along with a manager, butlers, assistants, housemen, gardeners, maintenance men, a chauffeur, 24-hour chefs, a culinary staff, a videotape engineer, and an animal keeper to tend the monkeys, flamingos, doves, pheasants, peacocks, ducks and—yes—rabbits, that inhabit the 5.3 acre estate.

Chicago-born Hefner told *Tribune* writer Cheryl Lavin, "If my life stands for anything, it is to show that there are possibilities beyond the particular road that you're told you should follow."

But suddenly it appeared that Mr. Playboy, who once admitted he had "tried everything, including swinging scenes both organized and spontaneous," had veered from that "particular road," and was advocating that his followers emulate him and practice safe sex.

It was a new Hugh Hefner, indeed, who greeted the 1990s. But like the old Hef who once turned a $600 loan into a multi-million dollar empire, he proved he was still no push-over. He made sure his new bride signed a prenuptial agreement.

Bessie Louise Pierce
(1890–1974)

The preeminent historian of Chicago, at least in the twentieth century, was University of Chicago professor Bessie Louise Pierce, author of the three-volume *A History of Chicago* and *As Others See Chicago*.

Historians consider her works as close to the final word as one gets in books on Chicago. She's it, she's the authority; not, however, on herself. She did not get her own personal history right in the facts she submitted to *Who's Who in the United States.* Miss Pierce made herself two years older than she was.

Was it simply a prank on her part, a spoof on her assigned role as the final word, rather than reason to consider her anything but the most reliable source of all on Chicagoans and their history?

A reporter caught this aberration from accuracy only because the then 83-year-old professor emeritus of history answered the question, "How old are you?" with the suggestion, "Look it up in *Who's Who.*" The wrong date was in *Who's Who in America* and *Who's Who in the Midwest,* but not in early versions of *Who's Who in Chicago.*

Courtesy of the University of Chicago.

In contrast, her books and her classes proved her thirst not only for the facts of Chicago history, but also for the city's spirit and life. Her approach to history demanded she verify facts, statements and stories from primary sources: the newspapers, documents and letters of the day. Doing much of her research during the Depression, she was able to use out-of-work Ph.D. historians and candidates to write monographs on various aspects of Chicago history, and then to condense that down to perhaps a few paragraphs or a page of text.

Tribune reporter Ruth Moss, after interviewing her in 1958, called her Chicago's Boswell who had captured Chicago's "breadth and passion, its culture and vision of life."

During Big Bill Thompson's term as mayor, she took on his fatuous charge that school textbooks were full of pro-British propaganda that was meant to make students disloyal to American ideas. She did a survey of 400 textbooks and stated:

> The conclusion must inevitably come that children are taught to honor and venerate their forefathers and the institutions they developed. As for England, no other country, with the possible exception of Germany at the time of the world war is treated so harshly.

Her three volumes on Chicago history were preceded by a book *As Others See Chicago,* a scholarly compilation of the writings about Chicago by those who had visited the city between 1673 and 1933, when the book was published.

Bessie Pierce was a visitor. She came in 1918 to get her master's and then doctorate at the University of Chicago. The diminutive and gentle Miss Pierce arrived here from Waverly, Iowa, and returned there to die in the early 1970s. In the intervening years, she taught the city its best history and tweaked its nose for asking her how old she was.

Jack Muller
(1923–   )

There was a time when an honest cop in Chicago seemed a rarity, which is why Jack Muller stuck out like a sore thumb.

During his 24 years on the force Muller gave new meaning to the term "flamboyant." He couldn't seem to keep the rules straight—like you're not supposed to give traffic tickets to politicians and other influential people.

Muller went right ahead and ticketed judges, foreign consuls, delegates to national political conventions, and federal and state officials, just as though they were ordinary citizens who broke the law.

"People kept asking me, 'Why don't you look the other way?' But I couldn't do that," he said.

Among his victims were Mayor Richard J. Daley's official limousine; Mayor Richard Hatcher of Gary; Governor William G. Stratton; Sheriff Joseph Lohman; and Cook County Board President Dan Ryan.

He once spotted Chicago's most industrious burglar, Joseph "Pops" Panczko, peering in a suspicious way into the window of a men's clothing store.

"I don't think you're standing here for your health, Pops," Muller said.

"You're right," Panczko nodded. "I'm looking for a suede jacket for my brother, Paul, for Christmas."

Muller, knowing full well that Paul "Peanuts" Panczko was doing 30 years in Leavenworth for robbery, hijacking, possession of counterfeit money and bribing a juror, replied, "I don't think he'll need it for several Christmases to come."

Muller searched Panczko and found a ring full of auto ignition keys in his pocket. He thought it strange, since Panczko did not own a car and did not have a driver's license. "You're under arrest for possession of burglar tools," Muller said.

Panczko offered Muller $200 to "forget it."

"You are also under arrest for bribing a police officer," Muller added.

"If you don't make an offer, you'll never know what might have happened," Panczko shrugged on the way to jail for the umpteenth time in his career.

Muller was once assigned to clean up the parking mess on Rush Street. He ticketed so many double-parked and illegally parked cars, and the nightclub owners screamed so loud, that he was reassigned to a beat on Western Avenue.

Meanwhile, Muller ticketed 18 federal employee cars parked around the Federal Building and 35 other cars parked around City Hall. He also ran as an independent candidate for sheriff, and got 300,000 votes.

Muller joined the force in 1946, after serving with the Navy during World War II. In 1949 he was shot in the face in a gun battle with an ex-convict.

After his grand ticket-writing spree and ill-fated run for sheriff, he was transferred to the auto theft unit, where he came up with a theft ring headed by four police officers. He was roundly criticized by fellow lawmen when he bypassed the Internal Investigation Division (IID) and went directly to the police superintendent with his findings.

"The IID is a giant washing machine," he said. "You throw the complaints in and the men come out clean."

Muller was sued for making derogatory remarks against the department, and he filed a counter-suit saying the department had violated his freedom of speech. He lost, and a written reprimand was placed in his file, but he refused to play dead. He took the matter to the United States Court of Appeals and won, and the reprimand was ordered expunged from his file.

"When a member of the department cannot speak out against corruption and graft, it's a bad day for taxpayers and the people of Chicago," he said.

In 1980, while washing his squad car, Muller found three marijuana joints in the ashtray. He destroyed them immediately, and reported the incident to his superiors. Incredibly, a check of records failed to turn up who had used the car before Muller.

In addition, the Internal Affairs Division slapped him with a reprimand for not saving the suspicious smokes as evidence.

"I was afraid I was being set up on a phony marijuana charge and didn't want to possess them for even a split second," he explained.

By 1981 Muller had had enough, and went on medical leave after being removed from his job as a burglary detective and put back in uniform walking a beat at age 57. His old bullet wound bothered him, he complained.

"I guess I was too critical of them hiding crime statistics and lying in their reports," he said. "It should have been 30 years of vaudeville and then a pension, but the job stopped being fun."

He moved out to his in-laws' 5 acre estate near Powers Lake, in Kenosha County, Wis.

"I won't give up the privilege of being a man just to be a police officer," he said. "One man with courage is a majority."

Ray Kroc
(1903–1984)

It took high school drop-out Ray Kroc more than half a century to decide what he wanted to be when he grew up. The former ambulance driver, dance band musician, real estate salesman, paper cup peddler and gizmo huckster was 52 years old before he discovered America's appetite for 15-cent hamburgers.

Even then, he hadn't originally intended to go into the fast food business.

By the way, if the multi-millionaire founder of

McDonald's Corp. were here right now he would admonish you right off not to refer to those places under the golden arches as restaurants. "McDonald's is not a restaurant," he'd say. "It's a hamburger business. It's a religion."

Young Ray Kroc, who grew up in Oak Park, dropped out of Oak Park-River Forest High School when he was 15, made his way to France, and found adventure as a World War I ambulance driver.

Another member of his Red Cross outfit was a 16-year-old Midwesterner named Walt Disney, whom Kroc thought rather strange. "While we chased girls, all he wanted to do was draw animals," Kroc recalled.

After the war Kroc landed a job as a piano player with small dance bands, and eventually hooked on with big names like Isham Jones and Harry Sosnik, who wound up leading the Hit Parade Band. By the time he was 19 he was earning a healthy $150 a week.

At the age of 20 he got married. That meant he had to give up life on the road, so he got a job selling paper cups. From there he went on to become musical director of Chicago radio station WGES. The real estate boom lured him to Florida, where he became a land salesman and quickly went broke.

"I sent my wife and daughter home on the train, and I drove to Chicago in a Model T Ford. I left in late September, 1926. I will never forget that drive as long as I live. I was stone broke. I didn't have an overcoat, a topcoat, or a pair of gloves," he recalled.

Back in Chicago, he resumed selling paper cups for a living, until 1937, when Kroc discovered the multimixer—a device that could mix five milk shakes at one time—which eventually led him to McDonald's.

Kroc peddled the multimixer for the next 18 years. Then, in 1955, he noticed that a hamburger stand in San Bernardino, Calif., was using eight of the mixers—more than any other place.

"This I have to see," he told himself. So he went to San Bernardino. "It was terrific," he said. "They had people in line, clamoring for more."

Kroc stayed on for three days, observing the mass production operation. His years of merchandising, going back to the paper cup days, convinced him there was a golden future in multimixers, and he suggested that Mac and Dick McDonald, the owners, branch out. But San Bernardino was their home, and they were happy where they were.

Kroc convinced them to let him franchise their short order operation for 0.5 percent of the gross, figuring he could make a mint placing multimixers in the new stands.

He opened the first McDonald's franchise in Des Plaines, and the rest is history. The drawing card, he quickly discovered, was not the multimixers but the 15-cent hamburgers—10 to a pound.

Kroc opened two more franchises in California that same year, and five years later bought out the McDonald brothers for $2.7 million.

By 1960 McDonald's Corp. grossed $6 million, and by the middle 1970s it was raking in more than $3 billion annually.

The one-time ambulance driver had a swank apartment on Chicago's Lake Shore Drive with its own piano, a 210 acre ranch in California, and a winter home in Fort Lauderdale.

The man who never had it made until he reached the age when most people are thinking about retirement was worth an estimated $500 million, and had just about everything a person could want—except his own ball club.

He tried to buy his favorite team, but the 1974 Chicago Cubs weren't for sale. The San Diego Padres were, however, and he picked up the team for $10 million. Then he closed his Fort Lauderdale digs and shifted his winter quarters to San Diego so he could be close to 28 of his favorite people: his three granddaughters and the Padres.

By the time of the former jazz pianist's death at the age of 81, McDonald's golden arches had sprouted in 32 countries, and baseball was alive and well in San Diego, thanks to Ray Kroc—who didn't know when to quit.

John Robert "Jack" Johnson
(1918–1985)

Bull-necked Jack Johnson, longtime warden of the Cook County Jail, was one of the most inwardly sensitive, thoughtful men anyone would ever want to meet. Yet the mere sight of this bear of a man, who carried some 250 pounds on his 6 foot, 2 inch frame, was enough to quiet the most belligerent prisoner in the teeming jail which had a prison population greater than San Quentin.

Johnson, who got the appointment at the age of 38, was the youngest warden in the history of the jail.

Much of his effectiveness as a warden came from a quiet understanding of inmate problems. He kept a chair beside his desk, and much of the time it was occupied by a prisoner discussing whatever was bothering him with "the old man."

One of Chicago's best-kept secrets was that Jack Johnson was also the official executioner.

It was a secret the handful of newspaper reporters who covered the Criminal Courts building in the 1950s and '60s helped him to keep. Jack had three young daughters in school, and it would not do for their classmates to know what their father did for his paycheck on certain occasions.

The myth reporters passed on to their editors and to the public was that there were four red-handled levers on a wall panel in the room behind the execution chamber in the basement of the county jail. Only one of the switches was actually wired up to the grim, black electric chair.

On the night of an execution, four guards who volunteered for the assignment pulled the handles in unison at a signal from the warden, and no man among them ever knew who activated the lethal switch.

Actually, that "anonymous" experiment was tried when the electric chair first replaced the hangman in 1929, but it didn't work. As the condemned man sat blindfolded and strapped into the chair, nervously awaiting his trip to eternity, the bye-bye nod was given and nothing happened.

Upon investigation, authorities discovered that one of the men could not go through with it, and only pretended to pull his handle. His switch, it turned out, was the live one.

"I absolutely do not believe in capital punishment," the warm-hearted Johnson confided to reporters he knew he could trust. "I just couldn't order any of my men to do a job like that—to kill another human being—so I must accept the responsibility myself.

"Sure, my conscience bothers me if I dwell on the fact that I'm breaking one of the Ten Commandments—Thou shalt not kill—so I have to rationalize that I am carrying out the will of society. I tell myself this is what the people wanted, so it must be all right."

In carrying out the will of society, Johnson always made it as easy as possible for the man who would be occupying the chair.

For a week prior to a scheduled execution his guards would methodically rehearse the grim drama to make sure each man knew his precise role right down to the second.

Using a volunteer of the same height and weight of the condemned man, they would march the "prisoner" the 15 steps from the death cell to the electrocution chamber, press him firmly into the chair, affix the black hood, strap down his forearms and legs, and attach the electrodes to his scalp and right calf.

It was all done as quickly and efficiently as humanly possible, to put the victim through as little mental and physical anguish as was necessary once the zero hour had arrived.

As soon as everything was in order the deputy warden gave the nod to Johnson, who was viewing the procedure through a one-way glass. Then he, and he alone, threw the switch that would send 1,900 bone-cracking volts coursing through the man's body until his blood boiled and his skin turned lobster red.

No liquor was allowed in the jail, but Johnson always saw to it that the condemned man got a generous shot of whisky to steady his nerves, if he wanted it, before taking his final walk to the chair. More than one convicted killer from Chicago met his maker with whisky on his breath.

Johnson, a tough ex-Marine, had been a captain in the sheriff's police before taking over as warden in 1955. The last man he executed—the last man to die in Chicago's electric chair before Cook County ceased killing its own murderers—was James Dukes at 12:10 a.m. August 24, 1962.

When Johnson asked Dukes whether he had any last words, the man who was about to die told him, "Warden, I wish I'd served with you in the Marines. The odds are I wouldn't be where I am now."

After an execution, Johnson would wind down by having a quiet post-midnight lunch in his private dining room with reporters assigned to cover the grim event. The meal would generally consist of whatever was left over from dinner in the county jail that day.

Johnson resigned as warden of the Cook County Jail in 1968 and took a job as an investigator for the Illinois Department of Revenue, where he remained until a heart condition forced his retirement in 1978.

Lenny Bruce
(1925–1966)

Walter Winchell called him "America's No. 1 Vomic." His mother called him Leonard. And almost everyone who wrote about him during his Chicago years referred to him as "foul mouthed Lenny Bruce," as though that were the nightclub comic's full name.

His biographer, Albert Goldman, wrote, "Using obscenity as a miner uses dynamite to blow up the deeply impacted prejudices and repressions of middle-class society, Lenny eventually provoked the wrath of the Catholic Church, the police and a lot of people who knew nothing at all about him except that he had a dirty mouth."

They didn't know his real name was Leonard Alfred Schneider. Born into a Jewish home in Mineola, N.Y., he was the son of a strip-tease dancer and a shoe clerk who were divorced when he was five.

Lenny's martinet father sent him off to a private school, but the boy dropped out in the 10th grade in 1942 and joined the Navy. He plotted, and got, a dishonorable discharge three years later posing as a homosexual.

He then married a girl, just like the girl who married dear old dad—a stripper named Hot Honey Harlow.

The hip-talking, irreverent Bruce worked as a movie usher, and in factories, while he studied acting in Hollywood.

Then he took his show on the road, bringing his glossary of hip and four-letter words into saloons, offbeat clubs and recording studios. By now Bruce was also a runaway junkie with a $600-a-week habit.

In Chicago he played the prestigious Mister Kelly's, the Black Orchid, the Tradewinds, the Maryland Hotel on the Near North Side, the Cloisters, as well as a lot of sleazy dumps. Night life critics variously described his act as "shocking," "outrageous" and "not in good taste."

"Chicago is so corrupt it's *thrilling*," he told his friends.

His career flowered in Chicago, and it died in Chicago, after his arrest on obscenity charges on Dec. 5, 1963.

The bust that began his decline came at the Gate of Horn, 1036 N. State St., where some of his most outrageous—and irreverent before-their-time—routines were first heard. The city lifted the Gate's liquor license when Bruce was arrested, and it never made a comeback.

Bruce's humor was universally branded as "sick."

"I'm not a comic and I'm not sick," he said. "The world is sick and I'm the doctor. I don't have an act, I just talk."

After being convicted in Chicago, he won an appeal to the Illinois Supreme Court. But the experience made him so paranoid that he never resumed the stride which once earned him $300,000 a year.

He was repeatedly arrested on drug or obscenity charges wherever his act played. His humor also got him banned from Britain, which deported him.

Back in Hollywood Bruce immersed himself in sex, drugs and nudity.

He had a thing about running around naked. Once, while serving as the MC in a burlesque house, he walked out on the stage "bare-assed naked."

On another occasion he toppled out of a third floor window of the Swiss-American Hotel overlooking Broadway, and landed in the street below, bare naked, with two broken ankles. When taken to the hospital for repairs, he made such obscene suggestions to the nuns on nurse duty that a doctor taped his mouth shut.

On Aug. 4, 1966, at the age of 40, he was found

dead on the bathroom floor of his Hollywood apartment. A syringe, a blackened bottle cap and burnt matches were nearby. The coroner's office listed the cause of death as an overdose of narcotics.

Bruce left the world the same way he came into it—stark naked. He had apparently toppled off the toilet seat and died while mainlining.

"I've been accused of bad taste and I'll go down to the grave accused of it and always by the same people," he once said. "The same people, the ones who eat in restaurants that reserve the right to refuse service to anyone."

Today the vocabulary of four-letter words that got Bruce thrown into jail in Chicago can be heard any time comics such as Redd Foxx, Eddie Murphy or Richard Pryor—and others—step onto the stage before a fawning audience.

More than anything else, perhaps, Lenny Bruce was a man ahead of his time.

Vincent DePaul Garrity
(1920–1972)

It seemed as though Vince Garrity was everywhere—at wakes and weddings, baptisms and bar mitzvahs, parades, picnics and parties, sporting events and political happenings. And if the truth were known, he was. The camera does not lie.

Pick up your morning paper and there on page one was Mayor Richard J. Daley talking to President Lyndon B. Johnson, with Garrity grinning between them. John Cardinal Cody with Garrity at his side. Harry Truman and Garrity. John F. Kennedy and Garrity. Dwight D. Eisenhower and Garrity. Joe Louis and Garrity. Judge Abraham Lincoln Marovitz chatting with a friend, and Garrity in the middle with his arms around the two of them.

"Vince was the city's loudest gamecock," according to Dave Condon, the famous sportswriter who was also Garrity's friend—but then, who wasn't?

Condon said he checked out a story that Garrity was at the Last Supper, with his hand on Christ's shoulder, and found it to be untrue. Had Garrity lived 2,000 years ago, however, he certainly would have been there long enough to get into the subsequent painting.

Vincent DePaul Garrity, one of 12 children, was named in honor of the church across the street from the home where he was born in 1920, St. Vincent DePaul.

One of his boyhood chums was Tommy Goss, who grew up to be the petulant TV personality Tom Duggan. Vince delivered *Booster* newspapers as a youngster, and played in the Charles H. Weber drum and bugle corps.

The job that most influenced his young life was that of batboy for the Chicago Cubs, starting in 1935, when the Cubs won the National League pennant. In 1938 he saw Gabby Hartnett hit the famous "homer in the gloamin' " against the Pirates to turn around the National League race, and traveled with the team to New York for the American League portion of the ill-fated World Series. That was the year Vince was named Chicago's "All American Boy in Sports."

The contacts he made in baseball led to an early career in radio and television, broadcasting sporting events from golf to network TV wrestling, and covering both Republican and Democrat political conventions. For nearly 20 years he had his own show on radio station WAAF, and later became vice president and director of WCIU, the city's first UHF television station.

The warmth of the spotlight beckoned Garrity into politics, and he won election to the board of the Sanitary District of Greater Metropolitan Chicago, serving as its vice president.

But it was as a photo-opportunity crasher that Garrity was the most creative. Whenever two famous people were being photographed, he had a knack for jumping between them just before the flashbulb popped, so the picture editors couldn't crop him out of the scene. One downtown newspaper once put its airbrush artist to work painting Garrity out of a picture in which he didn't belong.

Vince was never bashful. He once clambered aboard a moving limousine to shake hands with Fran-

klin D. Roosevelt, and on another occasion he buttonholed Truman at a political smoker and got the President
to call Vince's mother on the phone. Chief Justice Earl
Warren of the U.S. Supreme Court once inscribed a
gavel for Garrity saying, "For a little guy, you come on
strong."

He loved to see his picture in the papers so much
that the press gleefully obliged on occasions when he
was arrested for drunken driving and wife beating.

If Garrity could buy the good will of the press, he
was not above attempting it. He once buttonholed a
Daily News reporter at a political meeting, stuffed $15
into the newsman's shirt pocket, and told him, "Don't
ever be ashamed to accept money."

Garrity, always the good fellow, died in 1972 while
visiting a friend. He was 52.

Condon tells the story—passed on to him by
Garrity—of the time Vince booked sportscaster Bob
Elson for a speech in Kankakee, with the understanding
that they would split the speaker's "substantial fee"
50–50.

While Elson was speaking, the club president
handed Garrity an envelope containing four $50 bills.
Garrity skimmed one $50 bill off the top, sealed the
envelope, and slipped it to Elson after the dinner. On
the drive home Elson handed Garrity a $50 bill and told
him, "Here's your half. Those cheap blankety-blanks
only gave me a hundred bucks."

Lar "America First" Daly
(1912–1978)

Lar "America First" Daly looked a lot like Stan Laurel in
an Uncle Sam suit. He wore the red, white and blue
uniform, complete with star-spangled top hat, whenever he campaigned for public office—which was most
of the time.

He ran for President of the United States. He ran
for United States senator from Illinois. He ran for

governor. He ran for state superintendent of public instruction. He ran for Cook County superintendent of schools. He ran for mayor of Chicago. He ran for congress. And he ran for a whole lot of lesser offices.

Sometimes he was a Republican. Sometimes he was a Democrat.

Once he actually made it past the primary election. That was in 1973 when he won the GOP nomination in the 7th Congressional District, mainly because he ran unopposed. He lost in the general election to Democrat Cardiss Collins, who pulled 33,875 votes to his 1,329.

Daly's platform was always the epitome of simplicity. America First! Shoot dope dealers on sight! Castrate rapists—after a fair trial, of course.

"If they come out of prison and try again to force their attentions on women, you apply the Biblical law: You blind them," he declared.

The affable Irishman was born Lawrence Joseph Sarsfield Daly in Gary, Ind. His father was a Gary policeman. The family moved to Chicago when little Lawrence Joseph Sarsfield was 6. He shortened his name to Lar when he went into politics, hoping it might help garner the Swedish vote.

Although Daly never won an election, he won a victory of sorts in 1959 when the Federal Communications Commission ruled that as a bonafide candidate for mayor he was entitled to equal time on television news programs that ran footage on Mayor Richard J. Daley.

He also won a 47-minute shot on the Jack Paar television show in 1960 to compensate for a guest appearance by presidential candidate John F. Kennedy. The audience hooted and heckled him, but the perennial candidate, who could talk louder and faster than most humans, proved unflappable.

Daly loved people and he loved to play the fiddle. He was equally welcome at South Side wedding receptions and neighborhood saloons.

He sold bar stools for a living, and he lived to run for public office. In all, he offered himself to the public in more than 40 elections before he died in 1978, flat broke.

"Why do you keep running for office?" he was

once asked. "Isn't it apparent to you by now that the voters have rejected you?"

"Napoleon Bonaparte used to say that it is only one step from the sublime to the ridiculous," Daly responded. "That's an immutable axiom.

"Besides, I'm running because it's best for America, and Chicago, too."

His death, at age 66, left Chicago politics just a little bit duller.

Robert Sabonjian
(1916–   )

After returning from service with the Coast Guard during World War II, stocky, swarthy, two-fisted, four-letter-mouthed Bob Sabonjian opened a dry cleaning plant in his hometown of Waukegan. He called it the Dutch Mill, to get up high in the phone book.

"Why not call it the Armenian Mill and get higher?" he was asked.

"What!" he snorted. "And lose the Turkish trade?"

In the early 1950s the plant burned down. Sabonjian had no insurance. But nobody who had a suit or gown in his shop lost a dime. He struck a deal with a downtown men's store and a women's apparel shop.

Then he told his customers: "If you lost a pair of pants, you go down and buy a new pair of pants and put it on my bill. If you lost a dress, buy yourself a new one of comparable value and charge it to Bob Sabonjian. You trusted me with your clothes, now I'm trusting you with my wallet."

The trust test severely depleted his bank account, but to the best of his knowledge, nobody took advantage of him.

That somehow sums up the multi-faceted, bushy-eyed Armenian who went on to serve an unprecedented six terms as Waukegan's mayor, three as a Democrat and three as a Republican. He seemed unprepared for any eventuality, but when something did happen, he barged right ahead and dealt with it in his own way.

During the 1960s demonstrations by the Weatherman faction of the Students for a Democratic Society he denounced the students as "undesirable scum," and told a meeting of police officials: "There's a lot of talk about understanding these people. Understand, hell! Kick the hell out of them and they won't come back tomorrow! If they start throwing rocks, put your clubs back in your lockers and draw your pistols. You shoot, and tell them I said to do it. I'll go stand trial for you. Thank God for you men. Without you there would be chaos and revolution."

Yet when the Waukegan police force went out on strike for union recognition the following year, Sabonjian fired the whole bunch. He was a strict law-and-order man, as long as the cops maintained order by his law.

"In my town, if you wanna eat at my table, you gotta help set it," he once explained.

Sabonjian started out as a caddy at Skokie Country Club in Glencoe. He was later a bellhop at Northmoor Country Club in Highland Park, and a $7-a-week service station attendant. He was also an amateur boxer.

His political career started when he was elected alderman from Waukegan's Democratic South Side in 1951. He quit to become acting postmaster, a job he lost when the GOP took over Washington. He was re-elected alderman two years later.

A truly two-fisted representative of the people, he once exchanged blows on the city hall steps with Walter "Whitey" Hallen, a fellow Democratic alderman nearly twice his age.

When "The Rock," as Sabonjian called himself, decided to run for mayor in 1957, he borrowed a pass key to sneak into the city hall at 4 a.m. to beat two regular Democratic candidates in line.

It was a rip-roaring campaign in which it was difficult, at times, to be sure who Sabonjian was running against. He blasted Chicago's Mayor Richard J. Daley just as severely as he lambasted his Republican opponent in Waukegan.

"It's just a question of time before I take over," he threatened in the Republican-stronghold city hall on election night. When the votes were counted The Rock won, 8,518 to 6,799, with 2,500 Republicans splitting their ballots in his favor.

During his administration the mayor's door was always open, and anyone could walk in and talk to him, as long as one didn't mind being greeted with, "C'mon in, ya son-of-a-bitch."

He refused to negotiate with racial rioters in the city in 1966, calling them "junkheads and winos" and names that can't be printed, and blamed the disturbances on the NAACP.

When the local Democratic Party refused to endorse Sabonjian for a fourth term in 1968 he told them to "shove it" and ran as a Republican, being swept back into office by 75 percent of the vote. "I wanted to give the Republicans some class," he laughed.

Some people wondered how Sabonjian could drive a new Lincoln town car on the mayor's salary. The *Waukegan News-Sun* explained, "He freely talks about the gifts—boats, cars and free lunches—that businesses and industries have given him in return for things the city has done for them."

A five-month investigation by the Lake County Grand Jury into allegations of widespread official corruption, misconduct and sanctioned gambling concluded in 1971 that Sabonjian was technically in violation of conflict of interest laws, but nobody ever laid a glove on him, much less an indictment.

Instead the voters returned him to office two years later for a fifth term.

"I love being mayor, being there," he said. "I love the power—being in a position to help my friends out; to be able to walk down the street and have some guy yell, 'Hey Rock, what d'ya know?' I love it."

The romance ended in 1977 in his quest for a sixth term. A record number of 20,000 voters turned out and he lost by 880 votes. But don't count the ex-boxer out yet.

He came back strong in a 1985 rematch, beating incumbent Bill Morris in every ward but one. "Waukegan will come alive in '85," he hooted, returning to his old chair in City Hall.

After his sixth term he retired, at age 73 "at the top of my game, as Abraham Lincoln once said."

Since then Sabonjian has been selling insurance for a local firm that made him chairman of the board.

What does the ex-dry cleaner know about insurance?

"Not a thing! I bring in the customers, and the technicians take over. I'm making more money than I ever did in my life. I love every minute of it. I'm never going to retire."

And what is he driving these days?

"You know me. A brand new Lincoln Town Car. It's a beauty!"

Al Carter
(1915–1987)

In the beginning, there was Al Carter. He was the first man in line at the beginning of the A Century of Progress Exposition in 1933, and the last one out when the world's fair closed in 1934. He was the first person into the Chicago Railroad Fair of 1950, first one through the gates at the Seattle World's Fair in 1962, the New York World's Fair of 1964, Expo '67 in Montreal, the Knoxville World's Fair in 1982, . . . you name it, and Al was probably in front of the line.

Carter, a Chicago jazz drummer who made it his life's avocation to either be the first guy in or the last guy out, clearly was one of the city's zaniest characters of the twentieth century.

He was also a super-patriot, born on the Fourth of July, 1915.

He was not quite 18 when he decided to be the first customer at the A Century of Progress on Chicago's lakefront. But a pushy woman euchred him out of position at the last minute, and he had to settle for being the first male customer. He never let it happen again, and he got even by being the last one out when the fair closed its doors in 1934.

Over the years he built a handsome collection of affidavits and newspaper clippings attesting that he was first at all those other fairs, plus he was first through the turnstile at the San Antonio World's Fair in 1968; flew to Japan in 1970, clutching ticket No. 1 to the Japan World Exposition in Osaka; was the first paying customer at the Spokane Fair in 1974; and stood at the head of a line of 1,300 people to be first to enter the the 1975 International Ocean Exposition in Okinawa.

At Expo '67 in Montreal, he sat on a folding chair outside the main gate under a multilingual sign saying "Reserved for Al Carter" in English, French, Spanish and Arabic.

"I got newspaper clips from all over the world on that one," he said. "A friend on vacation even saw me on TV in Japan. They had me talking Japanese. Can you beat that?"

Advance publicity sometimes had its drawbacks, however. "Like at Niagara Falls in 1962, when I was waiting to be first at the opening of Seagram Tower over Horseshoe Falls," he recalled. "People read about me and kept driving by all night long, yelling 'Hi, Al,' and I didn't get any sleep."

All this firsting was somehow sandwiched in between beating the skins with Stan Paul's Orchestra in the Pump Room of the Ambassador East.

Al Carter fans will remember vividly how the balding drummer, driving a battered 1951 Chevrolet station wagon with its odometer on the second time around, was the first paying customer across the Mackinaw Bridge over the Straits of Mackinac in 1957, and how he became the first motorist on the Calumet Skyway in 1958 "after all those big shots."

And how he and his Chevrolet conquered the Tri-State Tollway, Northwest Tollway, Kennedy Expressway, the Eisenhower, the Dan Ryan and the Adlai Stevenson.

The resourceful Carter chartered standing room at the bow of a Canadian freighter to become the first person to travel through the new locks of the St. Lawrence Seaway; and when the "Show-Me" people of St. Louis, Mo., dedicated their 630-foot Gateway Arch hard by the Mississippi in 1966, you can bet your buttons it was Carter who showed the rest of the world how to be the first person to ride to the top.

Of course he was the first person atop Sears Tower when it was opened to the public in 1974.

Not all of Carter's rides were happy events. He took a depressing last ride on the North Shore electric line when it folded at midnight on Jan. 21, 1963, and he was the last person to ride on the last streetcar run on the last trolley line in Chicago on June 22, 1958.

That one took some doing.

Carter was clearly the last paying customer when he climbed aboard the streetcar at Vincennes Avenue and 79th Street and dropped his token into the box at 6:16 a.m., and conductor W.E. Rye autographed his transfer to that effect. But when the trolley rolled into the carbarn at 77th Street, everybody got sadly off except Carter and Chester Schleff of Gary, Ind.

There was an uncomfortable silence, a clearing of throats, a scuffling of feet—until finally a Chicago Transit Authority supervisor declared: "Hurry up, now, the crew's on overtime."

Still no movement, until CTA officials got the two contestants to agree that Chester would disembark from the front door while Al would alight from the middle exit. And off they stepped.

Oops! Carter, the seasoned pro, grabbed the handrail and pulled himself back, just as Schleff's feet touched the ground. Then, and only then, did Carter grandly debark, officially closing down 99 years of trolley tradition in Chicago.

"You gotta reconnoiter. Always reconnoiter, so you know what you're doing in case of competition," was his advice to newcomers to the game.

When not being first or last, Carter liked to debunk history. He once invaded the birthplace of George M. Cohan to prove by local records that Broadway's "Yankee Doodle Dandy" was not born on the Fourth of July, as he boasted in one of his songs, but on July 3.

Carter met serious defeat only once in his long career. On July 19, 1960, he set off to become the first civilian to see if all that gold in Fort Knox was really there. He got as far as the front gate, where he stated his business into a loud speaker arrangement. "They told me to scram!"

Throughout all his adventures, Carter always gave his age to the press as 40. It was not until he died on July 9, 1987, that a funeral director looked up his birth records and determined he was 72.

And the undertaker revealed something else about Carter that even his closest friends never knew. He was really a Chicago-born Lithuanian named Albert Vaitis. He took the name of Carter when he became a jazz drummer in the big-band era of the 1930s, "because Vaitis didn't have much of a beat to it."

Sylvester "Two-Gun Pete" Washington
(1906–1971)

Sylvester Washington was a kindly looking man with short hair, soft brown eyes and just a trace of a smile on his lips. He smoked a pipe and dressed right out of *Esquire.* Those who knew him claimed he was the meanest cop who ever walked the streets of Chicago. During his 18 years on the force he claimed to have made more than 20,000 arrests, was investigated by the grand jury, and is known to have killed 16 men—not to mention those he wounded.

He walked around with pearl-handled .357 Magnum revolvers strapped on each hip, and he was known as "Two-Gun Pete."

Washington was black. So were his "victims." When asked to explain how come he had never shot a white man, Washington pointed out that there were no white crooks in the part of town he patrolled. His beat was the South Side ghetto, and the streets he walked were those that other men of the law had hopelessly abandoned to the pushers, pimps, rapists, muggers and whores.

"This was a man who would make a Clint Eastwood 'Dirty Harry' movie seem like a Saturday morning cartoon," said his biographer, Jerry Jones. ". . . an incredibly complex man who was capable of great tenderness and awesome cruelty."

Once, when he came upon a man raping a 9-year-old girl in an alley, Washington shot him dead. Two years later the man's sailor brother, out for revenge, ambushed Washington, disarmed him and knocked him to the ground.

As the sailor commenced firing at Washington with his own guns, Washington pulled a derringer out of his boot and shot him between the eyes.

Charles Wellons, 35, met Washington when the lawman walked into the middle of a holdup he was performing in Kauffman's Dry Goods Store at 653 E. 63rd St. Washington said he was forced to shoot Wellons dead when the suspect resisted arrest.

Harold Lloyd, 18, made the mistake of trying to drive off in Washington's car. As the auto sped away Washington fired five shots at it, and Lloyd did not live long enough to enjoy his new possession.

Eural Richardson, 23, reportedly reached into his pocket when Washington stopped him for questioning outside a fish market at 554 E. 47th St., and ended up in the morgue. A coroner's inquest ruled the slaying was justifiable homicide, even though 10 witnesses testified that Washington put a second shot into Richardson's back as he lay on the ground.

Arthur Pierson, 33, was shot and killed by Washington in an East 53rd Street tavern after he reportedly

drew a revolver when the policeman tried to arrest him.

William Matthews, 33, a hotel bellboy who once captured a holdup man for police, died of a gunshot wound when he and Washington collided in a passageway near 55th Street and Calumet Avenue.

The list goes on.

Jones, in his book, *Two Gun Pete*, says he asked Washington how many men he killed.

"It might've been 11 men that I killed or it might've been more," Washington answered. "But let me say this—when you are stuck out there in them jungles all alone and somebody walks up and sticks a gun under your nose with the hammer cocked, you don't have no time to bargain on whether you should shoot him or shake his hand."

In 1951 Washington was one of five Wabash Avenue District police officers questioned by a Cook County grand jury investigating the policy racket. They were curious as to how Washington could wear custom-tailored suits, put down $20,000 in cash to buy a six-flat building and pay cash for a $3,600 Cadillac on an annual salary of $3,900.

He explained that friends loaned him the money for the building, he paid $300 a year for enough material to make six flashy suits, and that a tailor made the clothes for him free of charge.

Q—What is there to this persistent rumor that you have a valet?

A—Oh, that man just washes my dishes.

Q—Where did you get that big diamond ring?

A—A friend gave it to me.

Q—How about that gold belt buckle?

A—A bartender gave me that.

Q—Where did you get those handkerchiefs in your pocket, the ones embroidered "Sylvester Washington?"

A—The same bartender.

Q—Frank Costello wears handkerchiefs like that, doesn't he?

A—Costello is a hoodlum. I'm a law enforcement officer, the greatest.

Washington retired later that same year and opened a saloon on Oakwood Boulevard. Though a civilian, he tended bar with his revolvers strapped at his side.

Washington got the short end of it one cold January day in 1964 when his third wife, Roslyn, age 17, pulled her 58-year-old husband's revolver out of its holster and shot him in the abdomen.

It seems he had complained that the meal she was cooking didn't smell right. He somehow recovered and a judge freed her after she said the gun went off by accident.

Two-Gun Pete, much to the surprise of many who knew him, died in 1971 at the age of 65 of natural causes.

A retired police officer who had been close to Washington for years said, "He was the star of his own show."

Leo Durocher
(1905–   )

Leo "The Lip" Durocher, whose baseball career spanned six decades—from 1925 to 1973—claimed in his book, *Nice Guys Finish Last*, that no boss ever called him in and congratulated him for losing like a gentleman.

"Show me a good loser . . . and I'll show you an idiot," he declared.

Born on the kitchen table of his parents' three-flat in the French Catholic neighborhood of West Springfield, Mass., he pronounced his last name the French way, Doo-roe-SHAY, throughout his early years. He didn't become Duh-ROACH-er until he chucked his job as a millhand and got into baseball at the age of 19.

The first uniform he wore was that of a New York Yankee bench-warmer. He wasn't one bit happy as a $4,500 player trying to keep up with $80,000 guys like Babe Ruth. His career as a shortstop picked up in 1930 when the Cincinnati Reds claimed him on waivers. From there he went on to St. Louis, whose Cardinals were known as the Gas House Gang, "the roughest, rowdiest, most colorful team of all time," in Durocher's words. He was a member of the gang until 1938 when Brooklyn got him in a trade with the Cards. The following year he became the Dodgers' manager.

Tough, wily and arrogant as any man could be, Durocher never batted .300 in all his years as a player or playing manager, but he was considered the best short-stop of his time. Under his leadership the Dodgers won their first pennant in 21 years, and his regular mouthing off at umpires won him the nickname, "The Lip."

In 1948 he went over to the New York Giants, the Dodgers' mortal enemy. In three years he led them to a pennant, beating out the Dodgers in a playoff series. In 1954 his team swept the World Series in four straight games. In 1960 he went to what was by then the L.A. Dodgers as a coach.

Five years later he was hired by P.K. Wrigley as manager of the Chicago Cubs, the team of Ron Santo, Ernie Banks, and Billy Williams. He held the position for six and a half years

"Phil Wrigley is simply the finest man to work for in the world. The most decent man, probably, I have ever met," said Durocher, who put the Cubs back into the first division after 20 years. "The great disappointment of my career is that I wasn't able to win a pennant for him."

Durocher, who also had an eye for pretty women, had three wives—Grace Dozier, a dress designer, whom he married while playing with the Gas House Gang; movie actress Laraine Day, whom he wed while with the Dodgers; and Lynne Walker Goldblatt, whom he married in 1969 while managing the Cubs, at the age of 63. All three marriages ended in divorce.

While in Chicago Durocher battled with the press as much as he did with the umpires. He charged that an Unholy Six, led by broadcaster Jack Brickhouse and *Chicago Today* sports writer Jim Enright, were out to get him.

"Up yours too, Brickhouse. Screw you, Enright," he explained in his book.

The team was heading for a pennant, but collapsed late in the 1969 season and finished second. After an angry meeting with the team in the clubhouse, Durocher suggested to general manager John Holland, "You can take the uniform and shove it up your ass!"

He later recanted, giving in to pleas from Ron Santo, Joey Amalfitano, Ernie Banks and Holland himself.

In the spring of 1971 he was accused of associating with a known gambler, a charge which he described as "a set-up" by certain sportswriters. He left Chicago not long afterward, and in 1973 wound up with the Houston Astros. The new breed of player, however, was more than Durocher could comprehend, and at the end of the season he quit baseball for good.

"It isn't a sport any more," he said prophetically. "It's an industry."

After his retirement he settled down in Palm Springs, Calif., where he even passed the collection plate at Mass each week. It seems he was trying to make his peace with the only umpire who really mattered.

"The Lord," Durocher explained. "All those years I took his name in vain, a trillion times. Terrible. I'm not perfect now, but I'm 85 percent better than I was."

He was not good enough for the sports scribes, however, who were not yet ready to forgive him for his battles with the media. In 1990 he was nominated to the Baseball Hall of Fame, but the Lord didn't have enough pull with the Baseball Writers to get him voted in.

Ziggy
(1917–1975)

He was the biggest, baddest, bull elephant in captivity— an accused murderer—the only elephant who ever conducted a moonshine raid—he could play "Yes, Sir, That's My Baby" on a harmonica—and he could spit through his trunk with the accuracy of a sharpshooter.

Say hello to Ziggy, the Paderewski of the pachyderms. Ten feet, eight inches tall, with six-foot tusks, he was a 13,000-pound legend of ponderous proportions.

And he was all ours!

Show biz impresario Florenz Ziegfeld first spotted the baby Asian elephant being unloaded at a New York dock in 1920, and bought him off John Ringling, the circus man. The little fellow weighed only 250 pounds, and Ziegfeld took him home in a taxi—a surprise for his six-year-old daughter, Patricia.

Ziggy wore out his welcome the following summer during a greenhouse party in his honor on Ziegfeld's Long Island estate. Seeing the first real foliage since he'd left the wilds, Ziggy devoured every plant in sight and ended the affair by crashing through the greenhouse wall as the screaming children scattered in all directions.

Ziegfeld sold the elephant back to Ringling Bros., who eventually passed Ziggy on to Singer's Midgets Circus. Captain Charles Becker, the 41-inch-tall elephant handler, taught Ziggy to smoke cigarettes through a foot-long holder, and to play a giant harmonica.

Ziggy would also break into a thunderous, earth-shaking dance called the "lurch" whenever Captain Becker commanded, "Shake it up!"

During a tour of Spain Ziggy lurched so vigorously the stage collapsed under his weight, sending the midgets tumbling into the basement. The indomitable elephant just kept right on lurching amid the wreckage, however, until everyone calmed down.

Ziggy almost became a hero again in Milwaukee, when he battered down the wall of a doctor's stable where he was quartered for the night, and exposed a secret storeroom holding 130 cases of bootleg whisky worth $60,000 dollars.

The scandal rocked Milwaukee like Ziggy rocked the stable, but the stable's owner turned out to be the brother of Milwaukee's chief of detectives, who told the midgets to pack their elephant's trunk and get out of town.

Ziggy's circus career came to an end at the 1936 San Diego Exposition, when Captain Becker became ill and a substitute handler, Johnny Winters, tried to put him through his paces.

Ziggy indignantly broke loose from his ankle-stake and went AWOL in Balboa Park. A 1941 news account of the rampage reported that the enraged elephant scooped up a Marine trombone player who didn't get out of the way in time and hurled him to his death.

Phil Cihlar, Brookfield Zoo historian, argues this could have been a bum rap.

Another published report said Ziggy threw the musician 30 feet into the air, and landed him in a hospital.

Although at least three deaths caused by bull elephants were recorded in western states at that time, Cihlar could find none involving a musician in San Diego. He said one of the other fatalities might have erroneously been attributed to Ziggy.

Nevertheless, the rampage ended Ziggy's show business career. He was slated for execution, but the Brookfield Zoo, which was looking for a bull elephant, bought him for $800.

All hell broke loose in Kansas City on the rail trip to Chicago, when Ziggy extended his long trunk through a baggage car window and upset a train of baggage carts, strewing suitcases along the length of the station platform.

"We were looking for another Jumbo, but we got a Mauna Loa," Zoo Director Robert Bean winced afterward.

Reports that Ziggy killed the musician in San Diego, and another man in Europe, may or may not have been myths. But there is no question that he did try to kill his Chicago trainer, George "Slim" Lewis, who had lovingly polished his proud ivory tusks and curried his wrinkled hide for five devoted years. Ziggy returned the favors by playing "Yes, Sir, That's My Baby" for Lewis on a tiny eight-inch mouth harp.

Then, on April 26, 1941, Ziggy unexpectedly turned on Lewis, threw him to the ground and tried to gore him. Three times Ziggy charged head down, as the experienced bullhand rolled between the lethal tusks while spectators looked on in horror and photographers recorded the drama.

On the fourth try the elephant drove with such force his immense tusks became imbedded in the ground, with Lewis pinned between them. The keeper grabbed Ziggy's ear, pulled himself up and punched the elephant with all his might in his only weak spot, the eye—and scampered to safety as Ziggy trumpeted in pain.

That was the last outing for Ziggy for 30 long years.

For the next three decades the zoo's number one attraction was kept chained in a large indoor stall, where his magnificent ivory tusks grew to a length where they scraped on the floor, but no one dared enter his quarters to groom him.

Ziggy occasionally amused himself by hurling unwanted food or bowling-ball size elephant droppings at unwary spectators with uncanny accuracy.

On one occasion, his keepers recalled, the "most dangerous animal in America" stood wistfully watching a small mouse as it skittered around the stall. Ziggy seemed totally amused at the only living thing that had dared to enter his domain in years—until the foolhardy rodent paused to nibble at an apple that was intended for Ziggy's lunch.

With one hurricane blast from his trunk Ziggy blew the tiny visitor clear into the next cage.

In 1971, after interested citizens contributed enough money to build Ziggy a private, outdoor enclosure, he was paroled at last. George Lewis, the victim of the near goring and the only man alive who gave Ziggy commands he obeyed, flew back to Chicago from Seattle to call Ziggy out.

Ziggy responded, and found himself once again a free rogue.

To the delight of the crowds, Ziggy would perform for hours, tossing mud on his back and eating four loaves of bread, 25 carrots, and nearly a bale of hay—and going in and out of his stall whenever he felt like it.

Several attempts were made over the years to mate Ziggy. One would-be girlfriend, Judy, decided he just wasn't her type. When he tried to get amorous she butted him broadside and knocked him down, much to his mortification.

In 1974 Ziggy became a "ganesha," a one-tusked creature, when he wedged his right tusk into an opening in his cage door and broke off a massive, four-foot-long hunk of ivory.

The following March Ziggy became a real burden to his keepers. While attempting to give his current keeper, Ed Sykes, the back of his trunk— a trick he'd done many times before—he leaned too far out over the moat and lost his balance.

Nearly six and a half tons of pachyderm plunged

head-first, 10 feet down to the concrete moat, where he landed with a crash, snapping off what was left of his tusks. Ziggy flopped over onto his left side, where he lay bleeding and bruised and unable to move for 31 agonizing hours.

It took a heavy-duty tow truck to winch him upright, after which workmen poured 84,000 pounds of gravel into the moat to build a ramp so he could climb out. When he reached the surface, Widget, the lady elephant who lived next door, entwined her trunk with his as if to say, "Welcome back, old boy."

Ziggy got hundreds of get-well cards from school children, one of whom suggested sending his broken hunk of ivory to the "tusk fairy."

Seven months later, on Oct. 27, 1975, Ziggy quietly slumped to a sitting position in his stall in the Pachyderm House, then rolled over onto his right side, and took his final breath.

It was a dignified end after 58 years of adventure, not all to man's liking.

The Field Museum volunteered to take Ziggy's mammoth skeleton and to reconstruct it for display. Other parts of his anatomy were turned over to scientists, including Ziggy's tongue, larynx, jaw muscles and joints, salivary glands, and the tip of his trunk.

"These things are priceless," said D.E. Lloyd Du Brul, professor of oral anatomy at the University of Illinois Medical Center. "How often does one get to study an animal like this?"

Mathon Kyritsis
(1901–1973)

The night watchman is making his rounds in the Louvre to make sure everyone is out, when he discovers the rumple-suited young man asleep at the feet of Venus de Milo.

"Wake up, now! Be off with you! It's closing time," he says gruffly, shaking the man's shoulder.

Eighteen-year-old Korymathon Kyritsis shakes his

head to clear the cobwebs, takes one last look at the white marble statue without arms, and shuffles out of the Paris museum. It is 1919, and he is on his way to America.

Kyritsis was already homesick for his native island of Melos, Greece, when his route took him through Paris. He apprehensively went into the Louvre to be near his last contact with home when he dozed off at her feet. Venus of Melos—Venus de Milo—they had come from the same place.

A few weeks later Kyritsis arrived in Waukegan, Ill., frightened, alone and unable to speak a word of English. Thirty years later, in 1949, the people of Waukegan would honor him as the community's "Man of the Year."

Aided by members of the northern suburb's Greek community, Kyritsis hired on as a crew member on a Lake Michigan fishing tug. He shortened his first name for the sake of pronunciation, and forgot about his last. "Call me Mathon," he said.

But the roaring, raging, tossing icy waters of the Great Lakes were not for this son of the sunny Mediterranean. "I can't fish, I'm too seasick. And I'm cold all the time," he complained. "So are we," his fellow crewmen said. "But, what else is there to do?"

If there was one thing Mathon was determined to do, it was to keep his feet on dry land. So he scrimped and saved and opened a one-room lunch counter down by the harbor to provide steaming hot coffee and home cooked meals for the other fishermen when they came in off the lake. Word got around, and it soon became the "in" place for businessmen and professional people "up on the hill" to meet for fish fries, fresh out of the lake.

Mathon was forced to add a room to his diner to accommodate the noontime crowds, and another, and another. By the middle 1940s Mathon's Restaurant—"for ichthyophagists"—was listed in all the where-to-eat guides, catering to well-heeled sea food lovers from Chicago to Milwaukee.

The prosperous Mathon grew a goatee, acquired his own fishing tug, which he patriotically named the Franklin D. Roosevelt, and sent it out daily to bring in fresh catches for his restaurant.

He kept meticulous records of the fishing grounds —where his men made the best catches, and the depth of their nets. He soon discovered that the lake perch, in particular, seemed to seek deep water in the wake of unusually cold weather, and when they remained closer to shore the winters would be mild.

Mathon's restaurant by now had become a gathering place for the local press, since he never charged a newspaperman or a police officer for a meal. *Chicago Tribune* reporter John Hayes wandered down to the restaurant on a slow-news day in 1943, looking for something to keep people's minds off the war.

"Would you believe it if I told you I can talk to the fish?" Mathon teased, as they chatted over lunch. He then explained how he had charted the movements of the perch, which indicated the area was in for a severe winter.

Hayes knew a page one story when he heard one, and Mathon was on his way to building a nation-wide reputation as an odd-ball weather forecaster.

When FDR died he did not think it wise politics to call his boat the Harry Truman in heavily-Republican Lake County, so he renamed it the Mathon, and continued to send it out to seek fish and weather information.

When the blood-sucking lamprey eels made their way into the Great Lakes through the Welland Canal they decimated the fish population of the lake, threatening to put the entire fishing fleet out of business. Mathon helped organize and was named president of the Illinois Commercial Fishermen's Association, formed to battle the vampire-like parasite.

The self-styled P.T. Barnum of Waukegan carried the battle to Washington, where he marched onto the floor of Congress with a live lamprey dangling from his fist to drive home his point, and won a $466,000 appropriation to fight the menace.

Mathon, more than anyone else, was responsible for the return of trout and salmon sport fishing to Lake Michigan as we know it today.

He also latched onto the Great Lakes Unidentified Flying Objects Association, taking the group on regular midnight forays out onto Lake Michigan on nights of the full moon, in hopes of getting an unobstructed view of visiting space ships. They never made a confirmed sighting of a flying saucer, but their expeditions brought great media coverage for the restaurant.

Through all his new-found fame, Mathon never forgot the night he fell asleep at the feet of Venus de Milo. "It was an omen," he said. He spent thousands of dollars on two scuba diving expeditions to return to waters off the island of his youth to search for her missing arms.

The 2,300-year-old statue was found buried in a field on Melos in 1820, but its arms were broken off and lost in 80 feet of water offshore as local Greeks and French sailors scuffled over the relic.

Mathon's searches yielded one marble arm, a palm, wrist and forearm, and the front half of a bare foot. Unfortunately the Greet Antiquities Department ruled that none of the body parts had come from Venus.

He was still riding high as a weather forecaster, however, missing only twice, in 1948 and 1952, "when I did not listen to the perch."

In the fall of 1960, with a record of "89.9 percent accuracy," he predicted a mild winter. It was a horrible mistake. The winter of 1960–61 was so bitter that a group of Libertyville businessmen hung him in effigy in a downtown park, and officials at the U.S. Weather Bureau rejoiced at the publicity-seeking fisherman's sub-zero fumble.

It would never happen again. Mathon secretly subscribed to a professional weather forecasting service—the same one used by heating companies—for $50 a week. And every autumn after that, when the big city papers and TV stations called him for his forecast he would slyly consult the meteorological charts and announce, "The perch tell me that this winter is going to be. . . ."

"You're a fake, Mathon!" a news reporter who learned his secret chided him over free lunch one day at his lakefront restaurant.

"No, really I am not," Mathon explained. "You see, I am first and foremost a fisherman, and everybody knows that fishermen are liars—so if they know you are lying when you tell them something, it isn't really a lie."

The reporter kept Mathon's secret, and he went on issuing his famous forecasts "right from the perch's mouth" year after year after year—with far greater accuracy than restaurateur Jim Janek, who studied the fat of the bear, or Otis Lamar of downstate Rosiclare, who relied on the wooly-haired caterpillar.

Shortly before his death in 1973 at the age of 71, Mathon got a telephone call from a Chicago reporter asking for the latest weather prediction. After Mathon assured the scribe that the info he had just imparted came from the talkative perch, the young reporter asked the fisherman-restaurateur to verify the spelling of his name.

"No, no, no, it's not Nathan," he said impatiently into the phone. "Mathon, M-A-T-H-O-N. No, NOT Nathon. Mathon, with an 'M'—as in 'toMorrow' . . ."

Jack Brickhouse
(1916–   )

John Beasley Brickhouse arrived without a stitch of clothing in Peoria, Ill., on Jan. 24, 1916. He was the son of a wayfaring vaudeville promoter from the hills of Tennessee and a Welsh coal miner's daughter.

His father, Will, age 39, stood six feet, five inches and weighed 225 pounds. His mother, Daisy, a 15-year-old immigrant from Cardiff, weighed 90 pounds and was barely five feet tall. Their marriage lasted just about as long as it took to have Jack.

When a friend asked Daisy how she was able to raise the fatherless child on the $14 a week she earned behind the cigar counter of a Peoria traveling man's hotel she explained, "It's a poor hen that can't scratch for one chick."

Young Jack helped make ends meet by selling newspapers at the age of 11, but his true love was sports, and it is as a sports broadcaster that he made his mark in life.

Courtesy of WGN.

Jack Brickhouse first stepped nervously before the microphone at Station WMBD, Peoria, in 1934 at the tender age of 18. He finished fifth in a local "So You Want To Be An Announcer" contest, but the station honchos took a liking to him anyway, and let him work without pay. He eventually was given a salary of $17 a week, provided he sit in as switchboard operator when not on the air.

He broadcast Bradley University basketball and Illinois prep sports, and did "man-on-the-street" interviews.

In one memorable man-on-the-street broadcast he asked a farmer, "How do you explain this terrible drought?" Without missing a beat the farmer responded, "No rain!"

Brickhouse left WMBD and Peoria in 1940, to join WGN in Chicago. He remained with WGN until his retirement in 1981, except for brief defections to radio station WJJD and WBKB–TV (Channel 7), and two years as a Marine Corps private during World War II.

During his career in Chicago he served as play-by-play announcer for more than 5,300 Chicago baseball games, thus earning credit for having reported more losing ballgames then any other man in history.

"Jack Brickhouse has seen more bad baseball than any person, living or dead," Steve Daley once wrote in the *Chicago Tribune.*

Stanton Cook, chairman and former chief executive officer of the Tribune Company, which owns WGN and the Chicago Cubs, called him "the eternal optimist."

Although primarily recognized as a baseball announcer, he also broadcast college and professional football, wrestling, Golden Gloves and World Champion boxing matches, college and pro basketball, Democratic and Republican national conventions and Presidential inaugurations.

He claims an all-time record of having broadcast the play-by-play on eight no-hit, no-run games in the major leagues.

His broadcast trademark was "Hey-Hey," which he first uttered on the air one day in the 1950s, when Hank Sauer hit a homer for the Cubs. He's been saying it ever since.

Brickhouse was inducted into the Baseball Hall of Fame in Cooperstown in 1983, and in 1986 the Chicago Press Veterans Association honored him as Chicago Press Veteran of the Year.

Pictures of Jack with Pope Paul VI and with President Ronald Reagan are among the many trophies lining the walls of his Lake Shore Drive apartment.

Though he numbers many of the rich and famous among his close friends, Brickhouse also became known as the first person to extend the welcome hand to new

223

members of the baseball entourage, whether they were equipment managers, players or mere reporters.

"The nicest thing about Jack Brickhouse is that he is nice to everybody," Cubs super-star Ernie Banks said about him.

"Brickhouse" is a literal translation of the ancestral name of Von Steinhausen—which explains his family motto: People who live in brick houses shouldn't throw stones.

"Hey-Hey!"

1970s

John Cardinal Cody
(1907–1982)

On the day that John Patrick Cody, the archbishop of New Orleans, was reassigned to Chicago to succeed the late Albert Cardinal Meyer—June 16, 1965—the city editor of one of the downtown dailies told his religion writer, "Call the New Orleans papers and see what you can find out about our new archbishop."

The newsman made the call.

"Oh, you guys are gonna love Fat Jack," the voice of a New Orleans reporter drawled irreverently over the line. "He gives grrreat parties!"

Nine weeks later, on August 16, the under-six-feet-over-200-pound Cody arrived in Chicago with an entourage of 96 priests and chancery employees aboard a special seven-car train. He was greeted by a fanfare of trumpets at Holy Name Cathedral, where he was enthroned as archbishop of Chicago. Less than two years later, on May 29, 1967, Pope Paul VI elevated him to cardinal.

And it soon came to pass that the scribe from Mardi Gras land had told no lie. Once he got comfortable in his new surroundings Cody indeed proved an entertainer without peer in a newspaper town noted for its freeloaders. Reporters soon found engraved invitations in their mailboxes: "His Eminence, John Cardinal Cody, requests the honor of your presence . . ."

Not just religion editors, but police reporters, crime writers, labor beat men, the city hall press—you could see all your friends at the cardinal's parties. Mingling among them in his flowing white robe, a glass of clinking ice cubes in his hand, the prince of the church was just one of the boys.

Cody was born in St. Louis on Christmas Eve, 1907, the son of Irish immigrant parents. His father was a fireman. Three of his mother's sisters were nuns, and Cody himself was ordained into the priesthood in Rome at the age of 23.

He was assigned to the staff of the Vatican Secretariat of State, where he became close friends with two future popes, Eugenio Cardinal Pacelli, who would become Pope Pius XII, and Pacelli's assistant, Msgr. Giovanni Montini, who promoted Cody to cardinal after he became Pope Paul VI.

While in New Orleans Cody gained national attention by enforcing plans to integrate schools in the archdiocese, despite picket lines and threats from segregationists. As the new head of the nation's largest archdiocese, he brought that same zeal to Chicago, where in January of 1968 he announced the busing of black children to Catholic schools in white neighborhoods. A month later he banished a priest opposed to desegregation from the archdiocese.

On Christmas Eve of 1969 he observed his 62nd birthday by celebrating midnight mass in the newly remodeled (at a cost of $3 million) Holy Name Cathedral. During the offertory 50 people walked out of the church, protesting what they called his "pompous spending" of archdiocesan money.

While no reporter in his right mind ever turned down a free lunch in those days, any Chicago newsman worth his press card was inwardly suspicious of highly placed people who wined and dined the media.

"Why is he trying to get on the good side of us?" they asked themselves. "What is he trying to hide?"

In 1981 Cody's skeletons started rattling in the closet. During that year he entered the hospital six times for heart problems or diabetes, while the *Chicago Sun-Times* disclosed in a copyrighted report that a federal grand jury was investigating the possibility he had diverted as much as $1 million in tax-exempt church funds to benefit a childhood friend and cousin-by-marriage, Helen Dolan Wilson.

Could that have anything to do with the fact that the busy Cardinal was known to take time to go down to the post office at Grand and Dearborn to pick up his own mail?

The swirling controversy caused one former priest and longtime observer of Chicago Catholicism to opine, "If it's true he stole $1 million, then it's worth at least another $1 million for him to get out of it. If I were a betting man, I'd lay odds that Cody will survive it."

Cody died the following year, at the age of 74, and the investigation died with him, so all bets were off.

Shortly before his death he was asked to reflect on his tumultuous years in Chicago. "I did my duty and tried to make the most people happy. None of us is perfect," he said.

"We used to say that when the saints ran the church, the church was in bad condition."

John D. MacArthur
(1897–1978)

Back in the 1970s there were only two billionaires in America. One of them was Chicago's own John D. MacArthur, a Scotsman who had fine-tuned the art of penny-pinching to a science.*

He had no yachts, no race horses, no fancy cars, no jewelry, no country estates, and when he wanted a cup of coffee he went behind the counter in one of the many hotels he owned and poured his own.

MacArthur drank 20 cups of coffee and smoked three packs of cigarettes a day, which might explain why he only lived to be 80.

---

*The other billionaire was shipping and real estate magnate Daniel K. Ludwig.

"I do want to live to be 80," he said. He got that wish. He died in 1978, two months to the day before his 81st birthday.

Upon his death MacArthur ordered that his body be turned over to medical research, "to spare my friends and relatives the inconvenience" of attending his funeral.

While always hesitant to help his own family members ("If I gave them $1 million they would never do a goddam thing."), he left most of his fortune to the John D. and Catherine T. MacArthur Foundation for charitable purposes.

"I don't want anyone to feel sorry for me," he said when he learned he had inoperable cancer. "I've lived a good life and been reasonably happy all my life."

MacArthur was happy in his work, and he had plenty to keep himself occupied. Consider this, if you have the time:

MacArthur, who was in his 40s before he became financially independent, ran 12 major insurance companies in addition to Bankers Life of Chicago. He was the sole stockholder of Bankers Life, which alone was worth more than $863 million. He also owned more land than anyone else in the state of Florida, including the Collonades Hotel with 1,500 feet of ocean frontage, and the winter home of Ringling Bros. and Barnum & Bailey Circus. He had Citizens Bank and Trust Co. of Chicago and other banks, radio and television stations, numerous hotels, golf courses and country clubs, a trailer park, an advertising agency, farms and ranches, five paper recycling plants, a fleet of airplanes, utility, sewage, gas, printing, recording, brewing and terminal companies, not to mention vast holdings in Alaska, Canada, West Germany and Argentina.

The son of a Pennsylvania dirt farmer and evangelist, MacArthur came from a family of achievers. His brothers included Charlie, the newspaper reporter who with Ben Hecht wrote *The Front Page*; Alfred, chairman of the board of Central Life Insurance Co.; and Telfer, who headed Pioneer Publishing Co. General Douglas MacArthur was his cousin.

MacArthur, who never went beyond grade school, got his first job as a copyboy on his brother's paper, the

Examiner. He also ran a bakery and a gas station before he struck it rich by offering insurance by mail for $1 a month.

One of his early schemes involved an insurance package he called the White Cross Plan. When Blue Cross took him to court over the similarity in names, MacArthur raised his fist and declared, "Anyone who doesn't know the difference between a white cross and a blue cross deserves to be screwed!"

A man who often carried his lunch in a doggie bag, MacArthur was known as the "available millionaire." He was always available to reporters, and didn't even

mind being interviewed by long-distance, as long as the reporter paid for the call.

Because he would not spend money on air-conditioning, MacArthur was often seen conducting business in his Bankers Life headquarters during the heat of Chicago summers wearing only his underwear.

His home in Chicago was a two-story suburban style house built on the roof of one of his insurance company buildings. In later years he and his wife, Catherine, kept a modest two-bedroom apartment in his Collonades Hotel on Singer Island, and he conducted all business from a table in the hotel coffee shop.

On special occasions, such as his birthday, Mac-Arthur liked to don a green and yellow plaid jacket emblazoned with the family crest bearing the Latin phrase, *Fide et Opera*. Although he never learned Latin, he said it meant, "Be honest, and work like a son of a bitch."

Courtesy of the J. Roderick MacArthur Foundation.

J. Roderick MacArthur
(1920–1984)

If J. Roderick MacArthur was a bit of an odd ball it was because the flamboyant, self-made millionaire could afford to be, and he did it without much help from his filthy-rich father.

Plate collectors will know MacArthur from the Bradford Exchange, which he founded in 1973. The marketing exchange for collector's plates, which made him a millionaire several times over, is based in Niles, with branches in six countries.

He also owned Hammacher Schlemmer, the famous store with a branch on Michigan Avenue, which specializes in the unusual or best of anything.

MacArthur said his billionaire father, John D. Mac-Arthur, gave him financial help only twice in his life. Once, when they were together in Las Vegas, Mac-Arthur the elder gave his son $100 betting money, which he promptly blew; and once, when he was living in Paris in the late 1940s, attempting to write a novel while earning $60 a week with the United Press, his father gave him a stipend of $500 a month—which he cut off at the end of a year because the novel wasn't finished.

MacArthur had been a civilian ambulance driver in World War II and served with a French Resistance unit.

When he returned to the States in 1952 his father helped him get a job as a $125-a-week editor of *Theater Arts* magazine, but eight months later he was fired.

Then, at age 40, he went to work at Citizens Bank & Trust Co., of which his father was sole owner, for $190 a week. He once asked for a raise, but said the old man explained, "If you made more money, you would only have to pay more taxes."

He later became president of Marquette Life Insurance Co., a subsidiary of Bankers Life. "I sold more insurance than anybody else in that company," he claimed. "I don't know many people that sold half a million people insurance policies in 10 months."

MacArthur engaged in public feuds with his father, not the least of which was the highly-publicized battle over who had what to say in running the Bradford Exchange. The elder MacArthur, who had money invested in the operation, locked up the company's plates and mailing lists in an office. But the resourceful son staged a daylight raid, broke into the office and "rescued" the material, emerging as the undisputed victor.

MacArthur's greatest source of pride was his own J. Roderick MacArthur Foundation, which he formed in 1976 "as soon as I had the money to use in that respect." Long interested in the civil rights movement, he used the foundation to fund litigation and projects ranging from investigations into El Salvador death squads to racial discrimination in consumer credit.

When MacArthur died at the age of 63 after a yearlong battle with cancer, the *Chicago Tribune* wrote, "Despite his accomplishments, he was unable at times to shake the image of 'John D.'s son.' And there were many comparisons: Neither man became wealthy until middle age, and both earned it. Both loved the unconventional, and neither would back away from a good fight—even with each other."

Helen Brach
(1911–1977)

On Feb. 17, 1977, Helen Vorhees Brach, the heir to the Brach candy company fortune, checked out of the Mayo Clinic in Rochester, Minn., with a clean bill of health. As near as authorities can tell, she never arrived back at her home in the Chicago suburb of Glenview.

Seven years later, on May 23, 1984, she was declared legally dead.

Helen Marie was born Nov. 11, 1911, in Unionport, Ohio, four months and three days after the marriage of her parents, Walter Vorhees and Daisy Rowland. She could trace her ancestry back to her great-great-great-grandfather, Jacob Voorhees (the family later shortened the name), a German immigrant who settled in America around 1670.

A strikingly beautiful woman with reddish-gold hair, she was married and divorced by the time she was 21.

She met Frank V. Brach, president of the E.J. Brach and Sons Candy Co., while working as a hatcheck girl at a Miami Beach country club in 1950. She became his third wife the following year. The newly-weds—Helen was 39 and Frank was 61—settled on Brach's seven-acre estate north of Chicago. After Frank's death in 1970 she lived alone with her three dogs and a houseman, Frank Matlick.

She was known as a woman who loved animals, kept a diary, delved into psychic writing and dug big cars. She owned five, in fact—a dark lavender Rolls Royce convertible, a pink Cadillac convertible, a salmon-colored Cadillac sedan, a fire-engine red Caddy and a pearl pink Lincoln Continental.

Authorities investigating the disappearance learned that Mrs. Brach had been the victim of an embezzlement scheme in which someone forged her name to more than $13,000 worth of checks benefiting Matlick, an ex-convict.

An early suspect in her disappearance, the houseman claimed to have driven Mrs. Brach to O'Hare International Airport on the morning of Feb. 21, 1977—10 days after she was last seen alive by anyone else—to board a plane for Ft. Lauderdale.

Investigators could find no record of tickets purchased in her name to go to Florida or anywhere else, however. Nor could police find her diaries, which Matlick claimed he had burned at her request.

They also learned that the weekend before Mrs. Brach's disappearance Matlick had purchased a large meat grinder. Ernie Rizzo, a private detective who investigated the disappearance, theorized that the earth was too frozen to bury a body when Mrs. Brach disappeared, so her body might have been ground up and fed to her dogs.

In her book, *Thin Air*, author Pat Colander says, "Ernie Rizzo's final conclusion was that Mrs. Brach had become a missing person at the hands of Jack Matlick."

Although rewards of up to $250,000 were offered for information concerning her whereabouts, she was never heard from again. No one was ever charged in connection with her disappearance.

In 1988, a Mississippi convict, Maurice Ferguson, led authorities to the Minneapolis area, where he said he buried "the candy lady" at the behest of Silas Jayne, a prominent Chicago horseman.

Mrs. Brach was known to have purchased horses from Jayne's stable, and threatened to call police becauses she was unhappy with the transaction.

Jayne, who died in 1978, had once been a cellmate of Ferguson while serving a prison term in connection with the murder of his own brother.

The celebrated body hunt in Minnesota yielded nothing, however, and the case file remains open to this day.

Mrs. Brach, whose estate was valued at $45 million, is considered the wealthiest person who ever vanished without a trace.

Edward Martin Moran
(1912–1979)

St. Patrick's Day parades have never been quite the same

since the Good Lord called Edward Martin Moran home. He was an Irishman's Irishman. Alas, the final call came before he got to carry out his fondest wish—to march in the St. Patrick's Day parades of Dublin, New York City and Chicago all on the same day.

The millionaire plumbing supply contractor and blarney master from Elmhurst did accomplish a few other feats to leave his mark on the Windy City, however:

- He hired seaplanes and helicopters to deliver tools to plumbers so they wouldn't have to run back to the shop for supplies they "forgot."

- He imported an Irish boxer to win the Golden Gloves championship three years in a row.

- He tried to rent a submarine big enough to get a bathtub down the hatch.

- He offered a free home to anyone who would teach in a Catholic grade school in a town in Michigan.

- He established plumbing dealership rights on Mars.

- He campaigned tirelessly to make St. Patrick's Day a legal holiday.

- He spearheaded a movement to make Ireland the 51st state.

Moran got the idea to make Ireland the Shamrock State after visiting the land of his ancestors in 1953. After he publicized the proposal in 1960, committees were formed there to work toward the goal, and the idea was debated on radio from the University of Galway on Sunday afternoons.

In 1972, after hearing that the Iranian government had mistakenly manufactured 5,000 United States flags with 51 stars to fly over Tehran during President Richard M. Nixon's visit, Moran wrote to the Shah Reza Pahlavi offering to purchase one. Iranian Prime Minister Hoveyda sent him one free. Moran hung the giant banner in his plumbing supply shop to show what Old Glory would look like if Ireland were accepted for statehood.

The silver-haired Moran received responses to his idea—some favorable and some suggesting he was some kind of a nut—from 22 states and many foreign countries. One Chicago woman wrote him: "May God forbid!"

He reluctantly dropped the grand idea after the Irish consul general in Chicago told him to cease and desist having fun at the expense of the Irish government.

Another idea that never got off the ground was a suggestion that the South Side ball club change its name to the Chicago Green Sox.

"After all," Moran claimed, "the Irish invented baseball. My grandfather was in Wild McLain's pasture, outside Canaryville, County Clare, when a bunch of lads named Joey McCarthy, Gabby Hartnett, Eddie Walsh and Charlie Comiskey first thought up the game. They used a shillelah for a bat, a potato for a ball, and bricks from old Bob Carey's yard for bases. When they brought the game to America they introduced it to Abner Doubleday, because they mistakenly believed he was a Chicago police captain."

While some of his ideas never got to first base, other ventures were more successful.

Remember Little Christopher Rafter, the Irish flyweight, who won the Chicago Golden Gloves 112-pound championship? Former Illinois Attorney General William G. Clark told Moran in 1958 about the 22-year-old railroad porter from Ireland who wanted to come to America to fight.

"Hell, bring the boy over," Moran said. He paid the transportation, and got the fighter a job as a plumber's apprentice. Rafter married a Chicago girl, and fought with the U.S. Army in Korea.

In the summer of 1964 while attending mass in St. Peter's parish in Douglas, Mich., Moran was touched by the priest's plea from the pulpit for a teacher for the small parochial school there. He placed a newspaper ad offering his family's summer home near Saugatuck free during the school year to anyone who took the job, which only paid $4,000 a year. Moran's offer was well publicized, and St. Peter's got its teacher.

In 1953 Moran advertised in a number of papers for a submarine to take a party of 50 plumbing contractors to Michigan City, St. Joseph and Benton Harbor. He was elated when he got a call from a Mr. Harnischfeger of the Federal Shipbuilding and Drydock Co. in New Jersey offering the use of a government surplus sub. The sub never surfaced, however. When Moran tried to arrange for getting it to Chicago he discovered there was no Harnischfeger with the shipbuilding outfit and he—of all people—had been victimized by a practical joker.

The stunt would never have worked anyhow. The Greater Chicago Chapter of United States Submarine Veterans of World War II advised the former air corps veteran that a treaty with Canada forbids submarines on the Great Lakes except in time of war.

But all was not lost. Moran gave the $500 with which he had planned to rent the sub to Rear Admiral Daniel V. Gallery, who captured a Nazi submarine during World War II. The money helped bring the German U-505 to Chicago, to be placed on display at the Museum of Science and Industry.

Moran, a former Notre Dame University track star and president of Chicago's Notre Dame alumni club, won many honors in his time, but he was most gratified when he was named Notre Dame's Man of the Year in 1970.

For years Moran headed a committee to make St. Patrick's Day a national legal holiday, an event he compared to the discovery of the shamrock and the invention of the brick.

"It is even more sacred to the Irish than election day," he proclaimed. "If we could convince the government to acknowledge this legally, the banks would close and the bankers could join us at church on this magnificent occasion. The world would be improved if we could lure the bankers into church one day a year."

But his dream of marching in St. Patrick's Day parades in Dublin, New York and Chicago all on the same day was his most ambitious.

The plan was to fly to Dublin via Irish Airlines and, after a visit to Blarney Castle and kissing the Blarney Stone, to march in the grand parade down O'Connell Street. Then leap aboard a helicopter to be whisked to Shannon airport, and then a jet flight to New York.

"A jet would get us to New York City within 6

hours," Moran explained in 1966, after placing a news-paper ad for other interested dreamers of Irish heritage to join him.

"So, if we left Dublin at 11 a.m.—because of the six-hour time differential—we could still put down at John F. Kennedy Airport by 11 a.m. Manhattan time, in plenty of time to march with New York's finest."

An hour or so of that would be all the group would have time for. Another copter would airlift them back to Kennedy and get them aboard another jet for O'Hare International Airport. The hour's time difference, again, and a helicopter ride downtown, would get them there in time to join the rear echelon of the parade as the Irish marched through the Loop.

A minor problem was that the Irish held their parade at noon. Moran made one flight to Dublin to try to coax them to move up the starting time. When that failed he shrugged and said, "Well, we just might have to wait for faster jets."

His death at age 66 came before the advent of the SST, more's the pity, or he would have done it. Some-body will, one day, and the very least they could do would be to dedicate the feat to his memory.

Jane Byrne
(1934–   )

It was maple syrup and pancake day at the new park made of the no-longer needed Municipal TB Sanitarium and Jane Byrne was campaigning.

The year was 1983. She was ending a tempestuous four years as mayor of Chicago, the first woman to hold the office. She had just lost the Democratic primary to Harold Washington. The question was, should she run as independent in the general election? Very many Chicagoans thought she should not. Jane was not one of them.

Her just-finished, unsuccessful campaign for the Democratic nomination had seen her everywhere, shaking everybody's hand and using her stockpiled campaign funds to buy time on radio and TV. With Richard M. Daley also in the race, it was said that Washington had won because the two other candidates had split the white vote.

Jane had obviously enjoyed both the mayoralty and the opportunities it afforded her to be her rambunctious self. She had faced even worse odds four years earlier in first trying to get elected. All she would have to do now, she hoped, was put her head down and plow relentlessly forward, following the formula that had worked before. She was, after all, "Fighting Jane." A book about her even bore that title.

The woman standing in front of Jane with three small children easily recognized the would-be candidate and gave her a weak, sympathetic smile, but this mother was not looking at her favorite politician. The raspy tone of the mayor's frequent TV press interviews, the cynicism behind some of her actions and appointments as well as her association with the people she had once labeled a "cabal of evil men" were all working against Byrne with this former supporter.

Jane Byrne turned up her smile, an action that often helps more than a handshake in winning votes for candidates. Even those who called her "Calamity Jane" admitted she knew how to campaign. In 1960, a year after she had become a widow, Jane had entered politics to help John F. Kennedy get elected President. Her husband, William, a Marine Corps pilot, had been killed in a 1959 crash as he approached the fog-enshrouded Glenview Naval Air station.

For her efforts in the campaign, she had been rewarded with a seat in President Kennedy's box at the Army-Air Force game. Mayor Richard J. Daley had noticed her there and later ran into her at a dinner. "Why do I keep seeing you different places?" he asked her. For the young widow, it was the beginning of a long-term, productive relationship.

Daley assigned her to a position in the federally-sponsored War on Poverty program. There, association with Daley won her hostility from community individuals who resented "Boss" Daley and his Machine. She complained to him about the job but she persevered in the position.

In 1968, he surprised her and everyone else by appointing the unknown young woman head of consumer affairs for the city. In that position, Mayor Michael Bilandic inherited her when he succeeded Daley after the latter's death in 1976. Bilandic and Byrne feuded over negotiations with the city's cab drivers, who came under her jurisdiction as commissioner. Each took a lie-detector test to prove they were not lying. Both passed and Bilandic fired his consumer affairs commissioner.

In 1978, Jane, taking advantage of the publicity the feud engendered, announced her candidacy for mayor. She was pitted against Bilandic and the much-vaunted Chicago Machine. The city's political pundits yawned

"No way, Jane." Then a double whammy hit Bilandic. A 22-inch New Year's Eve snow fall was followed by another on Jan. 12. They paralyzed the city and proved the Machine's lieutenants were not what they had been under Daley. Bilandic, going to all the TV stations, assured the public all was under control. It was not. His plan, in particular, to run the "L" trains as expresses, bypassing the inner city stops, proved his downfall.

Jane Byrne walked from relative obscurity to the fifth floor office of mayor. She had, however, started as a fighter and she couldn't stop pushing and scraping. She saw the late mayor's son, Richard M. Daley, as her future opponent, fired many of those close to him, and supported his Republican opponent for state's attorney. She also waffled dramatically and embarrassingly at times, such as on Senator Ted Kennedy's candidacy for the Democratic Presidential nomination. The city's financial condition and its loss of revenues under the Reagan administration caused her to raise taxes despite promises not to do so.

One sympathetic suburban Democrat woman said:

> The point is that Jane Byrne—you don't defeat her. She attacks and attacks and attacks and this is the characteristic I think she shares with a lot of men that most women don't have.

Many Chicagoans were jubilant to see her "get hers."

Now, at this Chicago family outing, she was desperately trying to find a way to get the magic from four years before, to win back what she had lost.

Jane stuck out her hand to shake that of the mother in front of her. The woman, seeing a politician rather than a sister in front of her, refused to offer her hand in exchange. Instead, she put her hands in her pockets.

Nonplussed, the mayor pushed one last time. She followed the woman's hand right into her pocket and shook it there. Perhaps even she recognized the futility of the gesture. The next day, Jane Byrne announced she was dropping out of the race. Apparently she had finally learned that fighting and even shaking hands can take a candidate only so far.

Don Case
(1921–   )

Only one man in all creation was powerful enough to get Donald Trump, the multi-millionaire East Coast wheeler-dealer, unceremoniously thrown off the list of "The World's Ten Best Dressed Men."

That incredibly influential individual is none other than Chicago's own Don Case, one of the last of the old time door-to-door PR men and a master of the snap decision.

It happened in 1989 when Case, who numbers among his clients the International Association of Custom Tailors and Designers, released the exclusive list of Who's Who of Sartorial Splendor.

The list included Soviet President Mikhail Gorbachev; England's Prince Charles; Canadian Prime Minister Brian Mulroney; former President Ronald Reagan; Ron Brown, chairman of the National Democratic Party; actor Tom Selleck; New York developer Donald Trump; Vito Pascucci, head of the G. Leblanc Musical Instrument Corp. of Kenosha, Wis.; Phillip Miller, head of Marshall Field's in Chicago; Lee Flaherty, head of Flair Communications Agency in Chicago; and Italian actor Marcello Mastroianni.

Did you count them? Don Jensen did. Jensen, a *Kenosha News* reporter, was preparing a story reporting that a local businessman had once again made the coveted list when he noticed something that didn't add up.

Jensen put in a call to Case. "Uh, why are there 11 names on the list of the Best Dressed 10?" he asked.

Pause.

"Take off Trump," Case declared, barely hesitating.

That was it. Trump was bumped, and Jensen's story of how it came about was picked up by wire services and flashed around the world. Case, the custom tailors' press agent, couldn't have been happier.

If Rudolph Valentino were alive today, he'd probably look like Don Case—because when Valentino *was* alive, Don Case looked a lot like him.

So much, in fact, that Case—now one of Chicago's most dapper men about town—screen-tested for *The*

Valentino Story in Hollywood in 1947.

"I didn't get the part. They gave it to some guy as tall as my nose," Case recalled disdainfully. "He made the movie and it killed him completely. Nobody ever heard of him again."

That served Hollywood right. Because Case came to Chicago, where he gives us, in addition to the annual "10 Best Dressed Men" stories, those amusing before-and-after photos of sports jocks who get wigs.

"Hair pieces," Case gently corrects.

Case was born Donaldo Arturo Francesco Casanova in New York's Hell's Kitchen in 1921. Little wonder the Irish-Italian boy growing up in one of the toughest neighborhoods this side of the Atlantic changed his name to Don Case.

While good with his fists through necessity, Case also discovered he had a remarkable singing voice, and set his sights on becoming an opera singer. But his very wise father, a music critic himself, told the youth, "A voice is a delicate instrument, and can go out of focus at any time. Take up a second profession. It will be an excellent crutch in your ability to make a living."

"That's advice I'd give to any talented youngster today," Case said.

The boy from Hell's Kitchen studied journalism at Georgia Tech, where he also starred as a middleweight boxer. He was studying law at Columbia University when Uncle Sam beckoned during World War II.

Case was serving as an officer in the Army tank corps in North Africa when his singing ability was discovered, and he was posted to London. After the war, Case, who speaks fluent Italian, studied voice and repertoire at the Academy of San Cecelia in Rome. The lyric tenor with a baritone speaking voice was soon singing in opera houses throughout Europe.

His dreams of becoming another Caruso or Pavarotti were dashed with the onset of hay fever.

"It's a death wish for an opera singer," he said. "Without your B natural and high Cs, the best you can do is ultimately become a 'compremario'—a cast member with a minor role."

Case spent the next two years in Hollywood, under

contract to Paramount, which was seeking a singer to counter MGM's Mario Lanza. "I had minor parts in about a half dozen pictures," he related. "They thought I was a natural for the Valentino role, but this other guy got it.

"Maybe I was too good looking," he laughed. "Rudy had a bad complexion, you know. They had to use a lot of makeup. He also had one of those eyebrows that went all the way across the top of his nose."

So Case kissed Hollywood good-bye and came to Chicago, where he opened a Rush Street night club, "Singers Rendezvous," which became a gathering place for after-opera patrons and performers.

This led to a career in public relations, in which Case represented Jussi Bjoerling, Maria Callas, David Poleri and other greats who sang at the Lyric.

"Poleri, a tenor, once walked off the stage here while singing Don Jose in *Carmen*," Case recalled. "The soprano was so bad that Poleri, who was supposed to stab Carmen at the end of the performance, threw the dagger into the orchestra pit and yelled at the conductor: 'You kill her!' It was a PR man's dream, because it hit all the front pages."

Case also took a little-known violinist who was playing at the club, German-born Franz Benteler, and catapulted him into a national celebrity.

After Singers Rendezvous was sold in 1958, Case became a full-time publicist.

As PR man for the custom tailors, he personally selects the world's 10 best dressed men. Honest, folks, it's only a coincidence that some of his other clients, such as Pascucci, who used to play with the Glenn Miller band, Flaherty, and occasionally Benteler, find their way onto the list.

"Look at them!" Case asserted. "I challenge anybody to show me anybody who dresses any smarter than they do."

One of Case's greatest PR capers, which made the wires coast to coast, was the day Chicago Cubs infielder Carmen Fanzone walked up to the plate, pulled out a trumpet, and deftly played the Star Spangled Banner before a crowd of 36,000 in Wrigley Field.

This was a spin-off of Case's work for Pascucci's musical instrument company. Naturally the famed ball-player had serenaded the crowd—plus everyone who was watching on television—with a Leblanc trumpet.

Dining with Case is an exercise in name-dropping. With machine-gun precision he rattles off one anecdote after another about his former Hollywood friends and acquaintances, Lizzy (Taylor), Lana (Turner), Frank (Sinatra) and Tuck (Forrest Tucker).

"Did you know," he says, suspending his fork above his plate, "that Forrest was Polish?"

The Matar Brothers
(1940s–   )

The Matar brothers' idea of wishing one another Happy Birthday is to dump a ton of misery onto the other guy.

Twenty or so years ago, on July 14th, Sam Matar sent his brother John 25 birthday cards. Not to be outdone, John sent Sam 50 cards when his birthday rolled around on February 7th. The following July Sam sent John 75.

By 1974 things were getting serious. Sam, an auto dealer, sent two lovely models to deliver a huge birthday cake to John where he worked at Regenstein Press on Van Buren Street. John retaliated by sending three white-haired, elderly ladies to sing "Happy Birthday" to Sam at his auto agency in Seaside, Calif.

The following year Sam chartered a plane to fly over Regenstein Press trailing a giant aerial sign saying, "Happy Birthday, John."

On July 14, 1976, Sam gifted John with a 2,000-pound pet rock, dumped on his front lawn at 5219 S. Keating Ave. It was later hauled around to John's back yard, where it still sits. Meanwhile, John countered on February 7 by hiring four belly dancers to perform outside Sam's auto agency while a high school band paraded up and down the street.

"It was chaos. There was a big traffic jam. I'm gonna fix you, brother," Sam vowed.

On John's next birthday, July 14, 1977, he sat out on his front porch, waiting for the worst to happen. When a 2,800 pound pachyderm came plodding down the street and onto his fine lawn he simply looked up and said, "Hi, elephant." Actually, its name was Cathy.

John's next door neighbor yelled over, "This used to be a nice block."

The following year Sam, who is of Lebanese descent, looked out his office window and contemplated a giant billboard across the street. It said, "Happy Birthday, Sam," over a picture of Sam, in a Superman outfit, astride a camel. On John's birthday in July he found himself being serenaded by 20 youngsters from the Epiphany Church Choir, after which Sam sent them all off to summer camp for a week for their trouble.

And in 1979 Sam got the works again. A truck pulled up in front of his place and dumped 10 tons of rocks onto his auto lot, along with a message: "Sam, the pet rock you gave me was pregnant. You can keep the kids." The following February John dumped 27 tons of manure outside his brother's office building.

OK, John. You wanna get stinky, eh? When his next birthday rolled around in July of 1980, John's South Side neighborhood took on the aroma of the Stock Yards on a steamy day. And why not? Weren't there 10 shorthorn steers grazing on John's front lawn?

Sam followed up by sending John 50 bleating, snorting, nibbling goats on his next natal anniversary. An accompanying card said, "You have been trying to get my goat for years. O.K. Now you got 'em. Happy Birthday."

"He's out to ruin my lawn!" John moaned.

Do you get the impression that these guys are a little nuts? Or do they just love each other an awful lot?

In other years one showed his affection for the other with a hot air balloon piloted by strippers, an unassembled 1973 Volkswagen and a crashed airplane. But in 1983 Sam really nosed ahead in the competition when, as the city sweltered in 90-degree temperatures, John came home from work to find 100 skunks nibbling on his shrubbery. He didn't calm down until he was assured that the critters, rented from a Michigan wildlife farm, had all been de-perfumed.

The following February John sent Sam a 175-pound orangutan, followed by Joey, a 9-year-old kangaroo. Sam sent John 3,000 badly damaged golf balls, plus a golf lesson from Chi Chi Rodriguez. John sent Sam 100 snakes.

On his next birthday John found himself between a

rock and a hard place. Sam's gift was a two-and-a-half carat diamond, encased in a six-foot-square block of concrete. It took three hours of chipping with a sledge hammer before John got to the diamond in a plastic box. Then he had to clean up the mess.

He paid Sam back the following February with a truckload of balloons, along with four wilted carrots.

Who will do what to whom next? We're not sure we want to know.

It's a wonder the brothers can even remember one another's birthdays, because they certainly aren't sure how old they are.

In 1976, according to their press clippings, John Matar said he was 29. Two years later, in 1978, he claimed to be 40, while Sam owned up to being 35.

Fast-forward to 1981. John has picked up only one year, claiming to be 41, while Sam still sticks to being 35. By the time 1986 rolled around, John said he was 45, while Sam admitted to being 39. But a year later, in 1987, John told the press he was 43, and Sam subtracted three years, making himself 36.

Which either makes them two of the biggest liars Chicago has ever seen, or real slow at arithmetic.

Their mother, Lorena, once told her boys she thought they were a little crazy, so the brothers got together on her birthday and sent Mom 20 pairs of tennis shoes.

Harold Washington
(1922–1987)

There have been mayors, and there have been mayors. And then there was Harold.

There was something different about Harold Washington, and it wasn't just the pigmentation of his skin. The first person to push aside the color barrier to the mayor's office had a way about him that just naturally prompted people to call him by his first name.

To his thousands upon thousands of admirers he wasn't Mayor Washington. He was "Harold." And to his

detractors, of which there were many, he was "that son-of-a-bitch Harold."

He fought his way to the fifth floor of City Hall partly through what was described as a "clash of vanities" between then-Mayor Jane Byrne and future-Mayor Richard M. Daley, the late Mayor Richard J.'s son, who opposed one another in the 1983 Democratic primary and split the white vote. That produced a political arithmetic formula in which Washington worked out as the third factor.

To be sure, folks had their hearts in their mouths in some parts of the city when "the black guy" took the reins of government, but nothing terrible happened.

The city survived.

According to Louis Masotti, a Northwestern University professor of management and urban affairs, "The fact that Washington was as articulate as he was and as well liked as he was made it a lot easier for this very racial town to accept him as mayor."

But it still wasn't easy. Most of his first three years in office were spent battling a Caucasian-controlled City Council, led by Edward "Fast Eddie'" Vrdolyak of the 10th Ward, who frequently blocked his initiatives and programs.

Through it all he wore his Santa Claus grin, slowly wearing the opposition down. By the time Washington was elected to a second term four years later, there was no question about who was in control.

Harold was no stranger at overcoming adversity.

He won the mayor's office as a divorced, tax-dodging ex-convict whose law license had been lifted because he had cheated his clients. That would have been enough to keep a lesser man out of politics, but to the funny, witty and charismatic Harold, it was just something to shove back over his shoulder.

Born in Cook County Hospital, Harold was one of 11 children of Roy and Bertha Washington. After his parents were divorced, he lived with his father, a lawyer, Methodist minister and precinct captain.

He became a track star at Du Sable High School, winning the 1939 city championship in the 120-yard high hurdles, and placing second in the 200-yard low hurdles. He was also a middleweight boxer at Du Sable, and spent his summer months in a Civilian Conservation Corps (CCC) camp.

Washington's leadership ability came to the fore during World War II, where he rose to the rank of first sergeant in the Army Air Corps, helping build air strips in the South Pacific. After the war he attended Roosevelt University, where he was elected president of his senior class. He went on to earn his law degree at Northwestern University.

In 1970 Washington's law license was suspended after the Illinois Supreme Court's Attorney Registration and Disciplinary board found he had accepted retainers from five clients and failed to perform promised legal services.

The suspension was for one year, but by the time it was to have expired he was in tax trouble with the feds. As a result, his law license suspension remained in effect until 1975, when it was lifted by the state Supreme Court. Meanwhile, in 1972, while a State Representative, he was convicted in U.S. District Court for failing to file income tax returns for four years. Actually, the government asserted that Washington, a lawyer and legislator who should have known better, had filed no returns for 19 years, but he could only be prosecuted for four that did not fall under the statute of limitations.

The future mayor was sentenced to two years in prison. But Federal Judge Joseph Sam Perry—putting his "crimes" in perspective—suspended all but 40 days, of which he served 36 in the Cook County Jail.

Washington was a true enigma. Known as "Mr. Organized" in college, his friends asked themselves how he could forget to pay his bills, serve his clients, pay his income tax?

How should one judge such "crimes" compared to those of Teddy Kennedy, Otto Kerner, or Richard Nixon? The electorate decided that Washington had paid his dues, and promoted him to Congress.

Then, in 1982, a coalition of black leaders, led by activist Lu Palmer, an ex-newspaperman, convinced him the time was right to run for mayor.

Harold not only had a Santa Claus laugh, but a belly to go with it—ample testimony to his love affair with food. He carried 284 pounds around on his five foot, ten inch frame, and his doctors warned him that was too much.

Washington was in his fifth year as mayor when he was felled by a fatal heart attack on Nov. 25, 1987, while at work at his City Hall desk.

The jubilant glad-to-see-you voice that used to boom out from the podium, "Heeeere's Harold!" as thousands cheered the man who beat all odds would be heard no more.

The city cried, and then went about its business.

"The thing he'll go down in history for will be for

being a source of true, authentic racial pride to black people here and around the country," said the Rev. George Clements, a South Side Roman Catholic priest who knew what it was like battling overwhelming odds.

A black auto mechanic on the South side put it a bit more simply: "He'd have been a good person to know if he wasn't mayor."

W.R. "Andy" Anderson (1915–)

Every October 12th when the city's Italian-Americans parade through the Loop on the birthday of Christopher Columbus, just as sure as dogs do bark and wolves do howl, we can rely on W.R. "Andy" Anderson to resume making all that fuss about "those people" making all that fuss about Christopher Columbus discovering America in the name of Spain.

"Christoforo Colombo, the famous Italian weaver, died at sea in 1480," asserted Anderson, who has spent his adult life researching the proposition that historians have been making too much ado about the wrong man . . . er, men.

"So who 'discovered' America in 1492? Cristobal Colon, a Spanish ex-pirate, of course. But for nearly 500 years historians have combined the two under the name of Christopher Columbus."

It's hardly advisable to approach the pedantic Chicago Norseman on the subject if you have any other items on your agenda, because once the door is opened retreat is nigh impossible.

"Leif Ericson landed on this continent 500 years before Columbus," explained Anderson, a six foot, four inch Viking whose parents and wife, Gerd, came over from Norway themselves. "The only thing Columbus ever achieved is that he (they) brought an end to the long era of pre-Columbian exploration."

Anderson, a certified public accountant and insurance executive who lives on the North Side, even wrote a book to set the record straight. He called it *Viking*

Explorers and . . . the Columbus Fraud. The second half of the title, "the Columbus Fraud," is printed upside-down on the cover to emphasize the author's theory that revelations therein will turn history the same way.

Before you get the wrong idea, Anderson stresses that he has "absolutely nothing" against the mainstream Italian people, their other heroes, or their parades.

"I just think the Italians should celebrate the birthday of Michaelangelo, or Sophia Loren—or Martini & Rossi, for that matter—instead of a reprehensible Spanish pirate."

In 1964 Anderson, who is also president of the Leif Ericson Society, gained the attention of the Burlington Liars Club when he proposed Columbus posthumously for membership—in their club, not his. "His gasser about discovering America makes Baron Munchausen look like a truth-serum addict," he hooted.

A Liars Club membership card for Columbus came by return mail, along with a letter from Otis Hulett, the club's late president, asking, "Please clue me in on the Leif Ericson Society. It it an honest-to-goodness organization, or a bunch of foolishness like our club?"

Anderson foolishly forwarded Columbus' Liars Club card to the Joint Civic Committee of Italian Americans. Perhaps gleefully would be a better word.

What followed was an invitation from a group of concerned Italian-Americans to "bury the hatchet and break historical bread and wine."

The erudite Anderson could not wait to get to the Italian village restaurant where he was met by Anthony Paterno, president of the Joint Civic Committee; Joseph Barbara, president emeritus; two attorneys; "and one other man whose purpose I have forgotten."

As Anderson described the confrontation:

"After three martinis we enjoyed an excellent luncheon. The others had taken up the theme—the stigma of the many vowel-ending names on police records hung over their heads like Damoclean swords.

"I did my best then—as I have often since—to dismiss any associated guilt by changing the subject to the art of Michaelangelo and Cellini, the music of Verdi and Rossini. And the name of Loren may have entered the discussion, although it ends in a consonant.

"By the time coffee arrived, all six of us were in a friendly mood, and I was comfortably unprepared for the question, 'How many members do you have in your Society?'

"Alcohol sometimes has a disastrous effect on Indians and Norwegians. It dissolved my protective shield, exposing the naive honesty therein. I told the truth. At the time I had a 'membership' of perhaps 40, including a dozen freebies, but admitted that '90 percent of the Leif Ericson Society is above my ears.'

"You could almost hear five Italian jaws drop. Here they had wasted time and money on a one-man protest! Rarely have meetings adjourned more rapidly."

Unperturbed, Anderson carries on. He admits he isn't sure who really discovered America, but he knows it wasn't Christopher Columbus. So, until a better suggestion comes along, he is pushing Leif Ericson, "who valiantly explored the shores of the American continent in the year 1000."

To this end Anderson several years ago proposed the world's tallest building, the Leif Ericson Center, for downtown Chicago. But Sears, Roebuck stole his idea and named it after the company. So now he's working on a new idea—a 1,000-foot tall statue of Leif, straddling the Chicago River east of Michigan Avenue. But he can't do it by himself.

"We need someone of international renown to spearhead a major effort—someone of Norwegian ancestry. Aren't you weary of your desk job, WALTER MONDALE?" he asked.

Anderson pointed out that the Colossus of Rhodes, built about 280 B.C., stood a mere 120 feet in height. It should be no problem for today's architects to design a statue that would reach 1,000 feet into the air.

"You are only limited by the size of your own dreams. To see this dream realized is my Leif-long ambition," he quipped.

Joseph "Pops" Panczko
(1918–   )

Even the most dedicated criminal eventually goes straight or "burns out" with age, and so it was that Joseph "Pops" Panczko, the highly acclaimed dean emeritus of Chicago burglars, car thieves, trunk poppers, dognappers and lock pickers, declared at the age of 72 that he was through with crime.

"I'm gettin' too old," he growled. "Besides, my feet hurt."

The durable Panczko, with a record of well over 200 arrests under his belt, walked out of a half-way house for cons on Chicago's South Side on Feb. 2, 1990, and took his first breath of free air in years. He had just been paroled after serving a four-year term in the federal pen for removing $500,000 worth of jewelry from a salesman's car in South Bend. The FBI nabbed him when he made the mistake of fencing the jewels in Chicago. Doing business over state lines made it a federal offense.

Looking back on 60 years of almost uninterrupted crime he admitted it wasn't all good times and glory. Virtually every dishonest dollar he made—and it totaled in the millions—went to paying defense lawyers or paying off cops, he claimed.

"Pops" got his nickname on the only legitimate job he ever held, briefly driving a soda-pop truck between scores in the late 1930s. But he is best known as the patriarch of the Panczko burglary gang, in which he served as a role model for his younger brothers, Paul "Peanuts" and Eddie "Butch" Panczko.

"For nearly three decades, the saga of this larcenous trio has kept millions of Chicagoans laughing while driving thousands of others to the brink of bankruptcy," wrote Ovid Demaris in *Captive City* in 1969.

The fact that Panczko was still alive in 1990 to talk about it was a testament to lousy marksmanship, and his own tough skin.

He was first hit by a shotgun blast in the back at the age of 12 while liberating a 50-pound sack of flour from the trunk of a 1928 Model T Ford.

On New Year's Day, 1948, he was shot in the shoulder by a police officer who caught him transferring cases of liquor from a closed restaurant to his car. Accustomed to "making bail" at the scene of a crime, Pops dug into his pocket to give the cop $400 to "forget all about this," but the cop thought he was reaching for a gun.

A year later Panczko was shot in the groin when he was surprised by a private detective who was hiding in a truck loaded with furs when Pops pried open the doors.

And in 1957 a shotgun blast nearly took off his head when he broke into a Wilmette jewelry store to find police lying in wait. Surgeons at Evanston Hospital took six shotgun pellets out of his head and excised a wad of brain tissue that was too damaged to be of further use.

"Honest to God! The doc had (part of) my brain in his hand. I saw it," Panczko said. "Nowadays this doctor goes around to medical meetings and shows pictures of me, before and after he took my brains out."

While Panczko "hovered at death's door," his lawyer, George Bieber, won 15 continuances from six different judges before finally getting his battle-scarred client into what he hoped would be a friendly court. After the prosecution put on 17 witnesses who placed Panczko at the scene, Bieber called Pops to the stand.

"What is your occupation, Mr. Panczko?"

"I'm a teef."

"You mean you are a thief?"

"Yeah, I steal tings."

The jurors, visibly impressed by such unabashed honesty, leaned forward to catch the accused burglar's every word.

"Now, Mr. Panczko, please tell the jury exactly what happened on the day in question."

"That day I was out lookin' for a nice house to buy for my mother. I got hungry. I seen that shoppin' center and stopped, thinkin' to get a sandwich and a cup of coffee. I was gettin' outa the car and somebody shot me in the head and just about killed me."

The jury found Panczko innocent. The late Clem Lane, city editor of the old *Chicago Daily News*, liked to say, "Chicago is a Not Guilty town." Pops, of course, was a perfect example.

One of Panczko's zanier arrests came during the famous "screwdriver trial" in 1958. Police had earlier arrested him after spotting him in an alley outside a hosiery salesman's garage, with a large screwdriver protruding from his pocket. State's Attorney Ben Adamowski, knowing that Panczko could get more out of a common screwdriver than Stanley Tools ever dreamed possible, had him indicted for possession of a burglar tool.

During a recess in the trial Panczko stood in front of the Criminal Courts building complaining to reporters, "I can't do nuttin'. The cops are tailing me day and night."

"Aw, Pops, you're getting paranoid."

"I ain't either. See that car parked across the street with two guys in it? They're cops. They're watchin' me. Get a load of this!"

With that Panczko ran out into California Boulevard and clambered aboard the tailgate of a passing produce truck. Sure enough, the car containing the plainclothes cops made a U-turn and took off after the truck.

Gesticulating wildly at the unmarked police car, Panczko reached into a gunny sack on the back of the truck and began hurling onions at his pursuers, bouncing bermudas off their windshield. The cops curbed the truck and arrested Pops for hijacking.

"See, I tole you guys," he beamed triumphantly as he was slapped into handcuffs.

The hijack case was subsequently thrown out of court after the driver proved unable to positively identify the onions police picked off the pavement as having come from his load; nor was he able to testify as to exactly how many were missing from the sack.

Meanwhile the celebrated screwdriver case dragged on for 26 months through three trials before being thrown out when the intended victim got tired of showing up in court to testify.

Although Pops began his long criminal career by stealing other kids' coats from the cloakroom at grade school in Humboldt Park, he insists he did not turn professional until the age of 12, when he began swiping chickens from the Fulton Street market. It made his mother proud to see a boy of his tender age helping to put food on the table during the Depression.

Brother Butch is now dead, and Peanuts might as well be. He married a Chicago madam named Dolly and turned federal informant. He is now living at an undisclosed location under a new identity ("Walnuts" perhaps?) as a member of the federal witness protection program.

That leaves Pops with Chicago all to himself. After a lifetime of stealing everything from chickens to cement mixers, a king's ransom in gems to a bottle of aspirins, and pedigreed poodles to fur coats—he couldn't believe the first official document he got in the mail.

It was a notice from Cook County Circuit Court asking him to report for jury duty. "I wrote NOT GUILTY on it and sent it back," he said.

Mike Ditka
(1939–   )

If you want to drive the kind of car that Mike Ditka favors, go Toyota! That's the car he does commercials for on television, as every Chicagoan who has a TV set well knows.

Or say you just need wheels for the weekend. Go for Budget Rent A Car, if you want to make Iron Mike happy.

Need money? There's no place like Talman Home Federal Savings & Loan Association. That's where Mike goes—he says. Or if you prefer buying on credit, there's nothing like an American Express Card.

Taking a trip? Of course you know that when Mike Ditka takes to the air he flys Midway Airlines. And when he takes to the airwaves, he urges us all to soar forth and do likewise.

If you need a ride home from the airport, there's always Ditka's Iron Mike Limousine at your service.

Hungry? Try any of the Sara Lee goodies for between-meal snacks, or a nice wholesome bowl of Campbell's Soup. That's what keeps Ditka happy. And when a winter cold's got him down, he bounces back with Dristan. And so, apparently, do his Chicago Bears if they know what's good for them.

When dining out, naturally there's Ditka's North, or Ditka's City Lights on Ontario Street, depending on where you live.

Only Ditka knows whether Ditka really uses the myriad of products he endorses or has endorsed on television, but pitching them to the rest of us has certainly helped make him a millionaire.

Who says football players are dumb? Maybe Ditka's just making sport of us.

Sport has been Ditka's life since playing sandlot baseball as a youngster in Pennsylvania. He played basketball, baseball and football in high school and at the University of Pittsburgh, before signing on with the Chicago Bears in 1961 as the team's No. 1 draft choice for $12,000.

Ditka learned the rough-and-tumble game of pro football by George Halas' rules, and went on to play tight end for the 1963 NFL championship Bears.

In 1967, after being plagued by injuries, he was traded to the Philadelphia Eagles, which he called "purgatory on earth"—the low point of his life. He was rescued by Tom Landry, who brought him to the Dallas Cowboys in 1969. He played in the Cowboys' first two Super Bowls, 1970 and 1971, and when Landry offered Ditka a coaching job he jumped at the chance. He served as a Cowboy assistant coach until 1982, when Halas called him back to Chicago to take over his old team. For Ditka it meant finally coming home.

"Nobody loves the Bears any more than I do. I don't care who it is," Ditka said after his return to Chicago. "Not only that, I love the city . . . It's a great city with great people . . . It's a city that can do anything it wants to do if it wants to do it."

Proving his point, Ditka took the rag-tag team and built it into a class operation, bringing to Chicago a new breed of football players who knew how to decimate the enemy before a roaring crowd on Sunday afternoon, and still behave like gentlemen and be be a credit to their city when off the playing field.

By 1986 Chicago finally had a team of which it could genuinely be proud, when Ditka's Bears brought home the Super Bowl championship.

In his pre-game talk to the team before going onto the field for Super Bowl XX, Ditka told his players:

". . . we're in this together as a football team and we are going to play it for each other and we're going to win this game . . . That's what it's all about . . . This is your game . . . So let's go out there and play our kind of football . . . Heavenly Father, we are grateful for this opportunity and we thank you for the talents you have given us, the chance to prove that we are the very best . . . We pray as always in the name of Jesus Christ your son our Lord. Amen. Let's go."

With the explosive Ditka as head coach, there are always two shows in progress whenever the team takes to the gridiron—the Bears on the field and Ditka pacing on the sidelines, waving his arms, bellowing or hurling his clipboard.

Ditka's best line in *Ditka*, the 1986 autobiography he wrote with Don Pierson, is, "I had a temper when I was growing up, which is kind of unusual because I don't have one now."

Irv Kupcinet
(1912–)

He is Chicago's most durable columnist. A lot of people *read* the the other local and syndicated columnists, but they actually *know* Kup and he knows them. Dial his number at the *Sun-Times* and, like as not, he'll pick up the phone himself.

Irv Kupcinet is clearly a Chicago original. Born on the city's sweat-sox West Side he eventually made it all the way to the silk stocking Near North Side. And he is the only living person to have a bridge over the Chicago River named after him.

Courtesy Irv Kupcinet and the *Chicago Sun-Times.*

Kup is a big guy, built like a football player, because that's what he used to be.

After graduating from Harrison High School he went on to the University of North Dakota, where he earned a journalism degree in 1934. He was named to the 1935 College All-Star football team, along with future President Gerald Ford, and embarked on a professional football career with the Philadelphia Eagles.

A shoulder injury sent him from the playing field to the newsroom as a sports writer for the old *Chicago Times*. When the paper merged with the *Chicago Sun* he stayed on, steadily enlarging the scope and influence of the column he began in 1943.

Kup kept a hand in football by officiating at NFL games for 10 years, and later broadcasting Chicago Bears games on radio with Jack Brickhouse. Never mind that quarterback Bob Avellini sometimes came out "Avenelli," Kup was Kup.

Media critic Gary Deeb dedicated an entire column to making fun of Kup's broadcast gaffes, and then ended up on the *Sun-Times*, where he had to face Kup every day.

Kup never got even. He doesn't operate that way. The influence of his widely-read column can make or break a person, but when Kup criticizes anyone it is of a constructive nature, usually suggesting how something could be done better.

When a popular band leader publicly insulted Kup at a party, Kup could have come back in his column and accurately reported that the musician suffered from an alcohol abuse problem, but he didn't. He simply stopped using the man's name altogether, and as a result the drunk who insulted him is all but forgotten.

As if writing a column six days a week were not

enough, Kup inaugurated "Kup's Show" on local television in 1959, a show that ran for a record 27 years, won
the coveted Peabody Award, and 16 local Emmy awards.
He also appears three times a week on the local CBS
news on Channel 2, dishing out the latest dope there.

In 1945, with World War II painfully winding
down, Kup entertained a group of disabled veterans
from local VA hospitals on a day-long cruise on Lake
Michigan.

Kup's Purple Heart Cruise has become an annual
event, with 23,000 vets—many in wheelchairs or on
crutches—participating in the outing as of the summer
of 1990.

With Irv Kupcinet, the annual "thank you" to the
men and women who served their country is not just
done for show. He is truly a caring man.

When a reporter from a competing newspaper was
mugged and robbed on the lower level of Wacker Drive
one hot July afternoon, the first person to telephone his
paper to commiserate with him was Kup of the *Sun-
Times*.

At an age long past that which most men retire and
turn to the hammock, Kup still pounds out six columns
a week at the video display terminal that replaced his
battered typewriter.

He works well into the night, pursuing his never-
ending quest for things you might want to know from
Hollywood, New York, Miami Beach, Las Vegas,
Washington—and, of course, right here at home.

"Hey Kup, you're pushing 80. You're making the
rest of us look bad. When ya gonna retire?" he was
asked recently.

"Are you kidding?" he scoffed. "I want to be
'terminal' at my terminal."

Adeline Jay Geo-Karis
(1918–   )

The criminal trial was winding down before the one
Circuit Court judge then sitting in the Lake County

Courthouse in Waukegan in the fast-paced days following World War II.

The young defense lawyer was clearly getting the best of Assistant State's Attorney Charles E. Mason, the seasoned prosecutor.

Finally, in exasperation, the white-haired Mason wheeled around and bellowed at the young lawyer, "Why don't you take off your brassiere and fight like a man?"

Witnesses gleefully recounted the confrontation over cocktails, and word quickly spread through local legal circles that the dark-haired Greek lawyer, Adeline Jay Geo-Karis, was someone to reckon with.

"Geo," as she is known, had just returned from service as a Naval officer during World War II. "It wasn't fashionable to hire a lady lawyer in those days, so I started my own firm," she said.

It was not long afterward that State's Attorney Thomas J. Moran took her on as an assistant state's attorney, making her Lake County's first female prosecutor.

Greek-born Geo-Karis came from the town of Tegeas, the home of Herodotus, the fifth century historian known as the "Father of History." The youngest of 10 children, she was brought to the United States by her father, a successful banana merchant, when she was 4.

She grew up on Chicago's West Side, and joined the WAVES when World War II broke out. "I was taught that this was the greatest country on earth, and I wanted to do my patriotic duty," she said. She entered the Navy as an apprentice seaman, and was discharged as a lieutenant commander with a top secret clearance.

Geo-Karis made her first bid for public office in 1949, and was elected justice of the peace in Zion, where she now makes her home. She became the first female JP in Lake County, and served three terms.

She subsequently served three terms in the Illinois General Assembly. Then, in 1978, she unseated State Senator Larry Leonard.

Though a female, she proved anything but a shrinking violet in the male bastion. She was a strong supporter of the "death by injection" bill in Springfield, asserting, "I am tired of seeing vicious, murderous creeps who only spend their time in jail. They're beasts and brutes. I don't even think they're animals, because animals only kill for food."

Geo-Karis campaigned for office in her 1970 Buick, a rolling billboard with 164,000 miles on the odometer. She now drives a Lincoln Town Car, but still has the old Buick that got her where she is today.

In 1987 she took on a quadruple work load, when she got herself elected mayor of Zion—the first female ever to hold that position—in addition to continuing as state senator while keeping up her practice as a trial lawyer, and also serving as village attorney for Vernon Hills.

How does she do it?

"Easy. I put in 70 to 100 hours a week. I don't have time to get old, or to get into trouble."

To avoid even the appearance of conflict of interest, she keeps three separate offices.

Her duties as mayor are conducted from her office in the Zion City Hall. As the state senator representing the people of her district, she has an office on the west side of Sheridan Road in downtown Zion. Her law practice is conducted directly across the street in a building she owns.

The jobs of being a mayor and trial lawyer merged into one in 1990 when an atheist zealot won a federal court order enjoining the city of Zion from having a cross on its corporate seal.

Pointing out that Zion was founded by a religious order in 1902, Geo-Karis said the cross was a part of the city's history, and vowed to take the fight to keep it all the way to the U.S. Supreme Court.

A political writer once described Geo-Karis as "a political moderate with a flamboyant campaign style . . . and a zest for political combat."

Her own assessment: "I'm not afraid of anyone. I love a challenge."

Walter Jacobson
(1937–   )

As a former *Daily News* columnist, the highly respected Jack Mabley can claim credit for helping to create two of Chicago's journalistic giants—native sons Mike Royko and Walter Jacobson.

When Mabley quite the *Daily News* and went over to the *American*, bringing 29,000 readers with him, he left a column void that the hitherto unknown Royko eventually fell into, and crawled out with national celebrity written all over himself. Mabley brought Jacobson into the profession from out of left field a few years earlier.

"I was covering the Cubs when Walter was their batboy," Mabley recalled. "He came up to me and said he wanted to be a newspaperman. I liked his chutzpah and told him to call me when he got out of college."

Later, as a student at Grinnell College, Jacobson wrote to Mabley and got a summer job as his legman.

"As is so often the case, timing was all," Mabley related. "I was doing six columns a week and needed help. I talked Everett Norlander, the managing editor, into letting me take him on as an assistant."

It was 1957, and Jacobson was paid $75 a week. Meanwhile, the rather puritanical Mabley got an invitation in the mail to visit a nudist colony in Indiana.

"Public nudity was rare and considered quite titillating in the '50s, and I figured we could get a cutesy feature from it," Mabley said. "Inasmuch as I am not about to go public naked, even with my proud and noble physique, I naturally assigned Jacobson to the job—as I have always assigned the dirty and unpleasant jobs to my assistants, or associates, as I preferred to call them.

"I seem to recall his reaction was a combination of glee, apprehension, and lust."

So Jacobson went down to the nudist camp, took off his clothes, and set forth to cover his first big assignment wearing only a pencil and note pad.

"He did a good job," according to Mabley. "All I did was print his memo, edited for space. It was the most

Courtesy of WBBM-TV.

talked-about column I did that summer."

Among the highlights of Walter's story were his self-conscious walk through the cafeteria line, his confusion over where to place his napkin when he sat down to lunch, and the fact that the boards left indentations in everyone's behinds when they got up.

After graduating from Grinnell and earning a master's degree from Columbia School of Journalism, Jacobson went to work for *Chicago's American* where veteran reporter Sam Blair tagged him with the unfortunate nickname of "Skippy." He's never been able to shake it, and Governor Otto Kerner once used it as a put-down when Jacobson asked annoying questions at a news conference.

For about a year Jacobson covered the County Building for the *American*, opposite Royko, for the *Daily News*. Their competitive rivalry was intense, and to this day neither one passes up an opportunity to get in a dig at the other.

After becoming a syndicated columnist, Royko wrote that Jacobson once confided to him how demeaning it was to have been the Chicago Cubs batboy, because some of the more uncouth ballplayers would throw their jock straps and other soiled undergarments at him for the laundry.

"As Walter became the biggest midget in the circus he denied he ever told this to me," Royko now says.

In 1963 John Madigan, then news director for Channel 2, and a former *American* city editor, hired Jacobson as a general assignment reporter at the television station. He soon rose to co-anchorman on the evening newscasts, but is best known for his indignant nightly "Perspective" features.

Now a millionaire, he has a town house in Lincoln Park, and a summer cottage in Michigan.

Chicago magazine quoted Royko as saying, "If you could work out a mathematical formula between intelligence and income, Walter would probably be paid more per IQ point than anyone in the history of Chicago journalism."

And Jacobson was once quoted in the *Tribune* as saying, "The only thing that makes me feel bad, is that I know I am no more of a journalist than my colleagues in the print medium who are making one-fifth my salary."

He must have been needling Royko, because no mere reporter is making anywhere near one-fifth of what Walter makes on television.

Ever combative, ever competitive, Jacobson told a *Tribune* reporter, "There is no question that I'm considered a pain-in-the-ass among my colleagues. They think I'm a pompous, nit-picking big shot . . . As a matter of fact, the viewers think I'm pompous and arrogant too . . . But I believe I'm honest and fair and know some things about reporting and politics and this community.

"All I have going for me in this business is my credibility."

His one-time boss at Channel 2 once said, "There's no question in my mind that Walter is becoming one of the biggest single television factors in the country."

But let's get back to the dugout. True or false: Did

the great Hank Sauer, Dee Fondy, or any of the other Cubs ballplayers throw their sweaty underpinnings at poor Walter, the batboy?

"I really don't remember," Jacobson told *Tribune* writer Clifford Terry. "They were crude guys. And really racist. Especially someone like Eddie Miksis . . . There were some sweet guys, like Roy Smalley and a pitcher named Bob Kelly, but the others would do things like take me into the outfield, stuff tobacco in my mouth, and make me chew it . . . Yeah, they might have tossed their underwear at me. It's possible. Those guys were mean."

Royko, on the other hand, apparently harbors no grudge against his one-time competitor as he mellows with age. "I, for one, sure appreciate him," he said. "Next to the Muppets, he's my favorite television character."

Mike Royko
(1932–   )

The collaborators of this book were engaged in a weighty conversation.

"Would you mind doing the Royko chapter?"

"Are you kidding? That guy's got a Pulitzer, and he won the Heywood Broun, H.L. Mencken, Ernie Pyle, National Headliner, ABC, XYZ and Blah Blah Blah awards, AND the *Washington Journalism Review* says he's the best newspaper writer in America. Any other person would look like a fool, writing about him, and I'm no fool—I took early retirement, didn't I?"

"Yes, but you've known him for more than 30 years."

"I once invited him to a party at my house and he didn't come. You should write him. You're the obit editor."

"But he's not dead yet."

"When his liver explodes and his lungs rot, you'll have to do it. This would be valuable practice."

"What're you two yappin' about?" asked Slats Grobnik, stopping by the table.

"What are YOU doing in an ice cream parlor?"

"I hadda go real bad. Did I hear you mention that porch climber?"

"Mike Royko?"

"Yeah, dincha ever hear that story? One night Royko and his wife was out with another old *Daily News* reporter and his wife, and when the saloons closed they went over to Royko's two-flat on the Northwest Side. They climbed the rickety outside stairway to the second floor. Royko wasn't a famous columnist then and this upper was all he could afford. Anyway, they get up there, and Royko can't find his keys. So they all start banging on the door to wake up his 13-year-old nephew, who is babysitting for his two kids.

"They could see through the window that the nephew's laying on the couch, but he doesn't move. Now they're banging and kicking on the door and yelling at Chester or Stanley or whatever his name was, and the neighbors are yelling out their windows to shuddup and even worse things, so they can get back to sleep.

"Well, over on the side, about five feet from the porch maybe, is this kitchen window with the loose screen. Royko climbs over the railing, leans out as far as he can and makes a leap at the window, like a trapeze artist, and catches on the window sill with his hands. Then he knocks out the screen and starts scraping his feet against the side of the house, trying to pull himself up the wall.

"His wife yells, 'Please be careful. If you fall and kill yourself we won't be able to get in and go to the bathroom.' Finally he squeezes in through the window and unlocks the door from the inside and lets the rest of them in. Just in time, too.

"Meanwhile Royko makes sure that the kid on the couch isn't dead, just sleeping. He shakes him, pokes him, puts his foot against his butt and rocks him, but the nephew doesn't wake up. Royko wants to sit down, 'cause the other three people grabbed the only chairs.

"Then Royko feels obliged to entertain his guests, so he gets out his guitar. A lot of people don't know it, but he's a fantastic guitar player. He could be a folk

singer and make a lot of money. Anyway, he finally sits down on top of his nephew, starts playing the guitar and singing country songs. He's singing loud enough to wake up an alderman, but the nephew underneath keeps on snorin'.

"You never heard that story, how he broke into his own house? That's why we call him a porch climber."

"Gosh, have you known Royko long?"

"Since Micky and I were pinsetters at the bowling alley."

"Micky?"

"Yeah, that's what he usta call himself."

"Does Skippy Jacobson know that?"

"Not unless somebody reads this to him."

"Gee. How did Royk . . . er, Micky, get into the business?"

"After he came home from Korea he was workin' as a $52-a-week police reporter for the *Lincoln-Belmont Booster*. In '59 he tried to get on with the *Tribune*, the *American* and the *Sun-Times* and they all laughed in his face. But Stuffy Walters at the *Daily News* had a weird sense of humor and he hired him.

"Now the big columnist at the *Daily News* was then Jack Mabley, and when he defected to the *American*, John Justin Smith took over. Meanwhile, after a coupla years on nights, Royko ended up covering the County Building. The *Daily News* wanted to jazz up its weekend edition, so Ritz Fischer, the city editor, consulted his magic whatchacallit and decided to have each of the beatmen write a Saturday column about little tidbits that didn't make the news stories.

"Well, the City Hall guy was usin' the column to get his favorite pols' names in print, and the Criminal Courts guy was stickin' in puffs for defense lawyers and crap like that, but Royko was coming up with little vignettes about bookie joints in the County Building lobby, and how the goofy elevator operators could never stop at floor level, and stuff like that.

"Then Smith quits and goes to Channel 2, and the *Daily News* is lookin' for a columnist again. Fischer suggests giving Royko a shot at it, and the bosses ask him if he thinks he could write five a week. 'I can do six,' Royko tells 'em. He's been doin' it ever since, except at the *Tribune* he only has to do five, 'cause the *Trib* pays people more to do less."

"Royko walks through the newsroom with his head down like he's in a blizzard. He hardly ever says a word to anyone. Once, when he got mugged on the way home from the Billy Goat's, a reporter said to Brian Downes, the office manager, 'Did you know Royko was stuck up?' And Downes answered, 'Yeah, he never talks to me, either.'

"That's because Mike's got what you call a complex, because he doesn't have a college degree," Grobnik explained. "You got all these master's degree wizards in there, earning $500–$600 a week, and he doesn't know how to deal with them."

"What does Royko earn?"

"He takes home more than the editor, but the editor isn't syndicated in 615 papers," Grobnik winked. "That's the thing. Royko can't make eye-contact with all these young master-degree reporters, 'cause he's afraid he'll laugh in their face."

"He says he's going to quit writing when he hits 60. What'll he do then?"

"Don't be surprised if he gets an offer from Grand Ole Opry."

Epilogue

Did we leave anyone out?

How about Tom Duggan, Larry Schreiner, Ida B. Wells, Mickey Finn, Harry Romanoff, Walter McCarron, Colonel McCormick, Oprah Winfrey, W. Clement Stone, Harry Glos, Charlie Soo, Mad Man Muntz, Virginia Marmaduke. . . .?

Hey, we've got a list as long as Halsted Street! We're working on them, even as you read this. The parade of different drummers stretches as far as the eye can see. The cast for Act II is gathering in the wings, waiting for the curtain to go up.

Kenan Heise and Ed Baumann
Chicago, 1990

Bibliography

Chicago American

Chicago Tribune

Armstrong, Louis, *Satchmo: My Life in New Orleans*, Prentice-Hall, Inc., 1954

Asbury, Herbert, *Gem of the Prairie*, Alfred A. Knopf, Inc., 1940

Asinof, Eliot, *Eight Men Out*, Holt, Rinehart and Winston, 1963

Ballard, Everett Guy, *Captain Streeter Pioneer*, Emery Publishing Service, 1914

Barnard, Harry, *Eagle Forgotten*, Bobbs-Merrill, 1938

Beasley, Norman, *Frank Knox American*, Doubleday, Doran & Co., 1936

Berkow, Ira, *Maxwell Street*, Doubleday & Co., Inc., 1977

Boone, Robert S. and Grunska, Gerald, *Hack*, Highland Press, 1978

Brady, Frank, *Hefner*, MacMillan Publishing Co., Inc., 1974

Brickhouse, Jack, *Thanks for Listening*, Diamond Communications, Inc., 1986

Bibliography

Bright, John, *Hizzoner Big Bill Thompson*, Jonathan Cape & Harrison Smith, 1930

Bronte, Patricia, *Vittles and Vice*, Henry Regnery Co., 1952

Casey, Robert J., *Pioneer Railroad: The Story of the Chicago and North Western System*, McGraw-Hill, 1948

Colander, Pat, *Thin Air*, Contemporary Books, Inc., 1982

Collier, James Lincoln, *Louis Armstrong: An American Genius*, Oxford University Press, Inc., 1983

Connely, Willard, *Louis Sullivan as He Lived*, Horizon Press, Inc., 1960

Cortesi, Lawrence, *Jean duSable: Father of Chicago*, Chilton Book Co., 1972

Darby, Edwin, *The Fortune Builders*, Doubleday & Co., 1986

De Mare, Marie, *G.P.A. Healy, American Artist*, David McKay Co., 1954

Dedmon, Emmett, *Fabulous Chicago*, Random House, 1953

Demaris, Ovid, *Captive City*, Lyle Stuart, Inc., 1969

DiDonato, Pietro, *Immigrant Saint*, McGraw-Hill, 1960

Ditka, Mike, *Ditka: An Autobiography*, Bonus Books, 1986

Duncan, Hugh Dalzier, *Culture & Democracy*, Bedminster Press, 1965

Durocher, Leo, *Nice Guys Finish Last*, Simon and Schuster, 1975

Ellis, William T., *Billy Sunday: The Man and the Message*, Moody Press, 1959

Fehrenbacher, Don E., *Chicago Giant: A Biography of "Long John" Wentworth*, American History Research Center, Inc., 1957

Garden, Mary and Biancolli, Louis, *Mary Garden's Story*, Simon and Schuster, 1951

Gleason, Bill, *Daley of Chicago*, Simon and Schuster, 1970

Gleason, William F., *The Liquid Cross of Skid Row*, Bruce Publishing Co., 1966

Goldman, Albert, *Ladies and Gentlemen, Lenny Bruce*, Random House, 1971

Granger, Bill and Lori, *Fighting Jane: Mayor Jane Byrne and the Chicago Machine*, Dial Press, 1980

Green, Paul M. and Holli, Melvin G., *The Mayors*, SIU Press, 1987

Hecht, Ben, *A Child of the Century*, Simon and Schuster, 1954

Hecht, Ben, *Charlie*, Harper & Brothers, 1957

Heise, Kenan and Edgerton, Michael, *Chicago, Center for Enterprise*, Windsor Publications, 1982

Heise, Kenan, *The Chicagoization of America: 1893–1917*, Chicago Historical Bookworks, 1990

Heise, Kenan, *Is There Only One Chicago*, Westover Publishing Co., 1973

Heise, Kenan, *Resurrection Mary: A Novel*, Chicago Historical Bookworks, 1990

Hubbard, Gurdon Saltonstall, *The Autobiography of Gurdon Saltonstall Hubbard*, Citadel Press, Inc., 1969

Jones, Jerry, *Chicago's Two Gun Pete*, 1988

Bibliography

Jones, Max and Chilton, John, *Louis: The Louis Armstrong Story,* Little, Brown and Co., 1971

Kilian, Michael, Fletcher, Connie and Ciccone, F. Richard, *Who Runs Chicago?,* St. Martin's Press, 1979

Kobler, John, *Capone,* G.P. Putnam's Sons, 1971

Kogan, Herman, *The First Century: The Chicago Bar Association 1874–1974,* Rand McNally & Co., 1974

Kogan, Herman and Kogan, Rick, *Yesterday's Chicago,* E.A. Seemann, 1976

Kogan, Herman and Wendt, Lloyd, *Bet A Million!,* Bobbs-Merrill Co., 1948

Kogan, Herman and Wendt, Lloyd, *Give the Lady What She Wants!,* Rand McNally Co., 1952

Kogan, Herman and Wendt, Lloyd, *Lords of the Levee,* Bobbs-Merrill, 1943

Kogan, Herman and Wendt, Lloyd, *Chicago, A Pictorial History,* E.P. Dutton, 1958

Kupcinet, Irv, *Kup's Chicago,* World Publishing Co., 1962

Lewis, Lloyd and Smith, Henry Justin, *Chicago, the History of its Reputation,* Harcourt, Brace & Co., 1929

Lyle, John H., *The Dry and Lawless Years,* Prentice Hall, 1960

McPhaul, Jack, *Johnny Torrio,* Arlington House, 1970

Moore, Colleen, *Silent Star,* Doubleday & Co., 1968

Morgan, Gwen and Vesey, Arthur, *Halas by Halas,* McGraw-Hill, 1979

Morrison, Hugh, *Louis Sullivan: Prophet of Modern Architecture,* W.W. Norton & Co., Inc., 1935

Mundelein, George William, *Two Crowded Years*, Extension Press, 1918

Murray, George, *The Legacy of Al Capone*, G.P. Putnam's Sons, 1975

Murray, George, *The Madhouse on Madison Street*, Follett Publishing Co., 1965

Nash, Jay Robert, *People to See*, New Century Publishing, 1981

Pasley, Fred D., *Al Capone: The Biography of a Self-Made Man*, Garden City Publishing Co., 1930

Pierce, Bessie Louise, *As Others See Chicago: Impressions of Visitors 1673-1933*, University of Chicago Press, 1933

Poole, Ernest, *Giants Gone*, McGraw-Hill Co. Inc., 1943

Quaife, Milo M., *Checagou 1673-1835*, University of Chicago Press, 1933

Ross, Ishbel, *Silhouette In Diamonds: The Life of Mrs. Potter Palmer*, Harper & Brothers, Publishers, 1960

Royko, Mike, *Boss*, E.P. Dutton & Co., 1971

Sharpe, May Churchill, *Chicago May, Her Story*, Gold Label Books, Inc., 1928

Smith, H. Allen, *Life and Legend of Gene Fowler*, William Morrow & Co., 1977

Smith, Henry Justin, *A Chicago Portrait*, The Century Co., 1931

Stead, William T., *If Christ Came to Chicago*, Laird & Lee, Publishers, 1894. Reprinted by Chicago Historical Bookworks, 1990

Stone, Irving, *Clarence Darrow for the Defense*, Doubleday, Doran & Co., Inc., 1941

Sullivan, Louis H., *The Autobiography of an Idea*, Dover Publications, Inc., 1956

Terkel, Studs, *Chicago*, Pantheon Books, 1985

Twombly, Robert (Editor), *Louis Sullivan: The Public Papers*, University of Chicago Press, 1988

Vass, George, *George Halas and the Chicago Bears*, Henry Regnery, 1971

Washburn, Charles, *Come Into My Parlor: A Biography of the Aristocratic Everleigh Sisters of Chicago*, Nickerbocker Publishing Co., 1934

Weimann, Jeanne Madeline, *The Fair Women*, Academy Chicago, 1981

Weinberg, Arthur (Editor), *Clarence Darrow: Attorney for the Damned*, Simon and Schuster, 1957

Wendt, Lloyd, *Chicago Tribune: The Rise of a Great American Newspaper*, Rand McNally & Co., 1979

Wendt, Lloyd, *Swift Walker: An Informal Biography of Gurdon Saltonstall Hubbard*, Regnery Gateway Books, 1986

Wheeler, Adade Mitchell and Wortman, Marlene Stein, *The Roads They Made: Women in Illinois History*, Charles H. Kerr Publishing Co., 1977

Williams, Kenny J., *In the City of Men: Another Story of Chicago*, Townsend Press, 1974

Wilson, Howard E., *Mary McDowell: Neighbor,* University of Chicago Press, 1928

Index